Nabokov's Permanent
Mystery

Nabokov's Permanent Mystery
The Expression of Metaphysics in His Work

DAVID S. RUTLEDGE

McFarland & Company, Inc., Publishers
Jefferson, North Carolina, and London

LIBRARY OF CONGRESS CATALOGUING-IN-PUBLICATION DATA

Rutledge, David S., 1965–
　　Nabokov's permanent mystery : the expression of metaphysics in his work / David S. Rutledge.
　　　　p.　　cm.
　　Includes bibliographical references and index.

ISBN 978-0-7864-6076-2
softcover : 50# alkaline paper ∞

　　1. Nabokov, Vladimir Vladimirovich, 1899–1977 — Criticism and interpretation.　2. Nabokov, Vladimir Vladimirovich, 1877–1977 — Philosophy.　3. Nabokov, Vladimir Vladimirovich, 1877–1977 — Knowledge — Metaphysics.　4. Metaphysics in literature.　I. Title.
PS3527.A15Z8878　　2011
8013'.54 — dc22　　　　　　　　　　　　　　　　　　2010043955

British Library cataloguing data are available

© 2011 David S. Rutledge. All rights reserved

No part of this book may be reproduced or transmitted in any form or by any means, electronic or mechanical, including photocopying or recording, or by any information storage and retrieval system, without permission in writing from the publisher.

Front cover: Photograph of Vladimir Nabokov by Horst Tappe, 1964 (The Granger Collection)

Manufactured in the United States of America

McFarland & Company, Inc., Publishers
　Box 611, Jefferson, North Carolina 28640
　　www.mcfarlandpub.com

To my parents,
for constant support and love

Table of Contents

Acknowledgments ix
List of Abbreviations xi
Introduction 1

1. The Live Source of the Cliché 15
2. Time Frames 34
3. The Return Structure 43
4. The Metaphysics of Mistakes 51
5. The Problem of Biography 60
6. This Side 74
7. The Otherworldly Role of Water 90
8. Nabokov's Originals 97
9. The Metaphysics of the Zig-Zag 105
10. The Authorial Role 115
11. The Indivisible Pearl 122
12. Merging Souls, Inviolate Lives: Nabokov's Problematic Beyond 132
13. The Teleological Potential of Words 142
14. Not Quilty: The Problem of Persecution Mania 148
15. Ascending Structures 162

Table on Contents

16. The Conjurer's Rented Rabbit   175
17. The Metaphysics of Imagination   182

Chapter Notes   187
Works Cited   193
Index   197

Acknowledgments

Thanks to Gary Stonum and Roger Salomon of Case Western Reserve University, Cleveland, Ohio, for their encouragement and guidance at the outset of this project. Thanks, Gary, for many helpful suggestions and for your close reading. Thanks, Roger, for the same, and specifically for an idea that led to the title of this work.

Thanks to the University of New Orleans — specifically the English Department — for a sabbatical to work on this book. May we all survive the budget crunch. May this excellent city university survive despite the ... well, I'll save the editorial for elsewhere.

Thanks also to *The Nabokovian*— specifically Priscilla Meyer and Stephen Jan Parker — for editing and publishing a couple of pieces that found their way into this book. That kind of validation kept the momentum of this project going. And to The Vladimir Nabokov Society for selecting two of my papers, now in this book, for presentation at M.L.A. panels.

List of Abbreviations

Citations of Nabokov's writings are abbreviated as follows:

CE — *Conclusive Evidence*
EO — *Eugene Onegin*
IB — *Invitation to a Beheading*
LL — *Lectures on Literature*
LDQ — *Lectures on Don Quixote*
LRL — *Lectures on Russian Literature*
LATH — *Look at the Harlequins*
Butterflies — *Nabokov's Butterflies*
Nabokov-Wilson — *The Nabokov-Wilson Letters*
PF — *Pale Fire*
"*Plausible*" — "*Pushkin, or the Real and the Plausible*"
RLSK — *The Real Life of Sebastian Knight*
SL — *Selected Letters*
SM — *Speak, Memory*
SO — *Strong Opinions*
Stories — *The Stories of Vladimir Nabokov*

Introduction

Literary Techniques and Metaphysical Structures

The title of this book expresses a key concept in the art of Vladimir Nabokov: permanent mystery. Nabokov's literature has led to far too many arguments that attempt to provide answers to a given text. These arguments are severely reductive because they insist on a single solution to explain a complex work of literature. I have the advantage of being able to read these arguments, in regard to *Lolita, Pale Fire, The Real Life of Sebastian Knight,* and other works, and then stepping back to see the larger picture: the inclination to solve such works is misguided. I will argue that the many suggestions raised by a text — the many questions — are an integral part of the structure. Readers should avoid the complacency of an answer.

The narrator of *The Real Life of Sebastian Knight*, V., describes the response of one reader to Sebastian Knight's books, stating that Knight's books did not make him think; instead, "they left you puzzled and cross" (179). Some readers need to have the word filled in; otherwise, they are left "puzzled and cross." However, the missing word, the irresolvable puzzle, is a good way to think of Nabokov's best books.

In addition, this sense of permanent mystery reflects Nabokov's most profound metaphysical thoughts.

Yes, this book is an addition to the ever-growing number of studies of Nabokov's metaphysics. However, I do not plan to say much about the metaphysical beliefs themselves; rather, I intend to show how Nabokov expresses his metaphysics with certain literary devices and in the overall literary structures.[1] Nabokov's structures are built on a hierarchy of devices. At the bottom one will find his playing with clichés, his manipulating plot

Introduction

lines; the hierarchy builds up through the level of the narrator and the author, up to the highest point, where the structure suggests something beyond itself. This book is organized along that hierarchy: the reader will start at the lowest level, and gradually ascend to the top and to the suggestion of something beyond that top level. Of course, this is in no way intended to be comprehensive: Nabokov creates a great number of devices that will not be discussed here, even some that may not yet have been discovered. Such is the nature of Nabokov's art: no analysis can be exhaustive.

My goal is to explore some of the many nuances of Nabokovian structure. Each of these steps along this structure — each technique — will be relevant to a number of his structures, as will the overall hierarchy. Nabokov's set of beliefs are consistent over the course of his career. At no point are there any radical differences in the metaphysics, although the structures gain in complexity.

Was Nabokov aware of the many devices that I will be discussing? That, of course, is irrelevant, as long as the devices are there. In a 1966 letter to Carl Proffer, Nabokov states that the structure of a work may be determined by the author's intuition: "Many of the delightful combinations and clues, though quite acceptable, never entered my head or are the result of an author's intuition and inspiration, not calculation and craft" (*SL* 391). Many of Nabokov's structures are undoubtedly complex, and the "combinations and clues" which a reader might discover may never have been part of a conscious design. All of the structural complexities are, nonetheless, the work of "an author's intuition and inspiration."

The Teleological Intuition of Genius

Nabokov's sense of structure moves beyond the merely visible. In the first paragraph of his study of the structure of *Eugene Onegin*, he suggests that a literary structure could be planned by "the teleological intuition of genius" (vol. 1, 16). He does not directly state that Pushkin created his literary structure with this mysterious intuitive force. He merely suggests the idea. The suggestion, though, seems to point toward Nabokov's opin-

Introduction

ion of what forces motivated or inspired Pushkin's structure. The "teleological intuition of genius" may be a source for structural inspiration. The question then is what does Nabokov mean by that phrase?

The word "teleological" is an adjective which means related to the philosophical study of design or pattern. Nabokov seems to be saying that intuition could be a sense of teleology. One may be able to intuit natural or artistic patterns. Charles Kinbote of *Pale Fire* speaks to this idea when he suggests that the knight is capable of perceiving dimensions which transcend the familiar grid of everyday reality; he writes of "ghost consequences": "comparable to ... the fanning out of additional squares which a chess knight ... standing on a marginal file, 'feels' in phantom extensions beyond the board, but which have no effect on his real moves, on the real play" (*PF* 276). Teleological intuition, therefore, is the ability to comprehend patterns that extend into "ghost"—or non–material—dimensions.

Teleology also has to do with an ultimate purpose or design, an end. Nabokov uses the word in this way when describing a familiar childhood room with the lights out, in which the accumulation of detail works to convey a definite image: "the place acted upon my young senses in a curiously teleological way" (*SM* 89). Thus, the word "teleological," for Nabokov, refers to the gradual accumulation of a definite pattern, with the end result being a "permanent" image. Humbert Humbert also uses the word to refer to an accumulation of experience when describing his first cross-country excursion with Lolita: "a hard, twisted, teleological growth" (*Lolita* 154). In this sense, teleological intuition would seem to be an intuitive sense of a completed image or pattern which builds from one's sensory experiences.

In his lecture on *Quixote*, Nabokov comments on the common perception of human knowledge, stating that most people believe in "a set of senses reduced to five" (1). The sense of "teleological intuition" is certainly not one which could be categorized within those common five. As shown in Nabokov's ideas about rereading, the human sense which appreciates the art of the written word is also not one of those five, not quite the eye one uses to perceive painting: "We have no physical organ (as we have the eye in regard to painting) that takes in the whole picture and then can enjoy its details" (*LL* 3). Teleological intuition may be that extra sense

Introduction

which comprehends the essence of a literary structure, an innate ability to perceive literary patterns.

Next one must ask how the word "genius" works in this term. The "intuition of genius" could mean either a superior intuition, an intuition at genius level, or the intuitive sense of the existence of genius.[2] The former implies a hierarchy of intuitive ability: some are geniuses of intuition, others are intuition impaired. Nabokov, of course, claims a top spot on the hierarchy, beginning his collection of interviews with the claim, "I think like a genius" (*SO* xv). This is no casual self-compliment: later in the same book he states, "I still feel appalled and puzzled at seeing 'genius' applied to any important storyteller.... Genius still means to me, in my Russian fastidiousness of phrase, a unique, dazzling gift" (146–147). Because of this same "fastidiousness of phrase" we can assume that the "teleological intuition of genius" is also not a random application. Nabokov directly tells us that he has at least one of the qualities contained in the term, that of "genius." We can safely assume he would claim an equally high intuition quotient as well.

The second possible meaning of "intuition of genius" suggests the existence of a quality called "genius" which lies outside of oneself, a "genius" which one might intuitively perceive. In this sense, "genius" is similar to Wallace Stevens' use of the word: "She sang beyond the genius of the sea" (128). Here "genius" means something like "essence" or "spirit" or "intrinsic nature." One might even argue that Stevens' "The Idea of Order at Key West" is a poem about the "teleological intuition of genius," an intuitive impulse to order natural forces coinciding with an ability to perceive them. Geoffrey Hartman explains that in Romantic poetry "genius" could signify either the spirit of a place ("genius loci") or an individual mind. He discusses the precarious "marriage" of the two: "The marriage of genius and genius loci (of imagination and nature)" (333).[3] Nabokov probably intended both the interior and exterior sense of the word "genius." Genius is both a quality of mind and a quality of the outside world. Perhaps one's teleological intuition may be capable of making connections between the two, of matching patterns of the mind with those of the natural world.

The following exchange occurs in Nabokov's last completed novel:

Introduction

"'What do *you* call "genius"?' 'Well, seeing things others don't see. Or rather the invisible links between things'" (*LATH* 40). The idea that "genius" is that quality which sees "the invisible links" suggests a closer connection between teleology and genius: genius is the quality which perceives teleological mysteries. Genius perceives "invisible links," moving beyond material perception, beyond those common five senses. The greater one's genius, this quote suggests, the greater one's sense of a patterned structure. Pekka Tammi writes of "one of the predominant themes in VN's work": "a belief in the essential comprehensibility of human existence through its latent patterns" (20). It is precisely the "latent" nature of those patterns that can only be detected by the most teleologically perceptive mind. One may even be able to perceive a pattern which moves beyond the visible.

Nabokov never attempts to explain the term "teleological intuition of genius," although it may be more precise to say he wrote a four-volume translation of Pushkin to attempt to do so. Nabokov's *Eugene Onegin* is, in part, a detailed attempt to convey in English the results of Pushkin's "teleological intuition of genius," the structural-poetic depths of Pushkin's art, including the invisible structural links. Nabokov's *Onegin* attempts to make those invisible links visible.

Rather than focus on the term, as I have done, Nabokov seemingly dismisses it, but the manner in which he does so is significant. The full context of the term comes in Nabokov's insistence that only a final, published literary work should be studied for structure. The sentence reads, "We can invoke a change in plan, or an absence of plan, and — instead — the teleological intuition of genius; but these are matters of a metaphysical order" (16). Nabokov's apparent dismissal of the issue is entirely consistent with his metaphysical sense: he considers his own metaphysics to be akin to that of Pushkin, and one should not attempt to define this sense shared by all artists of "genius." The teleological intuition of genius is the perception of something beyond words. Of equal importance is the fact that this apparent dismissal of the topic directly connects the study of literary structure to metaphysics. Nabokov believes literary structures — visible structures which lead to and suggest the invisible, the intangible — can embody metaphysical values.

Introduction

Limitations of Language

One of the great difficulties in writing about Nabokov's metaphysical sense is choosing one's words. Nabokov famously states, in answer to the direct question of whether he believes in God, "I know more than I can express in words" (*SO* 45). His response, much discussed by Nabokov scholars, stresses the inability of language to capture this mystic presence, but it also stresses knowledge. He claims to "know" the answer, not simply to believe. Christine Rydel points out that in this response Nabokov "never even utters the word 'God.'" Perhaps "God," like "reality," is a word which must always be placed in quotes, each person's perspective determining his or her sense of the word.[4] Nabokov refuses to adopt the interviewer's term because that might imply an acceptance of the interviewer's sense of "God." That is, a simple "yes" or "no," or an equivalent, could suggest that the word "God" has the same meaning for both the questioner and Nabokov. However, this does not mean he is reducing the issue to mere relativism. Instead, his reply emphasizes both the mystery and the definite existence of some supreme being or force. (Similarly, Nabokov writes in a letter of advice to his brother: "every person sees things in an individual way and must find *his own* words for them" [*SL* 8, italics in the original].) Thus that statement — "I know more than I can express in words" — artfully combines mystery and knowledge and allows Nabokov to answer the question in and on his own terms.

Nabokov's metaphysical sense is beyond words. According to his autobiography, he appears to have shared this sense with his mother. Her sense of belief also combines a definite knowledge with an inability to fully comprehend the mystery from this side: "having equal faith in the existence of another world and in the impossibility of comprehending it in terms of earthly life" (*SM* 39). "Earthly life," in the metaphysics of both Nabokov and his mother, only allows one glimpses of what may be ahead, yet one nonetheless has an "intense" faith that something does exist beyond. Nabokov's knowledge may seem stronger than his mother's firm faith, but both maintain a certainty in a beyond which cannot be fully expressed or comprehended in the "terms" of this life.

Of course, scholars writing about Nabokov and his metaphysics have

Introduction

had to search for words to express that sense. D. Barton Johnson, in his book *Worlds in Regression*, writes, "Nabokov's games are a prominent part of the intricate web of allusion, coincidence, and pattern that mark the presence of the other world in the novels" (3). Vladimir Alexandrov similarly states that the "central theme" of Nabokov's art is the "otherworld":

> This term is my (not wholly satisfactory) translation of the Russian word *potustoronnost,*'a noun derived from an adjective denoting a quality or state that pertains to the "other side" of the boundary separating life and death; additional possible translations are "the hereafter" and "the beyond" [*Otherworld* 3].

Véra Nabokov uses the same word —*potustoronnost'*— and says that it is a "key undercurrent in Nabokov's work ... which permeates all that he has written" (qtd. in Dmitri Nabokov 174). Dmitri Nabokov translates it as the "hereafter" (174). Tammi focuses on the same word, saying that it is "not an easily translatable Russian noun, approximating 'the world on the other side,' 'the world beyond the grave,' or 'another world'" (22).

I want to argue that any word, even one endorsed by Véra, is inadequate, and potentially misleading. Nabokov's metaphysics are beyond words. This is one reason why a study of his sense of structure — which will not focus on a specific word to label his thoughts — can help to shed some new light on his metaphysical sense.

The metaphysics are beyond words, but, nonetheless, Nabokov came up with some of his own. Kinbote is one of the few Nabokovian characters who attempt to attach this sense to a word. He writes, "In trying to find the right name for that Universal Mind, or First Cause, or the Absolute, or Nature, I submit that the Name of God has priority" (227). The "Name of God," of course, does not even have priority in his own sentence. Kinbote is misguided by his belief that the metaphysical sense (Universal Mind, Nature, God) can be so easily named. He stands in sharp contrast to Nabokov's mother: the purest faith cannot be reduced to a word.

Another problem with searching for an apt word for Nabokovian metaphysics is that his metaphysical sense is intimately involved in this world, not only an "other" one. Zoran Kuzmanovich discusses the importance of "ground[ing] Nabokov's metaphysics firmly in the here and now, in the stuff of the real" (28). This approach may suggest a limitation on the ability of the word "otherworld" to represent this metaphysics. The

Introduction

metaphysical is in part physical; the "little shiver" which Nabokov says all good readers should feel when reading great writers is a metaphysical sense: "That little shiver behind is quite certainly the highest form of emotion that humanity has attained when evolving pure art and pure science.... We are vertebrates tipped at the head with a divine flame" (*LL* 64). Thus the "divine" is not solely a quality of an other side, but an essential aspect of a sufficiently evolved human being. There is an interaction between this world and the "other" world, but that interaction has no rational, wordable explanation. The best invented term to summarize this idea of a spiritual intermingling of sides may be Nabokov's own: "the here–and–there–after" (*Ada* 315).

Another term Nabokov uses to convey this earthly aspect of the "other" world is "celestial essence." In Nabokov's spiritual realm, artists are in touch with a "celestial" quality: "the gods delegate to our world certain beings composed of celestial essence whom in their incarnation we call poets" (*EO*, vol. 2, 234). This idea comes in his analysis of a poem by Küchelbecker, but it is an apt expression of Nabokov's own idea of divinity: "poets" are both in contact with and made up of a divine "essence." He uses the same term in the story "Tyrants Destroyed":

> When the gods used to assume earthly form and, clad in violet-tinted raiment, demurely but powerfully stepping with muscular feet in still dustless sandals, appeared to field laborers or mountain shepherds, their divinity was not in the least diminished for it; on the contrary, the charm of humanness enwafting them was a most eloquent reconfirmation of their celestial essence [*Stories* 435–436].

This passage illustrates that "celestial essence" is not lessened by an "earthly form": a god's "muscular feet," firmly planted on this planet, are only an "eloquent reconfirmation" of a divine nature. There is no strict division between this life and the beyond. In fact, Nabokov says, one may complement the other.

Vladislav Khodasevich recognized the importance of the "otherworld" in Nabokovian metaphysics as early as 1937. Khodasevich argued that the source for this "celestial essence" is the other side of the boundary between life and death. However, Nabokov's art demonstrates that plentiful examples of celestial influence can undoubtedly be found on this side of the boundary. Though the ultimate source may be celestial, Nabokov believes

Introduction

that celestial essence can be recognized in this world, and that literature can be one means for conveying it.

Another reason why Nabokov does not directly state his metaphysical or philosophical ideas in his fiction is that he simply considers such didactic forms of fiction to be inartistic. Brian Boyd writes, "Nabokov is passionately concerned with philosophical questions, but he thinks that art at full stretch may get closer to plucking the truth than philosophy can" (*Ada* 228). Concerning epistemological and moral questions, Michael Wood explains, "Nabokov doesn't write about them; he writes them" (111). Nabokov consistently expresses his tedium as a reader for characters caught in the midst of philosophic throes. This at least partially explains his dislike for Dostoevsky and his impatience with Sartre. Here is a passage from Tolstoy's *Anna Karenin* (Nabokov's translation of the title) which he read in his class lecture on that novel, published as follows with Nabokov's commentary in brackets: "'Well, what is perplexing me?' Lyovin said to himself. 'I am wondering about the relationship to God of all the different religions of all mankind. But why do I bother?' [Why indeed, murmurs the good reader.]" (*LRL* 170). There is a real problem, Nabokov feels, with fiction which deals too bluntly with metaphysical concepts, fiction which becomes too heavy-handed or overtly ponderous. In these bluntly phrased philosophic musings of Lyovin, Nabokov believed he could hear Tolstoy's voice pushing through the pattern of the fiction. The author has unsubtly imposed his ideas into his created world. The same is true of Sartre's *Nausea*, in which Nabokov says the "author inflicts his idle and arbitrary philosophic fancy on a helpless person whom he has invented for that purpose" (*SO* 230). The problem is not that a writer has philosophic or metaphysical ideas, but that the author inartistically forces these ideas into the fiction.

When asked to explain the pleasure he felt from "butterfly hunting and writing," Nabokov replied: "Neither is easy to describe to a person who has not experienced it, and each is so obvious to the one who has that a description would sound crude and redundant" (*SO* 40). The experience cannot be expressed, yet it is definite. When interviewed for his seventy-second birthday, Nabokov ascribed at least some of his longevity to "fabulous (and on the whole rather bracing) scientific enigmas incapable of being stated, let alone solved" (*SO* 177). Here, as in his answer about

Introduction

"God," he conveys the idea of something which unquestionably exists, but which cannot be put into words, cannot be "solved." That boundary between life and death is not a puzzle waiting for our simple human solutions. For Nabokov, the word "scientific" does not mean capable of being solved by rational thought: "the greater one's science, the deeper the sense of mystery" (*SO* 44). Here again, he intertwines knowledge and mystery in an effort to convey his idea of the most profound form of thought.

His point is that the metaphysical sense — whether lepidopterological or literary — should not be discussed reductively: "Aphoristicism is a sign of arteriosclerosis" (*SO* 79). Nabokov, in this aphorism, again stresses the shortcomings of language. Just as he insists on not reducing his metaphysical knowledge to a pat answer, he responds in this way to a question about the "view of life" in his novels: "I can't find any so-called main ideas, such as that of fate, in my novels, or at least none that would be expressed lucidly in less than the number of words I used for this or that book" (*SO* 117). The entirety of any given book best expresses Nabokov's metaphysical ideas: "a precis would be an opaque shadow" (*SO* 178).

Celestial essence, here–and–there–after, divine flame, *potustoronnost'*: though Nabokov believes no word or phrase can adequately capture his sense of metaphysics (or, stronger than mere sense, as he would insist, metaphysical knowledge), the limitations of language did not prevent him from creating a few apt phrases. None of these phrases, however, is sufficient. The perfect words cannot be found. As Woody Allen said in regard to religion and "divine matters," "I know exactly what I think about all this, but I can never find the words to put it in. Maybe if I get a little drunk I could dance it for you." Nabokov does not do a drunken dance, but he does find an element of his art — an element composed of words, yet leading beyond words — which is able to convey his metaphysical certainty: the literary structure.

This idea of "permanent mystery" is one that is integral to many works of art, not only those of Nabokov. *Hamlet* comes to mind.[5] Perhaps it says something about the essence of art itself. That, however, is a much larger topic than I intend to take on here. But I do want to offer one poem, "Butterfly of Light," by Juan Ramón Jiménez, a poem that captures this and other Nabokovian themes:

Introduction

> Butterfly of light,
> beauty flees when I arrive
> at your rose.
> I race, blind, after her ...
> I half-grasp her here and there ...
> All that remains in my hand
> is the outline of her flight!⁶

In this poem the butterfly has an uncapturable quality of beauty. The speaker has no doubt about this butterfly's existence, but a taxonomical classification of this insect would not allow one to hold its essence in hand. The ellipses at the end of lines four and five (in the original) represent the sense of the unfinished chase, the inconclusive quest. The metaphysical sense, for Nabokov, just as the "beauty" for Jiménez, can be perceived but not captured. Nonetheless, there is a certainty that such beauty exists.

In dealing with such a grand topic as Nabokovian metaphysics, one would be wise to read this thought from Khodasevich: "You speak of the significant, of the profound, and/ it comes out small; I speak of the small, and the profound is/ revealed" (qtd. in Bethea vii). Anyone who speaks of the profound in Nabokov's art does run the risk of making it sound small. Therefore, I plan to discuss Nabokov's metaphysics by working with even some of the smallest details of his literary structures, without systematically attempting a complete (and therefore false) definition of that metaphysics. Emily Dickinson wrote of some members of the public: "they talk of Hallowed things, aloud — and embarrass my Dog" (178). Nabokov would sympathize with Dickinson's dog. He too disliked public talk of "Hallowed" topics, mocking those who participate in metaphysical debate with *Pale Fire*'s Institution of Preparation for the Hereafter — I.P.H.: "big if!" (52). The method of this work, showing that the small is integral to the profound, the particular artistic detail to the larger metaphysical concept, is a method which should not offend sensitive pets or poets.

"The Art of Translation"

The essay "The Art of Translation" provides a nice, relatively simple example of Nabokov's intimate linking of structure and metaphysical con-

Introduction

tent. In this essay, Nabokov creates a structure which conveys the "perfect" essence of a translation. The structure of this short essay is nowhere near as involved as that of any of his novels, but it is a concise instance in which Nabokov makes a direct connection between not only structure and content, but between structure and the suggestion (rather than definition) of a metaphysical content.

Though "The Art of Translation" may initially appear to be little more than a commentary on good and bad translations, primarily the latter, the essay is in fact framed around some important metaphysical concepts. The first sentence of the essay introduces the concept of "verbal transmigration." With this phrase Nabokov immediately places the idea of translation on a higher plane than that of merely changing languages. The phrase suggests that the essence of translation is the transference of a writer's soul, not from one body to another, but from one language to another. The key to a good translation is the ability to keep that soul intact in a new language.

Nabokov goes on to explain some of the potential evils of translation and gives examples of various "step[s] to Hell" (*LRL* 315). Bad translation is not simple incompetence, but blasphemy, a lack of respect for the poet's soul. This first section of the essay ends with the suggestion of infinite evil: "and so on, *ad malinfinitum*" (318). The potential depths of Hell, the possibilities of mistranslations, are endless.

However, he does not end the essay with this injunction against would-be translators. Instead, he begins to describe the more positive possibilities of "verbal transmigration." The first of these upper circles holds those who are learned and diligent but "devoid of any semblance of creative genius." The next best is the "authentic poet," someone who casually translates a few lines, but is incapable of achieving true "transmigration": "Instead of dressing up like the real author, he dresses up the author as himself" (319). This "translator" (Nabokov sometimes puts the word in quotes in his notes on *Onegin*, as though inferior work is unworthy of the name) does not succeed in transferring the poet's soul to a new medium, only in putting his own clothes — his own style — over the poet.[7]

The top rung on the hierarchy of translators, where one can find those few who are truly able to adapt the creative soul of the original poet to a

Introduction

new language, is represented in this essay, of course, by Nabokov himself. On this top level the translator is truly a "creative genius" (319). Nabokov proceeds to detail the process of translating a line of Pushkin, a line which in the original Russian "is the perfect beginning of the perfect poem" (320). He goes on to explain some of the problematic details of translating this line into English, keeping in mind the possibility of achieving the "perfect" translation of this "perfect" line.

The conclusion of the essay represents a perfect example of Nabokovian metaphysics. After setting up the contrast between the "evil" results of bad translation and the potential ideal of perfect translation, he gradually develops the essay through his own process of translating one line, building toward an example of his own, then concludes the essay with this paragraph:

> Thus I was confronted by that opening line, so full of Pushkin, so individual and harmonious; and after examining it gingerly from the various angles here suggested, I tackled it. The tackling process lasted the worst part of the night. I did translate it at last; but to give my version at this point might lead the reader to doubt that perfection be attainable by merely following a few perfect rules [321].

With this conclusion, the entire structure of the essay is designed to point toward the possibility of the perfect translation. Note that Nabokov does not withhold his translated line because, as a "genius" translator, that might make the work of true translation look too easy. No: he chooses not to write it because seeing this line "might lead the reader *to doubt* that perfection" is possible. That is, putting into words what he feels to be the "perfect" translation might cause the reader to doubt that very sense of perfection.

There are other places in Nabokov's writing where he expresses the ideal translation in terms of a personal sense of "perfection." Here is his comment on the tedious work of translating his last large novel: "it is to the French *Ada* that I am giving the blood of my brain, and I will not be spurred on by anything short of a private illusion of perfection" (*SL* 359). Here again the perfect translation is not expressed as something attainable, but as an "illusion" for which one should strive. And this illusion is a "private" one: the publication of the translated text may or may not convey the same satisfying sense of "perfection" to readers.

Introduction

In addition, Nabokov planned for "The Art of Translation" to be the concluding chapter of a book of criticism called *The Poetry of Prose* (*SL* 128). This book was to have consisted of ten chapters, the first nine of which were to have been essays on Cervantes, Jane Austen, Pushkin, Dickens, Gogol and Proust (together), Flaubert, Tolstoy, Chehov (his spelling) and Kafka. (Much of this one intended book is now published separately as his lectures.) Placing "The Art of Translation" in the concluding position of the book would further stress its invisible ending. The reader of *The Poetry of Prose* was to have been left with the impression of a bodiless soul, perfect though unprinted on the page.

That is one of Nabokov's metaphysical themes: the expression of one's sense of perfection, putting into words one's sense of metaphysical certainty, immediately invites doubts about that very sense. Words can only reach for perfection, while simultaneously incurring the possibility of doubt. An outline of one's metaphysical sense will necessarily cause someone to doubt that sense. Thus the structure of "The Art of Translation" — in order to avoid those doubts — points toward the idea of perfection, rather than attempting to place perfection on the page. Nabokov's art shows that this sense of structure — a hierarchy that leads toward a sense of perfection that is beyond the visible structure, beyond the book — is the ideal method for accurately conveying his metaphysical sense.

Chapter 1

The Live Source of the Cliché

The Detective Quest and Clichés of Revealed Identity

One might think that Vladimir Nabokov, among the most sensitive of aesthetic thinkers, would have no time for clichés. However, the truth is that he seems to be intrigued by them. They are not only the primary mode of expression of a *poshlust'* culture; they also represent a way of thinking that creates a barrier between language and real experience. Nabokov likes to take clichés and demonstrate their limitations, at times even showing them to be fossils of some long-extinct creative thought.

Nabokov explains the purpose for creating a character whose thoughts are composed of clichés in his analysis of the Gerty MacDowell scene in *Ulysses*; here he defines what he means by "cliché, stereotype, trite pseudoelegant phrase." He says that originally, the phrase that has become a cliché had "a vivid meaning." Because it was originally an effective use of words, "the phrase was used over and over again until it became a stereotype, a cliché." What began as "vivid" and alive, has, over time, become "hackneyed" and deprived of life: "We can thus define clichés as bits of dead prose and of rotting poetry." He says that what James Joyce does in creating Gerty MacDowell is take that dead language and make it "reveal ... its live source, its primary freshness" (*LL* 346).

A stereotype is dead language, dead because it is repeatedly overused to the point where any original significance is lost. Michael Moriarty, writing on *S/Z*, explains Roland Barthes' concept of the stereotype in literature in a manner that matches Nabokov's sense: "The stereotype is by nature repetition. But the [stereotypic] text further refers to its status as a particular kind of repetition, which deepens the gap between it and any non-textual reality to which it might be held to refer. What the text copies is not reality, but other artefacts" (133).[1] The formula for the stereotype, then, is based on repetitive steps away from the original creative source. Stereotypes reproduce themselves by losing touch with "reality": a stereotypic text is one whose only context is other texts. At the same time, Nabokov argues, there is a "live source" at the incipient stage of each cliché, before it has been repeated to death.

We can see Nabokov working with clichés in an effort to reveal their live source in novels such as *The Real Life of Sebastian Knight*.[2] On the surface, this novel appears to be a type of detective novel, where the narrator, named only V., searches for clues to his half-brother's past, clues to the life of Sebastian Knight. While readers of Nabokov know that this novel is no more a simple detective story than, say, *Lolita*, the storyline never entirely abandons this first, surface level. The detective level is ever-present as a contrast to other, initially less tangible levels of narrative. In fact, Nabokov uses the idea of a detective novel to play upon structural expectations, heightening the sense of narrative unreliability by undercutting some of the clichés of that genre.

Some of these clichés center on the idea of a firm conclusion, a satisfactory solution to the detective's quest. One scene ends with a "voice in the mist," apparently preparing to tell V. some of "the real story" about his half-brother Knight (49–50). The following scene begins, "The stranger who uttered these words now approached — Oh, how I sometimes yearn for the easy swing of a well-oiled novel!" (50). Thus, the expected presence of an easy novelistic solution is undercut, and we are meant to understand that rather than a "well-oiled novel," this is one with rustier hinges. After the clichéd structure is shown to be no more than wishful thinking, a simple hope for an easy answer, Nabokov draws attention to the clichéd image by capitalizing the "Voice in the Mist" (50). Such common constructs will not work in this novel.

An experienced reader of Nabokov will not, of course, literally "expect" the cliché. Nabokov's method is to undermine the uncreative, standard sense of reality, regardless of whether or not the reader is surprised

1. The Live Source of the Cliché

by the technique. Stanley Fish writes, "Everything a reader does, even if he later undoes it, is a part of the 'meaning experience' and should not be discarded" (3–4). In this case it is the undoing itself—the collapse of the cliché—which creates the meaning. Even on a rereading, one should see that the standard structure is not where one will find the ultimate significance of this text.

Novelistic clichés are again connected to a door in this passage, where V. unsuccessfully exits without gaining any information from a hotel manager: "I ... slammed the door after me,—at least, I tried to slam it,—it was one of those confounded pneumatic doors which resist" (122). The pat finish is frustrated; even on this small scale, the expected plot is confounded. V. wishes for the quick swing of a non-pneumatic door, just as he wishes for the "easy swing of a well-oiled novel," but *Sebastian Knight* does not allow for such compact closures. These frustrated clichés are clues that this novel will resist all the efforts one might make to slam it shut with a solution.

The idea that this broken cliché concerns closure can be made more clear by comparing it to a similar moment in *Laughter in the Dark*: "Margot pushed open the door without looking round.... The door would have banged, had it not been of the reluctant, compressed-air kind" (136–7). Here there is no frustration on the part of the character. For Margot, the door can close any way it likes, and the scene is instead an example of her indifference to her surroundings. In *Sebastian Knight* the scene is presented through V.'s perspective, demonstrating his frustration. We are witness to V.'s frustration at the fact that the doors won't swing the way he wishes.

V. needs the clichés. Unlike Nabokov, his author, V. wishes the stereotypic descriptions would function as simply as they do in novels. Nabokov firmly believes stereotypes about people tend to set up too-strict expectations, not allowing for the vicissitudes of truth: "one meets now and then pale-faced butchers and forgetful elephants" ("Mr. Williams' Shakespeare" 702). In contrast, V. often seems able to understand the surrounding world only through the clichés of detective stories, in much the same way that Don Quixote tries to understand his through old stories of chivalry. In both books, a mind dependent on previous texts is shown to be one which stands a few steps away from reality.

Nabokov's Permanent Mystery

In one scene, V. tricks Madame Lecerf into revealing that she understands Russian, and his reaction parodies the dramatic, all-explaining speech a clichéd sleuth would make to provide perfect closure to a mystery. After that supposed speech, he reveals that it took place only in his mind, and that he did not make that clichéd speech at all (171). Once again, clichés are the comfortable category of V.'s mind and the level on which Nabokov ironically places the plot.[3] As in the previous examples, the reader is briefly led to accept the clichéd scene before it is revealed that what the narrator has written has only taken place in his imagination. This is the same method that W. W. Rowe sees at work in Nabokov's "honest deceptions," where "the reader is momentarily invited to believe" that some information provided is correct, then discovers it is not (Rowe, "Honesty" 173). David Packman sees a similar structure at work and connects Nabokov's "tinkering" with the detective genre to his tactic of game playing: "The writer's game involves deceiving the reader's expectations about the old form" (24). This deception, however, has a real purpose: we are first told of the cliché, then told that it did not really occur, thereby causing us to question on which level we should be reading to find the "reality" of the novel.

The cliché is an overused construct which falls flat in a creative world, like a note carried over from some previous composition. In this way "real" life is contrasted to novelistic life, showing that actual events don't fit as easily into place as they do in predictable books. Like Quixote or Joyce's Gerty MacDowell, V. views his own story as framed by stories he has read, though the reader can see that the real story of Sebastian Knight slips the standard frame.

Nabokov's use of detective story stereotypes is not simply an attempt to ridicule formulaic structures and images found in popular literature. In fact, Knight's opinion of popular detective narratives corresponds to that of Nabokov. Writing of those readers who he least respects, Knight makes clear, albeit a bit condescendingly, that he is not thinking of those who read detective stories (53). Nabokov writes, "Obvious trash, curiously enough, contains sometimes a wholesome ingredient, readily appreciated by children and simple souls" (*Gogol* 68). However, Knight and Nabokov both firmly believe that repetition deprives an idea of life. Repetition,

1. The Live Source of the Cliché

rather than any particular genre, creates the cliché. Knight believes that the "adopted method of a detective story" is equivalent to a "malodorous corpse" (89). Nabokov calls the cliché "dead prose"; Knight calls it a "malodorous corpse." Thus Knight's "detective" story, *The Prismatic Bezel*, is "not a parody of the Sherlock Holmes vogue but a parody of the modern reaction from it" (92). Like Knight, Nabokov parodies clichéd detective structures in an effort to reinvigorate the original image. His purpose is equivalent to what he sees as Joyce's purpose: to reveal the "primary freshness" of such standard structures. The "reaction," the "adopted" method, is to be avoided. Clearly, an individual work within the detective genre can be original and creative; the narratives derived from these originals, however, tend toward the lifeless, and the narratives derived from the derivatives are dead texts.

Accordingly, Nabokov argues that Cervantes' *Don Quixote* is not an attack against the institution of chivalry, in which he sees a link to "what we call democracy," or an attack against original books of chivalry, such as Malory's *Le Morte d'Arthur* (which V. finds on Knight's bookshelf). Rather, "Cervantes attacked — if he attacked anything at all — second-rate romances of chivalry" (*LDQ* 43). In regard to *Le Morte d'Arthur*, which he uses as an example of a fifteenth-century precursor to *Quixote*, Nabokov writes, "In *Don Quixote* you will easily discover parallel scenes and the same atmosphere" (46). Thus Nabokov states that Cervantes was returning to the original sources of chivalry, the original texts, and providing a critique of the romantic derivatives. Still, he says that Cervantes secretly believed "the books [of second-rate chivalry] were not worth attacking with a novel of a thousand pages" (49). And Nabokov agrees with the opinion of his version of Cervantes. Cervantes even adopts the methods of chivalric romances, Nabokov writes, to the point where he is hardly criticizing them at all. Nonetheless, the clichés of these books invade Quixote's mind to the point of madness. Nabokov discusses all of this under "Structural Matters."

Clichés seem to cling to V. almost against his will (like Quixote, like Gerty). In the scenes which undermine the clichés we can see Nabokov trying to brush them away, to work through them and attain that "live source." V. wishes he could exist in a text that worked, which would mean — for him — one in which the clichés function as they are supposed to. He does, however, realize that the clichés are failing him (unlike Quixote, unlike Gerty). V. is often frustrated by the malfunctioning clichés — the "confounded" pneumatic door, the non-existent Voice in the Mist. John Burt Foster, Jr., regarding Hermann's "trite ... fictional machinery" in *Despair*, writes that Nabokov is able to make "tired novelistic conventions gain a fresh psychological relevance ... and the reader passes abruptly from one level to the other ... in this case from the already written to the personal" (94). The same can be said of V.'s clichés in *Sebastian Knight*. What Foster calls the "already written" could be seen as a potential structural level below that of the plot, consisting solely of previous plots and repeated clichés. The malfunctioning of this "machinery" brings the written words to the personal level of the narrator. Like Alice demanding her looking-glass world conform to the regular rules of "reality," V. wishes he could rely on an easy world ruled by a law of stereotypes, a simple and predictable world, but finds that he cannot.

The following example should show how these clichés are connected to the deeper philosophy of this novel; V. uses a clichéd detective technique in attempting to trick a concierge into describing a woman for whom he has been searching, the woman who may have been Knight's last love. He asks his "informant" if the woman had dark hair; this "informant" replies in the affirmative. V.'s attempted trick is to have the man reply no and quickly offer the correct information; V. refers to this as an "old Sherlock Holmes stratagem" (151). Of course, the "stratagem" backfires; the clichéd structure of discovery is unsuccessful. Even referring to this man as his "informant" is a cliché. V. feels he should be conforming to some recalled scene in a detective novel, so he feels the need to label this concierge "informant," while in fact the man gives no information at all: V. filters the real world through his recollections of previous texts.

In this small scene the repetitive detective method, the standard structure, centers around the expectedly simple trick of revealing an identity. In the world of this novel, however, identities are never so easily revealed. The slickest detective trick will not unmask one's "real" self. In this way, the problem of clichés is connected to the problem of biography. It turns out this woman is not the clichéd "dark handsome woman" at all. Instead,

1. The Live Source of the Cliché

she is "a fat elderly woman with waved bright orange hair, purplish jowls and some dark fluff over her painted lip" (151). However unattractive, the reality is no cliché.

Adding to all this uncertainty surrounding identity, we later receive a possible hint that this woman dismissed by V. as far too ugly to have attracted Knight, Lydia Bohemsky, may have had a connection to him after all. In Knight's last book there is a "bohemian woman," perhaps referring to Bohemsky, identified by the "fast color of her cheaply dyed hair," which certainly could be Bohemsky's "bright orange." V. does not make the connection between Knight's fictional character and the woman he encountered, and the possibility that one inspired the other — in Knight's novel — is only suggested, inconclusively, by the text. Charles Nicol, however, sees more significance in the connection between these two characters, as explained in his discussion of some ways in which Knight's works seem to impinge on V.'s "real life" ("Mirrors" 92).[4] Such enigmatic "clues" pervade Nabokov's novel. This technique shows that real life identities cannot be encapsulated in a cliché.

There is a "real" and there is, at least theoretically, a way of phrasing which would express reality more adequately than the clichés. Accurate perception — detailed perception — is the appropriate method for striving to achieve the "real"; nonetheless, one cannot entirely trust a text to fix the "real" in place. At one point we are told of a bosom, a vein, and some lashes. (This is V.'s description of Madame Lecerf [166].) The bosom heaves, the vein throbs on her neck, and the lashes flutter. V. adds some parenthetical commentary as to which of these three is cliché. The heaving bosom is real, V. informs us, even though Knight once stated that such bosoms are strictly literary; the blue vein may not be real, perhaps extending too far into the realm of clichés; the fluttering lashes are left uncommented upon. While some stereotypes can be quickly dismissed as unreal, this does not mean that Nabokov has provided a simple solution to the puzzle of what is "real." Much is left up to the reader. Plus, that live source can re-enliven a cliché. Lashes can flutter, after all, and bosoms can heave.[5] In addition, the dismantling of clichés suggests that there is some unstated "real" which exists beyond the power of clichés. If the stereotype, the "trite pseudoelegant phrase," is an inadequate description of reality, there is nonetheless an implication that the "real" does exist and that a more creative aesthetic approach may come closer to it.

Madame Bovary is another example which Nabokov connects to clichés, as he describes Flaubert's strategy for creating her character by listing all of her favorite "romantic clichés": "his cunning choice of these cheap images and their cadenced arrangement along the curving phrase produce an effect of harmony and art" (*LL* 138). Even someone whose innermost soul is composed of "cheap images" can be portrayed sympathetically by the author. Madame Bovary may view her world through received romantic clichés, but her "heart" is no less real. Nabokov does something similar in his depiction of Lolita, where clichés — as in *Sebastian Knight*— are contrasted to "real life."

The Real Life of Lolita

Nabokov insists that the "dead and rotten stuff" of trite phrases and stereotypes have a "live source," a "primary freshness" at their inception. Repetition of a phrase creates a dead aesthetic; originality of expression is a necessary ingredient of art. In *Lolita*, Nabokov keeps in mind the "live source" for words which have, through repeated use, become dead expressions, clichés. At one point, Humbert depicts the sense of the "live source" which is obscured by the repeated cliché: he explains that he had always believed "wringing one's hands" was something people only did in fiction; however, he discovers that this is precisely what he feels like doing (83). This baroque sentence — all fifty-six words of it — provides a rather roundabout method of stating, simply, that he felt like wringing his hands. To have stated that idea as directly as possible, however, would have been to rely on an overused, clichéd expression. This passage reinvigorates the cliché by returning it to its live, human source: "wringing one's hands" is not merely a gesture found in fiction and detached from reality. The cliché is a mindless application of an overused expression. Humbert here insists that the expression has a real source, and thereby resuscitates a dead phrase. On a higher structural level, Nabokov brings Humbert to life by bringing the phrase back to life, by reattaching the words to a live source. That is,

1. The Live Source of the Cliché

on one level, Humbert brings the cliché to life; on another, Nabokov brings Humbert to life through the enlivened cliché.

There are more examples of the use of clichés in *Lolita*. I will show some additional ways in which Humbert's use of clichés coincides with that of Nabokov before contemplating the significance of clichés for the conclusion of this novel. It is only in the conclusion that Humbert sees through his frame of clichés and catches a glimpse of the real life of Lolita.

After marrying Humbert, Charlotte insists upon hearing about all of his past romances. Humbert states that he fabricated a past that followed the standards of American advertising, where clichéd scenes are set up to satisfy the consumer: "So I presented my women ... the languorous blond, the fiery brunette, the sensual copperhead..." (79–80). To satisfy his bride, Humbert comprises his past of the expected clichés. Mrs. Humbert does the same, though with a distinct difference: her clichés are not fictional concoctions, but true confessions. Humbert tells us that she described her "love-life" with "sincerity and artlessness." The interesting point, though, is that the history she retells is interchangeable — on the surface, that is, in the words, images, and characters — from the false history that Humbert concocts. Both find their material in the expected sources of popular culture. While the two may seem strikingly similar, the history that she tells differs "ethically" from Humbert's stories (80). Appropriately, Humbert's mention of ethics has to do with the ethics of expression, rather than ethical behavior. He obviously does not condemn Charlotte for this "love-life" (a term that is set apart as a cliché with quote marks — not a word that Humbert would use without irony), but he does specifically state that his composition of clichés, while made up of the exact same material as hers, has a distinct ethical difference. Humbert collects the clichés and gives them life; Charlotte, in contrast, uses the lifeless clichés to explain her real life. As Humbert says, "Her autobiography was as devoid of interest as her autopsy would have been." Thus it is a more ethical mode of expression to give fictional life to overused phrases than to use such moribund phrases to explain one's real life. Creating from clichés is an ethical act, whereas substituting clichés for reality is not.

Clichés, however, are one of the means by which Humbert obscures the presence of the real Lolita in the text (and in his mind). One might even argue that the character of Lolita is composed of the clichés of mid-twentieth century American girlhood. At moments when his lust is at an ebb, Humbert refers to her as a "disgustingly conventional little girl" (148). Edmund Wilson, for one, specifically critiqued the book on the grounds of the believability of Lolita: "The little girl ... seems ... rather implausible to me" (*Nabokov-Wilson* 287). Though she is clearly a distinct character from the rest of her classmates and the other children in the book, to Humbert's mind she is a definite product of her culture: "She it was to whom ads were dedicated: the ideal consumer, the subject and object of every foul poster" (148). Humbert sees her as a very average little girl and, therefore, portrays her as a rather mediocre-minded and not especially interesting person: "my conventional Lolita" (287). He criticizes her for liking musicals, that "grief-proof sphere of existence wherefrom death and truth were banned," as though it is incomprehensible why she should want some form of escapist entertainment (170). Humbert, who has virtually no empathy, simply portrays her as the average result of her environment. Nabokov, on the other hand, does not believe in averages, that "tissue of statistics" (*LDQ* 1). The structural emphasis on the narrator might explain why a reader like Wilson would find Lolita "implausible": Humbert allows her very little life. However, study of the novel's overall literary structure reveals that Lolita only appears to be composed of clichés because Humbert is not able to recognize the real life of Lolita, until — perhaps — the end of his narrative.

By reducing Lolita to a simple reflection of her culture, Humbert is violating Nabokovian metaphysics and aesthetics. Unlike Humbert, Nabokov believes that no human being can be considered solely a product of his or her culture; according to Nabokov, a human being has an "essentially human urge to reshape the earth": "unless he is a born Marxist or a corpse and meekly waits for the environment to fashion *him*" (*SM* 302). The Marxist and the corpse lose the essence of what it means to be human. Nabokov's stance is consistent: if one believes that the material level dominates human life, then aesthetics will be reduced to the standard material of clichés and people will be devoid of any essence which differentiates them from their surroundings. Real life is a quality that is separate from one's environment, according to Nabokov; he states that there are three

1. The Live Source of the Cliché

influences in the formation of each person: "heredity, environment, and the unknown agent X." He says that environment is the least influential, and that the last one — that mysterious and indefinable force that he has labeled "agent X" — is "by far the most influential" (*LL* 126). The force which originates a real life is essentially mysterious. Humbert is unable to appreciate the presence of this mysterious "agent X" in Lolita, and thereby reduces his sense of her to the level of cliché.

Toward the end of *Lolita*, however, there are some passages where Humbert seems to recall that there was a real girl obscured by the clichés. He remembers a moment when he realized that he "simply did not know a thing about my darling's mind." His sense that there is a real Lolita, beyond his controlling and limiting definitions of her, is a sense that she transcends clichés: "behind the awful juvenile clichés, there was in her a garden and a twilight." He also senses that these terms — "garden" and "twilight" — are inadequate, that they do not convey anything of the real little girl, because those "regions ... happened to be lucidly and absolutely forbidden to me" (284). Beyond the clichés there is an original life, a live source. Notably, Humbert does not use the name "Lolita" during this moment of understanding. The word "lucidly" in this passage means "translucently": the idea that the source of Lolita's real life is "lucidly ... forbidden" to him means that he can undoubtedly perceive the existence of that light, but cannot fully capture it. This is the nature of the butterfly of light, the celestial essence, and Humbert, towards the end of the novel, does seem to sense this presence.

Another example of Humbert's minimal ability to perceive the "real" Lolita, from the same chapter, involves Lolita asking where her "murdered mummy" is buried. Humbert tells her that she already knows where the grave is, and adds, "If you really wish to triumph in your mind over the idea of death —" The sentence ends there, with Lolita leaving the room. Just as Nabokov refuses to explicate his metaphysical ideas, Humbert here does not go on to explain exactly how one might triumph over the "idea of death." This is not to say, however, that Nabokov simply uses Humbert as a puppet for his own metaphysics, for his sense that the ultimate answer is beyond words. While this sentence is left open-ended in exactly the same way that Nabokov leaves metaphysical thoughts open-ended elsewhere (*Invitation*'s "there is amongst us a —," Sebastian Knight's unrevealed last word, Nabokov's "I know more than I can express in words"), all evidence suggests that Humbert's sense of how that sentence might continue would not coincide with that of Nabokov. Is he going to tell Lolita that if she wishes to triumph in her mind over the idea of death she must find a sexual obsession which creates the illusion of transcended time? Nabokov almost gives Humbert a Nabokovian metaphysical device, but Humbert always veers at least a degree in the wrong direction.

Significantly, however, this scene ends with Humbert attaining something of a revelation by looking at the book that Lolita had been reading. He states that it was "trash." Though he relegates Lolita's literature to the realm of cliché, the passage he reads demonstrates that the breaking of a cliché is crucial to the text's effectiveness. The book presents an unhappy girl protagonist and "her stepmother"; this stepmother breaks the clichés of literary stepmothers by turning out to be "against all expectations, a young, gay, understanding redhead" (286–287). Of course, the stereotyped stepmother, as in the Cinderella story (often referred to in *Pnin*), is a dark woman who is cruel to the adopted daughter.[6] The shattering of this cliché—this breaking of expectations—prompts a real reaction from Lolita, real thoughts about her own deceased mother. The stepmother is never supposed to be a "young, gay, understanding redhead," and Lolita is never supposed to have real thoughts of her own. Humbert is forced to recognize that there is something in Lolita that lives beyond the clichés with which he has limited his view of her. (Also, while Humbert dismisses this book as "trash," we should recall that Nabokov says that in "obvious trash" one can often discover a "wholesome ingredient, readily appreciated by children" [*Gogol* 68].) Earlier, in the "palace gate" example, Humbert could fleetingly recognize that there was something to Lolita that was obstructed from his view because of his lust. Thus, the breaking of stereotypical expectations is representative of Lolita breaking away from the cage of clichés in which Humbert has framed her. She slips beyond his perception and remains untrapped by his controlling prose.

Structurally, the lowest level—a world composed of clichés—is revealed to be insufficient to contain real life, and through this revelation one is at least able to perceive the presence of a higher level—the level of

1. The Live Source of the Cliché

real life, the live source. Humbert catches a couple of glimpses of the real life of Lolita through the bars of his cage. The real life of another is always only glimpsed. We learn, however, that stepmothers can be young, good-natured and thoughtful, and Lolitas can have thoughts which are beyond the grasp of Humberts.

This idea shows another important difference between Nabokov and Humbert in regard to metaphysics and clichés. Though both believe that clichés have a live source as methods of expression, Nabokov thinks of the cliché as an aesthetic failure, and therefore a failure of original thought. In *Sebastian Knight* the fumbling narrator often expects the predictable cliché to proceed as planned. The same is true for Humbert, who, at least in regard to Lolita, tends to expect nothing more than the cliché. Prompted by her reading about the red-headed stepmother, Lolita has broken Humbert's expectations, and thereby revealed something of herself, or at least revealed that she has something which escapes Humbert's best attempts at solipsizing her.

As far as the chronology of the storyline, these realizations occur long before the point at which Humbert places them in the text.[7] Humbert thus creates the illusion of a realization by placing the moments when he claims to have caught glimpses of the real Lolita toward the end of his text. What appear to be the final moments of the novel actually come much earlier in the course of events. However, the use of illusion and deception, in Nabokov's worldview, is not a reason to reject Humbert's claim: an appreciation of illusion may actually be an insight. Nabokov believes that deception lies at the heart of nature and art: "all art is deception and so is nature; all is deception in that good cheat..." (*SO* 11). Perhaps it took Humbert most of the fifty-six days of writing his text for him to understand this idea, to understand that Lolita did have a hidden real life, beyond the cultural camouflage of clichés. Cincinnatus writes in his cell, Fyodor of *The Gift* enclosed in the exile of his little room, Kinbote alone in his motel room, Humbert in his mental ward, and Nabokov — composing *Sebastian Knight*— "on the implement called *bidet* as a writing desk — because we lived in one room and I had to use our small bathroom as a study": the romantic ideal of the solitary artist seems to be one of Nabokov's guiding principles (*Nabokov-Wilson* 51). He believes that the act of isolated writing can lead to personal insights.

Where Humbert's realizations occur in "real" time is less relevant than the fact that they exist at all. This alone does not make for the "moral apotheosis" that John Ray Jr. attributes to Humbert in the foreword. But within these descriptions Humbert does see through the clichés, at least achieving a minimal recognition that there is a real Lolita. To create the reunion scene with Dolly Schiller, Humbert must build on this sense of the real person who he has named Lolita, or what he calls "the signs made to me by something in Lolita — the real child Lolita" (125).

Breaking Clichéd Structures

This concept of the "real" Lolita — beyond the clichés — is therefore structurally relevant to the manner in which this novel concludes. The final pages of *Lolita* are structurally consistent with Nabokov's other conclusions: they represent a new level of reality, prompted by Humbert's imagined attempt at redemption, as he sits in the seclusion of his mental ward. Scholars of Nabokov have engaged in much debate about the dates of *Lolita* and just how "real" the concluding pages are as compared with the rest of the text (more on that in the next chapter). Although Boyd disagrees with the idea that the ending of *Lolita* is less real — more based on imagination — than the rest of the text, he notes in his biography that "the device of the false continuation" is one which Nabokov used in even his earliest work, calling it "a Nabokov hallmark." This device "fashions the end of a story as a trapdoor dropping us from one plane of being to another" (*Russian Years* 232). Nabokov moves the narrative to a different level in these scenes, creating a fantasy conclusion, an ending which cannot be called "real" in the same way that the rest of the novel is "real."

In this way the idea of breaking through clichés to reach the real is built into the structure of the novel: the clichés around Lolita accumulate until the conclusion, where they are at last shattered. Alfred Appel, Jr., writes that "the simplicity of *Lolita*'s 'story,' such as it is — 'plot,' in the conventional sense, may be paraphrased in three sentences" (*Annotated* 346). But here we see that plot, in a less conventional sense, extends into the realm of metaphysics. These clichés, one of the devices which motivate

1. The Live Source of the Cliché

Nabokov's plot, can be read on *every* level of the literary structure. In his final scene with Dolly Schiller, Humbert's imagination has broken through the clichéd expectations of a three-sentence plot.

One person who would disagree with such an interpretation of this scene is Michael Wood. Wood writes of this reunion scene, "Humbert seems to glimpse the attraction of the acceptable and the familiar, of the way other people daily talk and live — the realm of shared feeling which inhabits cliché, and which cliché serves" (142). This is a misreading of Nabokov's sense of cliché. Nabokov never argues that "the acceptable and the familiar" are an ideal for which one should strive. Clichés, to Nabokov, are not a realm of "shared feeling," but an overly repeated mode of expression that has lost contact with all real feeling. Clichés are the realm of a shared absence of feeling. Nabokov never portrays common perception, or its mate, common expression, as enviable. Rather it is the shattering of the commonplace through the strength of an original imagination, and the coinciding breaking of clichés to get through to the "live source" of artistic and metaphysical insight, that Nabokov believes to be the highest possible achievement.

Nonetheless, he seems almost as interested in those stranded at the aesthetic level of clichés as he is in those who break them. He describes his earliest efforts at writing as a battle with clichés — specifically a clichéd structure or "frame." In *Speak, Memory*, he writes of the primary problem he encountered while writing his earliest poetry: "The frame impelled the picture, the husk shaped the pulp" (*SM* 221). Even here, when he considered himself "an innocent beginner," he writes of structure and content as inextricably bound together: "The hackneyed order of words ... engendered the hackneyed disorder of thought." He uses the same word, "hackneyed," to link directly the problems of structure to the problems of content, the poor order of words on the page to the disorder of thought. The problem was, he explains, that his own hackneyed structure would force a particular, much-overused rhyme at the end of a line. The word "engendered" also emphasizes the absolute link, the symbiotic relationship, between structure and content. The "hackneyed" husk demanded an unoriginal pulp; the clichéd frame forced an inappropriate picture. Part of Nabokov's growth as a writer involves his creating less and less clichéd frames for his work, culminating—structurally—with *Pale Fire*, which is the furthest from a clichéd frame. A major part of Nabokov's growth as a writer involves his gaining control over the frames.

Nabokov ends the paragraph in *Speak, Memory* that begins with his discussion of his earliest writing and his struggle with "hackneyed" frames with the image of a "paling" from a circus which he saw years afterward. He describes the fence as having various animals painted on it "by a versatile barker," but the fence had been reconstructed in a way that created "disjointed" animals (221). Here Nabokov is making an analogy between his first, unsuccessful attempts at writing and a literal structure, a fence, the pieces of which have been poorly assembled. Nabokov compares the process of a young writer struggling to find a personal voice to the process of rebuilding a fence with borrowed boards. What is especially interesting about this image is not the fact that as a beginner his poetry turned out "disjointed," constructed from the reused parts of previous poets (that, after all, may be typical of a first-time poet), but that the implied structure which should have been attained, and wasn't, did exist. In some sense the proper construction of the poem, just as the proper placement of the fence's boards, was conceivable, even though the young Nabokov found himself unable to put this conception into words. He felt it was necessary to find a unique structure capable of framing his already present, though as yet unexpressed, unique artistic vision.

This image of the fence from *Speak, Memory* suggests that not only words and images preexist, but an entire idea of structure preexists as well. Attributing the painted animals to a "versatile barker" also shows that the creative realm, from which even this fence comes, necessarily involves the imagination: the painting on the fence could as easily have been made by a creative clown or a talented acrobat. Nabokov always stresses the agent of any created work, though the actual agent here, as often, can only be imagined. Additionally, the misplaced palings suggest the possibility of a more perfect structure. Just as that fence should have been put together a certain way, to bring the pictured animals into alignment, Nabokov sensed that there was a correct imaginative pattern for his own work. He only needed to restructure the boards the right way to attain the desired artistic effect.

1. The Live Source of the Cliché

The protagonist of *The Gift*, Fyodor, describes this same "remarkable fence" and directly connects its "senseless order" to a metaphysical message. His assessment of this fence is: "life's promise of a life to come had been kept with respect to the fence, but the rupture of the earthly images on it destroyed the earthly value of immortality" (176). Thus, because these circus images were rendered unintelligible by their "senseless" arrangement, their metaphysical message had become meaningless, or at least the "earthly" value of that metaphysical message had become meaningless. Fyodor further complicates this image by describing "the shadows of leaves" that one can see on this fence at night; in contrast to the convoluted animals of the daytime, these leaves are "in perfect order." Thus, he makes this structure more complex by adding another dimension — a "perfect" dimension. Fyodor and Nabokov not only share this fence, they also share a sense of structure. Fyodor says in regard to one story, "[T]he mere presence of such a suspiciously neat structure ... would never have permitted me to make it into a short story or a novel" (42–43).

Nabokov's ethical use of clichés, the breaking of expected reading patterns, is central to his sense of structure. He is well aware that some readers will begin *Lolita* with the expectation of finding plain pornography (that is, a book whose primary purpose is erotic titillation rather than aesthetic or metaphysical significance). In his afterword to the novel, Nabokov discusses the expectations of a typical reader of pornography, the expectation for standard pornographic clichés in order to achieve "simple sexual stimulation." He then connects this expectation of clichés to the idea of a clichéd literary structure, saying that in pornographic fiction "action has to be limited to the copulation of clichés. Style, structure, imagery should never distract the reader..." (313). Here as elsewhere he stresses that a creative "structure" is essential to his sense of worthwhile literature. In Nabokov's view of stereotypic pornography it is the dead phrases themselves which copulate, creating a sort of narrative necrophilia. His criticism of pornography has nothing to do with content, but with clichéd methods of expression and, as inevitably follows, clichéd literary structures. Such pornography is not immoral because it depicts sexual situations; it is immoral because it lacks all originality.

Nabokov specifically mentions two aspects of uncreative pornographic structures: the transitions between scenes and the "crescendo line" leading to the conclusion. Both of these aspects of structure are precisely the opposite of Nabokov's structures. He describes the transitions between the scenes in standard pornography: "logical bridges of the simplest design, brief expositions and explanations, which the reader will probably skip…" (313). This type of reading is in exact opposition to Nabokov's sense of structure, where the transitions between scenes are much more than "logical bridges of the simplest design" linking each point of the story. A Nabokovian plot is never a straight line, and one must appreciate the zig-zag sidetracks to appreciate his art.

In his lectures, Nabokov points out Tolstoy's blunt transitions and Flaubert's more fluid movement between scenes. Transitions are crucial to his general sense of literary structure. The transitions between scenes in typical pornography, however, are the most minimal acknowledgment that, for the story to seem "true," one needs some sort of transitions. Nabokov, on the other hand, selects these moments between the more overt points of the story for "special delectation," stating that one such scene took him an entire month to write (316). In striving for timelessness, Nabokov believes that the steady progression of a storyline means nothing alongside such frozen moments of artistic truth.

The second structural point in which Nabokov tells us *Lolita* differs from the clichés of modern pornography is in the conclusion. He critiques the stereotypical pornographic structure which steadily introduces "new variations, new combinations, new sexes" as the plot moves toward the conclusion. The final chapters, he says, must have more and more sex, much more than in the opening chapters. In contrast, the structure of *Lolita* leads toward Humbert's attempt for imaginative redemption, rather than a final erotic fulfillment. Instead of a clichéd crescendo, we have Humbert's gradual descent, followed by his private effort to salvage something through art. Thus Nabokov's novel is structurally antithetical to his sense of standard pornography. He specifically states that the accumulation of clichés will only lead one to a clichéd conclusion. In contrast, neither clichés or standard conclusions are part of Nabokov's created worlds.

Nabokov breaks the clichés in order to show that there are no easy answers. The slammed-door solution to the expected detective novel does

1. The Live Source of the Cliché

not work; the attempt to understand someone through the accumulated clichés of their culture will not suffice. Real life is always more complex, more rewarding, and — like Nabokov's novels — never reducible to a single solution. Clichés — expected modes of expression — may be the opposite of Nabokov's ideal of mystery; therefore, he plays with them and interrogates them in order to show that there is something much more in life than that which can be contained in average language.

Chapter 2

Time Frames

Frames and Dates in Speak, Memory

Another plot device which Nabokov uses to comment on mundane concepts of "reality"—comparable to his use of clichés—is an ironic reliance on dates. The opening sentence of *Sebastian Knight* contains one example, with the date of Knight's birth announced as the final day of 1899. Here there is an especially remarkable date without any special mention. Nabokov uses this same method to highlight dates in *The Gift* (April 1) and *Lolita* (July 4, December 25) and elsewhere. He often refers to time ironically, highlighting the idea that dates—like clichés—are another misguided means for measuring real life.

A reader of *Speak, Memory*, however, might argue that Nabokov does place a great emphasis on dates, that he does value precise chronology. The changes which Nabokov made between the earlier version of his autobiography, *Conclusive Evidence*, and *Speak, Memory*, show a close, though not clearly methodical, attention to dates. Whereas *Conclusive Evidence* dates one event on "that twenty-first of July, 1902," *Speak, Memory* revises the recollection to "that August day 1903" (*CE* 4; *SM* 22). A trip in *Conclusive Evidence* inconclusively takes place "in 1903, I think," but Nabokov seems more certain in *Speak, Memory*, dating the same trip "in the fall of 1903" (*CE* 6; *SM* 24). Other date changes are scattered throughout the two books (though primarily in the earlier chapters): "autumn, 1910" becomes "August 1910"; "part of the winter of 1907" becomes "part of the winter of 1907–1908" (*CE* 143, 109; *SM* 204, 157). There is, as I said, no apparent method to these changes: some dates become more specific, some less; some change years, others months or seasons. Nabokov may even show some self-mockery about his great concern over the details of dates:

2. Time Frames

the plain "well into August" of *Conclusive Evidence* becomes in *Speak, Memory* "August — August 9, 1915, to be Petrarchally exact, at half past four of that season's fairest afternoon" (*CE* 167; *SM* 230). Nabokov seems almost overly concerned with delineating these dates. Despite this concern, none of the changes has any substantial effect on the autobiography. In fact, the many insubstantial changes may only result — whether intentionally or not — in raising doubts about the validity of any of the dates.

While one structural purpose of *Speak, Memory* is "to fix correctly, in terms of time," (25) the early events of his life, Nabokov also writes, "I do not believe in time" (139). *Sebastian Knight* and *Speak, Memory* both develop a structural contrast between creative time and clock time. In the novel, V. believes in standard measurements of time, whereas Sebastian Knight tends towards timelessness.[1] The purpose for creating such a contrast may be to raise the metaphysical question of where "real life" resides.

The point is not that one sense of time is "real" and the other is not, only that one — clock time, dates, the outward frame — is limiting if it is taken to be a final determinant of what is "real." V. is not entirely wrong, after all, to believe in time. Michael Wood writes, "Time, we might say, doesn't care whether we believe in it or not, doesn't depend on our belief" (83). V. is not wrong to believe in time, but he is wrong to believe in it all the time. Wood sees a movement in *Speak, Memory* which applies equally to *Sebastian Knight*: "the voice saying it doesn't believe in time is harshly and awkwardly caught between time's brilliant but momentary abolition and its imminent and inevitable return" (84). This is the cause of the "doubts" which Wood attributes to the "magician." The transcendent sense is always threatened with an imminent return to earth. Time can be imaginatively transcended, but not permanently. The difference between the structures of *Speak, Memory* and *Sebastian Knight* is that the voice is split in the novel, so that abolished time, creativity, tends to be the voice of Sebastian Knight, and time's return is most often voiced by V. In *Speak, Memory* both aspects of the voice belong to Nabokov, hence the seeming contradiction as to whether his purpose is to situate himself "in terms of time" or to demonstrate that he does not "believe in time."

The time frame of past events, however, is only one type of frame that catches the attention of Nabokov. Many other types of frames are present in *Speak, Memory*, and taken together, these frames extend the structural significance of the idea of a "frame" to include many kinds of material settings. A close look at the other framing devices in the autobiography can shed further light on Nabokov's philosophy. All of these frames have a structural and metaphysical significance. First, there are literal frames: "oval frames," "empty frames" and one "fancy frame" (236, 235, 108).[2] The "colored panes" through which young Nabokov looks to see the world vividly tinted are "inset in a whitewashed frame" (106). More pertinent to the topic of dates are the framed historical moments (23, 295). Both of these examples relate "frames" to periods of history.

Nabokov's autobiography is full of frames. A frame may also be one's body, as when a mother uses her hand "to propel one's reluctant frame" (83). Like one's material body, by extension, a present setting, in this case Cambridge, can form the outward frame of a hidden interior life: "...Cambridge and all its famed features ... existed merely to frame and support my rich nostalgia" (261). No matter how "famed" the features, they are only the "frame" for private thoughts. Therefore, "real life" is not defined by these frames. Frames are merely one's solid surroundings: one's history, body, or locale. They are only the outward setting of one's "real life."

Frames represent all sorts of necessary containers, structures, which are often contrasted to less tangible, less measurable qualities. "Note the frames, the receptacles," Van Veen writes in *The Texture of Time* (*Ada* 540). Nabokov most often notes the frames in order to highlight by contrast that which is contained in them. The frames are necessary, though not essential.

In *Conclusive Evidence*, Nabokov describes the "dim little photographs" which his mother kept in "disintegrating frames" (28). In *Speak, Memory* the "disintegrating frames" become "crumbling frames" and are placed next to "émigré writers' books, so prone to disintegration in their cheap paper covers" (49). However, his mother's crumbling frames — and one should think of the many possible meanings of that word — do not represent a loss of memory, a loss of the past. Although these tangible objects — books in crumbling covers, photographs in disintegrating frames — are incapable of permanently recapturing the past, this did not matter because her "soul" was the true and ineradicable dwelling place of that past: "nothing had been lost." One might also make the conjecture that perhaps the "soul" will not be lost once the many frames have finally disintegrated. *Speak, Memory* shows us that real life exists beyond the frames.

Chronometric Concepts in Sebastian Knight

Dates are also a misguided means for measuring real life in *Sebastian Knight*. As with the use of clichés, this is a plot device which the narrator, V., uses for different purposes than the author, Nabokov, and their differing—even opposing—reasons for using dates highlights a major contrast between narrator and author.

Throughout the novel, V. orients himself, and his version of Knight's life, with definite dates. Clearly, this is a standard technique for anyone writing a biography. V. uses dates as biographical grounding, as firm facts on which he can base his narrative. Nabokov, however, uses the same dates to create an ironic contrast between such a handy factual device and a more imaginative, less time-centered sense of reality. The result is that dates turn out to be two-dimensional measurements of a multi-dimensional world.

Nabokov juxtaposes the seeming solidity of dates with endless stretches of the imagination. V., however, firmly feels that dates can help create an apt frame for his version of Sebastian Knight's "real life." He does not go overboard with his reliance on dates, like Mr. Goodman (Knight's other biographer), who believes that all of Knight's thoughts can be reduced to the ideas of his era, his "generation." V.'s use of dates does not quite reach the point of clichéd generalities. Still, his more typical belief that calendars can successfully measure a life is juxtaposed to Nabokov's sense of the immeasurability of one man's imagination.

In regard to Mr. Goodman's concept of time, V. explains that his goal is to describe his pitiable subject, Sebastian Knight, as "a product and victim" of their era. V. then wonders why such biographers are so desirous of having readers—and subjects—suit their "chronometric concepts" (60). Here V.'s ideas are in agreement with those of Nabokov, who stands firmly opposed to the idea that one is entirely created by one's environment, by one's time. V.'s "chronometric concepts" are less stereotyped than those of Goodman, but still they do not coincide with Knight's concepts. V. often starts a chapter by situating his subject "chronometrically." That is, a chapter will begin with a particular date (22, 119); other chronological situating techniques place one event in regard to another, and these statements are also often found at the start of a chapter (69, 31). Structurally, these statements create apparently solid, logical starting points for a narrative which turns out to be anything but direct or linear.

V. also makes certain to supply the dates, as accurately as he can, of both the publication and the production of all of Sebastian Knight's books, and a reader might be tempted to skip over the precise record of a fictional author's books. Nothing significant about *Sebastian Knight* would change if all of the dates were altered. Regarding the dates of Knight's vacation to Germany, V. even presents possible dates of which he is not certain (62). Here, too, a reader might not pay much attention to the question of which year — if either — is the correct one. The actual point of such passages is not the exact date on which Knight wrote or published any particular book or took a particular trip. The real purpose for presenting these dates is to show V.'s typical attempts to present the life of someone now deceased. Like any good biographer, V. is attempting to grasp something retrievable from the intangible past. He does not realize that real life is not retrieved by a recitation of dates.

The use of dates in *Sebastian Knight* also makes for some clunky transitions between chapters and paragraphs. The abrupt transitions from creative samples of Knight's prose to the factual data of V.'s quest add to the sense that V. is stumbling about with limited vision. V. is intimately caught in a zig-zag atmosphere while wishing for a linear solution. Knight's mind is attracted to such imaginative reversals as this: "physical growth considered upside down as the lengthening of a suspended drop; at last falling into nothing" (175). V., however, while often attempting to demonstrate that he appreciates Knight's art, seems to feel that it is important to know on what date this line was written. Nabokov uses the contrast of these two characters to create a sort of bas-relief: V.'s frame of dates sets off the multi-leveled, multiply contoured mind of Knight; Knight's creative insights show the flat limitations of V.'s more temporal methods.

2. *Time Frames*

Ultimately, as it becomes clear that Knight's mind is the more complex, and comes closer to Nabokov's thoughts (who also appreciates reversals: "The plump, soft particles of snow rustled against the windowpanes, falling, falling without end. If one watched them for long, one had the impression the entire hotel was slowly drifting upward" ("Wingstroke," *Stories* 33), the novel's apparent emphasis on dates becomes more obviously ironic. Knight (with Nabokov) appreciates the Russian Formalist technique of "making strange"; the thoroughly earth-bound V. is much more interested in trying to "make familiar."

The transitions, once again, often lead the reader to proceed bumpily between narrative levels. This ungraceful sort of transition, however, is ungraceful in a different way than, say, those of Tolstoy, who, according to Nabokov, "used any old kind of transition" (*LRL* 198). Rather, these transitions show V. trying vigorously to hold the prose to a proper time frame, trying to situate himself. V. tries to keep his feet set firmly on dates because of the difficulty he has in grounding Knight's soaring thoughts (or, in reverse, V. is a suspended drop in fear of falling into an uncontrolled realm of imaginative timelessness).[3] Meanwhile, the reader rises along the written inspiration of Knight, only to clunk back down to V. and a date.

V., in contrast, would not like to admit to the dissolubility of dates, the breakdown of frames. This inability to relinquish linear measurements, like an inability to look beyond the simplest concept of plot, restrains him from actually recapturing the spirit of the past.

The Debated Dates of Lolita

Nabokov does pay great attention to dates, although his reasons for doing so might not be what they initially appear to be. The dates of *Lolita* are a topic that has already received much attention. Christina Tekiner, in her essay "Time in *Lolita*," was among the first to take seriously the idea that the dates of Humbert's narrative do not add up. Specifically, Humbert reports that it took him "fifty-six days" to write *Lolita*. He supposedly received the letters from John Farlow and "Mrs. Richard F. Schiller" (aka Lolita) on September 22. Finally, John Ray, Jr., reports in his foreword that the date of Humbert's death was "November 16, 1952," exactly fifty-six days from September 22. While one might argue that Humbert's calculations could be off by a few days, Nabokov's numbers are perfectly chosen to suggest the possibility that from the moment Humbert receives those two letters, all of his final fifty-six days are spent writing in, first, "the psychopathic ward," then, in what he calls "this heated, albeit tombal, seclusion" (308). In effect, this detaches the conclusion from the rest of the narrative.

Tekiner writes, "If the chronology is correct, then it implies that the events which Humbert claims had occurred prior to September 22 have some basis in the 'reality' of his life, but the events which he tells us occurred after September 22 are his fabrication" (466). While some readers have chosen to resolve this mystery, others have chosen simply to read it away, as though these precise numbers were an error in the text. Nonetheless, the chronology is there as one of the clearly stated facts of this imagined world. There is nothing in the text to tell us these numbers are *not* correct.

The second volume of *Nabokov Studies* includes three essays which debate the significance of these dates. The first two, by Alexander Dolinin and Julian Connolly, explore some of the possibilities invoked by these dates. The third, by Brian Boyd, argues that these dates are actually a mistake by Nabokov and should not even be considered in one's reading of the novel. Boyd suggests,

> [Nabokov] — or the typesetter — put "November 16" rather than the intended "November 19" for Humbert's death, making no more than the very common slip of 6 for 9. If the text now read "November 19," the argument for Humbert's having invented the last fifty pages of *Lolita* would immediately collapse. Surely it is too much to base a major reinterpretation of a novel on a single typographical character? [76].

Boyd attempts to defend the text against any interpretation of those dates as they are written. He calls those who pursue the significance of these dates "revisionists," while basing his defense on what he labels as "one revisable digit" (80, 86). The dates as they stand in the text lend themselves to a potentially rich and unexpected reading which emphasizes Humbert's imaginative abilities and, perhaps, his attempt to absolve himself, as much as possible, through art. I believe, along with Dolinin and Connolly, that

2. *Time Frames*

the significance of the dates should be considered. I also want to emphasize that these dates add an additional complexity to the text, not a solution.

One might also note that Humbert's thoughts about Lolita which move beyond the clichés, discussed in the previous chapter, occur within that time period of the novel that is in question. At what level of reality should those thoughts be understood? Perhaps one should understand them as taking place within a realm that is not defined by standard time, a place where Humbert is able to think beyond the bars of his cage. Perhaps. That is only one approach to this topic, one angle for understanding this issue.

Many readers have found Humbert's meeting with the pregnant Dolly Schiller, his last moments with the older (though only seventeen) Lolita, to provide the most poignant scene of the novel. A reader who is truly moved by this scene, or one who feels it is crucial to the conclusion of the storyline, may feel defensive about the idea that the reunion never takes place, that Humbert fabricates the entire scene. Julian Connolly writes that "the greatest objection to the theory that Humbert has invented his reunion with Dolly ... may lie in the fact that ... the reader would lose the certainty of the discovery that Dolly has emerged as a plucky survivor." He states, "Humbert's invention might seem less satisfying to the reader than a 'real' encounter with a more mature Dolly" ("Nature's Reality" 44). One can understand a reader reacting defensively to the idea that the conclusion of this novel is not "real" in the same way as the rest of the text, but that reader certainly does not wish this scene to be real any more than does Humbert himself. That is, one's insistence that the scene *does* occur, that it is a *real* aspect of Humbert's experience, might place one directly in the position of Humbert. No longer is there a tension between Humbert's desire and the reader's own wishes. By this point, most readers have unexpectedly found themselves coinciding with Humbert's manipulative mind, thoroughly buying into his fabrication, his illusion.

A reader's wish for a scene to be "real" is antagonistic to Nabokov's sense of fiction. Humbert here has reached a point where he is able to imagine the real life of Lolita, or at least a real life of Lolita, and imagination is the key to salvation within Nabokov's metaphysics. The pages represent the peak of Humbert's creativity and perhaps (only perhaps) a final positive transformation of his disturbed character. Humbert's artistic imagination builds on the mere glimpse he had attained of Lolita's real life, the sense that there was a private garden beyond the clichés, and he has created a plausible Dolores. This Dolores is purely the work of Humbert's imagination. The narrative, therefore, creates a relatively smooth transition from memory to imagination, the two of which are intimately linked in Nabokov's view: "both memory and imagination are a negation of time" (*SO* 78).

Time does not contain the experience of real life. In the short story "Spring in Fialta," Nabokov suggests that a "life story" might be limited "to the dash between two dates" (*Stories* 416). That "dash" (both a hyphen and a quick sprint) might signify the totality of a life, but it does not reveal much about the deceased individual. The significance of "real life" is beyond those who are too focused on the frames, the external settings. Nabokov uses dates and other external frames to suggest an added complexity that is beyond those dates and frames, something less tangible. Those external frames of the present — that tangible reality — may even be less real than the realm of imagination. Nabokov shows this in his first novel, *Mary*, where Ganin's present life is presented as a dream and his "real life" is only in his memory: "the ghosts of his dream-life in exile ... would talk about his real life — about Mary" (52). Dates and other elements of tangible reality are the firm ground from which Nabokov can make imaginative leaps to a more compelling place.

Chapter 3

The Return Structure

The Metaphysical About-Face

From his first novel, *Mary*, Nabokov shows a great interest in the individual's relation to the past. Specifically, he is interested in characters who strive to recapture the past, along with the necessary limitations that they run up against. Boyd writes, "*Mary* is a novel about time: about the reality of the past, even though we can only reach it within the present" (*Russian Years* 248). It is only when the protagonist Ganin realizes that the past cannot be relived that he is able to accept the present: "Only when Ganin changes his mind on the last page of the book does he in fact turn his story toward triumph, when he realizes he has all his past already with him and need not befoul the present" (247). Here we can see that Nabokov's sense of the past is similar to his sense of "real life": the past has a definite reality that cannot be captured. There are some Nabokovian characters, however, who become obsessed with the attempt to return, to go back to the past.

This theme is hinted at in the "second thought" structure of the first paragraph of *Sebastian Knight*. V. begins by telling us that the woman whose diary informed him about the weather on the day of Knight's birth asked him not to reveal her name. At the end of the paragraph, however, he writes that "[o]n second thought" he feels no real need to keep her name a secret from the reader. In the final sentence, then, he tells us her name. The structure of the paragraph is based on this return, this "second thought." One might even say that this is the purpose of the paragraph. (The reader has no reason to care about that name or if it is revealed.) V. is often involved in such returns, such reconsiderations. This structure points to the indecisiveness of V.'s nature, perhaps one cause of his lack of narrative control. In addition, the return-structure has metaphysical implications in Nabokov's work.

Minor examples of the "second thought" structure of the plot can be found throughout the novel. At one point, he mentions a time when he saw Knight in a nearby café, but he does not go in and continues on his way; he then returns and goes into the café "on second thought" (69). V.'s constant reconsiderations add to the sense of his uncertainty about any sort of knowledge, a crucial problem for someone writing a biography. This is another trait which shows V.'s lack of grounding, his groping for a definite thought. V.'s second thoughts are often followed by a series of questions, doubts, which also heighten the sense that he is not certain about anything. It might be wise, however, to compare V.'s uncertainty to Goodman's pompous certainty: V. is definitely more honest and does not latch on to one all-encompassing answer at the expense of other possibilities. V. has at least some appreciation for the nature of permanent mystery, unlike Mr. Goodman who seems obsessed with some sort of permanent solution. In fact, V.'s doubts are crucial to a Nabokovian sense of true understanding. His flaw, however, is that such doubts do not coincide with a successful "quest."

In addition to mental returns, reconsiderations, V. physically returns to locations. He draws attention to this fact when one woman asks him to return and he recalls that one of Knight's friends had also asked him to return (58). V. is vaguely aware of being drawn back, but he makes no comment on the possible significance of these returns. He seems to believe that by physically returning to the locations of Knight's life, he can recapture the past.

In fact, the entire plot of *Sebastian Knight* is a return, and I do not simply mean the plot represents V.'s attempts to return to Knight's life (which it does). The structure of the novel is ultimately a chronological return to the moments before Knight's death: the apparent conclusion on the final pages of the novel is actually the start of his story, even though these pages are written as though they were the end of the quest. The entire literary structure is, in a phrase written by Knight that sounds much like F. Scott Fitzgerald, a "backward glide into the past" (97). V.'s quest actually must begin, chronologically, with the final event in the novel's

3. The Return Structure

plot: Knight's death. Gennady Barabtarlo explains (in a comparison with the "reverse causality" in the overall structure of *Pnin*): "V. begins the book after Knight's death and leads the narration up to that death, a logical starting point of his quest, which is the end of the story about that quest" (*Aerial* 169, 165). Despite the appearance that the novel is being spontaneously written, without editing, at the time of the quest, the revelations in the final pages must occur before the quest begins. If V. actually learned anything in those final pages, they were learned *before* he begins his narrative. The quest, therefore, is actually a return to daily details, after the apparent revelations on the final pages, a return to the places and objects of the present.

Similarly, Humbert Humbert, in composing his text, is mentally returning to the events of his past. Earlier I discussed Humbert's apparent revelations, showing that the actual events that he discusses occur much earlier chronologically. Perhaps he places them toward the end in order to emphasize his insights, being the manipulative narrator that he is; on the other hand, perhaps those insights only occur to him as he returns to those moments in his mind, while writing. Humbert may be a successful guide for this technique of the return, showing just how one can go back to the past: through memory and imagination. Sitting in jail or an asylum, he has no other option, but he still demonstrates a successful method for recapturing the past. That is a key metaphysical lesson in Nabokov's art.

Nabokov's interest in the metaphysical implications of the return-structure are more explicitly discussed in *Look at the Harlequins!* The narrator of this novel, Vadim Vadimovich, complains of being unable to imagine himself making the simplest of physical returns:

> I imagine myself walking the twenty paces needed to reach the opposite sidewalk, then stopping with an unprintable curse and deciding to go back for the umbrella I left in the shop.... There is ... something dreadfully wrong with my sense of direction, or rather my power over conceived space, because at this juncture I am unable to execute mentally ... the simple about-face ... which would allow me to picture instantly in my mind the once already traversed asphalt as now being *before* me [105–6].

That is, Vadim is unable to imagine a return. V., on the other hand, might be diagnosed with an opposite problem: an inability not to return, a constant process of second thoughts and reconsiderations. V. seems almost obsessed with trivial returns, such as deciding whether or not to reveal the name of the lady who showed him her diary. V. not only returns, but seems to be swiveling about without control, returning all over the place. Despite all of his returns, however, the ultimate retrieval — a recapturing of the "real life" of Sebastian Knight — cannot be achieved by any physical return. V. can note the weather conditions and Knight's date of birth, but that has nothing to do with the state of mind one needs to recapture the "real life" of the past. He cannot make the mental return any more than Vadim, but unlike Vadim, V. is unable even to accurately diagnose the difficulty of such a return.

Alexandrov writes that Nabokov's essay "Pushkin, or the Real and the Plausible," delivered in 1937 (with James Joyce in the audience), "is crucial for understanding" *The Real Life of Sebastian Knight*. In this lecture Nabokov raises many questions about how one can know a previous life and what limits, if any, should be placed on the biographer. Alexandrov writes, "Nabokov is in fact implying that the intuitions, conjectures, and extrapolations that contribute to a fictionalized biography carry with them the potential for their own validation" (*Otherworld* 137–8). Nabokov recommends intuition and imagination as tools for the biographer, to create "plausible" realities which one might think should be excluded from a factual account of a life. A biographer should imaginatively extrapolate possibilities of the past. V. believes that the truth of Knight's life is waiting somewhere to be (re)discovered, but Nabokov believes that exploring "the plausible" is a necessary creative endeavor for truly understanding one's biographee.[1] Alexandrov points out that for Nabokov "fictitious" is not equated with "falsehood" (*Otherworlds* 144).

Discussing Pushkin, Nabokov writes, "those of us who really know him revere him with unparalleled fervor and purity, and experience a radiant feeling when the richness of his life overflows into the present to flood our spirit" ("Plausible" 39). At times we can see V. attempting to achieve this type of inspired understanding. Nabokov, however, ultimately states that no creative projections — regardless of how apparently revealing — can be definitive: "Let us admit defeat, and turn our attention to the contemplation of his work" (41). When the inspiration has passed, the weather returns, and present-day objects re-assert themselves. The works survive

3. *The Return Structure*

and should be appreciated; the "real life" cannot be resurrected. Alexandrov writes that "support for the seemingly unconscionable and unreliable methods that V. uses to infer information about Sebastian can be found" in Nabokov's lecture (*Otherworld* 137). However, the real point of the lecture is that plausible conjectures, if properly inspired, can perhaps be insightful, but ultimately such methods prove little or nothing.

This "plausible" portrayal is very similar to what Humbert strives for in the conclusion of his narrative, when he finally shows some respect for the real life of Lolita. Humbert has created a plausible Dolores, regardless of whether or not that depiction is "real." Nabokov writes about his own biographical depictions of Pushkin in "Pushkin, or the Real and the Plausible":

> It is not my fault if I get carried away by these images, images common to Russians who know their Pushkin, and a part of our intellectual life in the same inextricable sense as multiplication tables or any other mental habit. These images are probably false.... Yet if I inject in them a bit of the same love that I feel when reading his poems, is not what I am doing with this imaginary life somehow akin to the poet's work, if not to the poet himself? [40].

It is significant that Nabokov says these "images" are part of one's life in the "same" way as multiplication tables: one's intellectual life contains imaginative projections which are no less real than mathematics. "Imagine me," Humbert earlier begs of his readers, "I shall not exist if you do not imagine me" (129). Equally, Lolita also does not honestly exist for Humbert until he has imagined her.

In keeping with Nabokov's penchant for somewhere inserting a parody of his own conclusion, Quilty's play *The Enchanted Hunters* concludes with "the play's profound message, namely, that mirage and reality merge in love" (201). In "The Real and the Plausible" we see Nabokov stating more directly that if one injects one's images with "the same love" one feels for one's subject, then one's work is "akin to the poet's work." Therefore, if we feel that Humbert has injected a sufficient degree of love into his fictional depiction of pregnant seventeen-year-old Dolores, then he has become a poet. "Mirage and reality" have merged in this final depiction of Lolita/Dolly Schiller, and Humbert is able to express a form of love of which he was never before capable. This does nothing to alleviate any of the "real" Lolita's past or present suffering, but this — an imaginative depiction suffused with actual love (mirage and reality merged) — is the best, at this point, that the secluded Humbert can do. Thus, when Humbert says that his misery can only be treated by the "palliative" of art, he is not reciting the idea of art for art's sake, but recognizing the real limitations which he faces at the time of writing.

While I believe Nabokov would agree that Humbert has reached his minimal best here, his closest moments of much-delayed enlightenment, I also believe that Nabokov would say that art can be much more than a "palliative" for those who have not collapsed into the irrevocable state of misery in which Humbert finally finds himself. The best art is stronger than a palliative and can transcend the local. For Nabokov, the merger of mirage and reality is perhaps the best means for conveying one's sense of the celestial source.

This may help explain why, when comparing Humbert to Hermann, the murderer in his novel *Despair*, Nabokov writes, "Both are neurotic scoundrels, yet there is a green lane in Paradise where Humbert is permitted to wander at dusk once a year; but Hell shall never parole Hermann" (xiii). Humbert gets his one-day break from eternal damnation because of his final poetic repentance. One day, after all, is the most one can get for an imaginary repentance, that is, a repentance which has no effect whatsoever on the world beyond his private asylum: a purely personal repentance as expressed through art. Nothing of Humbert's crime can be undone. Never will we open the book to see Lolita enjoying a carefree American childhood. He has merely earned an annual reprieve for having appreciated something of the real life of Lolita, beyond the clichés in which he had encaged her.

It seems that only the imagination — the soul — can bring the past back to life, but even then the past that is brought back is not entirely reliable. Such inspired projections are only satisfying to the person who knows that such projections were prompted by the artist's work, by something that feels as though it was in touch with that previous life. In this regard, V. is inconsistent: he sometimes has some luck, but then he continues hunting for something more tangible.

Clearly, the past is not a physical location: it is something only retrievable in the mind. This is essentially the argument that Boyd makes in his discussion of "the myth of return" in Nabokov's work, although he discusses

3. *The Return Structure*

different examples than I have discussed here ("Nabokov as Storyteller" 44, but really throughout that chapter). Though occasionally able to admit the need for an affinity with Knight's mind in order to comprehend Knight's life, V. acts as though he believes if he keeps moving from place to place, where Knight lived, worked, loved, he will eventually run into his past. All of these topics are present in the first paragraph, though they would most likely only be noticed with the reader's return, with a rereading.

"One can only reread"

In fact, one cannot read a novel by Nabokov only once and expect to comprehend it fully. Nabokov himself states this even more strongly: "one cannot *read* a book: one can only reread it" (*LL* 3). He believes that "artistic appreciation" can only come through rereading (*LL* 3). Though this is a general concept which he would apply to all "artistic" literature, for his own fiction the necessity of rereading takes on a special significance. In fact, Nabokov worked to make certain that one's first reading of his novels could not possibly capture the many nuances of artistic truth which he had included.

One reason Nabokov stresses the necessity for rereading is because of the problem of time. That "divine flame" is better sparked as one becomes more closely acquainted with the world of a given book. As one reenters a world, one is better able to overcome the demands of the linear intake of written words. He argues that one must become acquainted with a book, and return to it, in order to appreciate it in its entirety. Only then can our brains comprehend literature in something like the way our eyes can appreciate a painting: "at a second, or third, or fourth reading we do, in a sense, behave toward a book as we do towards a painting" (*LL* 3). Roland Barthes makes a similar point at the beginning of *S/Z*, and his explanation can help to clarify Nabokov's idea that with subsequent readings we begin to "behave toward a book as we do towards a painting": "rereading draws the text out of its internal chronology ('this happens *before* or *after* that') and recaptures a mythic time (without *before* or *after*)" (16). Thus for both

Nabokov's Permanent Mystery

Barthes and Nabokov, linear time in literature is an obstacle which must be overcome with multiple readings.

In attempting to explain the physical apparatus we have for perceiving literature, Barthes prefers an analogy with music: "habit creates a reading process just as conditioned as our hearing: one might say there is a *reading eye* as there is a tonal ear" (30). Neither Barthes or Nabokov are completely happy with their analogies; both include mild disclaimers: Nabokov says that "in a sense" a book becomes like a painting; Barthes, "one might say" it is like music. Nabokov goes on to state that it is precisely not the eye which finally perceives literature: "let us not confuse the physical eye, that monstrous masterpiece of evolution, with the mind.... The mind, the brain, the top of the tingling spine, is, or should be, the only instrument used upon a book" (*LL* 3–4). Once again, literary art must spark a divine flame. Both Barthes and Nabokov make the point that there is an aspect of literature which is more than the initial meaning of the words on the page. If one simply understands the words, it does not suggest that one appreciates the art. Nabokov gives this theory a metaphysical dimension: words cannot adequately convey one's sense of a beyond. Rereading, therefore, is something like an ideal model for recapturing the past—returning in an effort to overcome time. Rereading is also the best means one has for overcoming the limitations of language.

Chapter 4

The Metaphysics of Mistakes

The Possibility of Perfection

In his introduction to the structure of Pushkin's *Eugene Onegin*, Nabokov states that errors in a text may be intentional. It would be a critical mistake, he writes, simply to correct apparent errors in a text, as though the author had actually intended to write better sentences: "Even obvious misprints should be treated gingerly; after all, they may be supposed to have been left uncorrected by the author. Why and wherefore he did this or that is beside the point" (*EO*, vol. 1, 15–16). Nabokov's interest in errors extends into his own texts and provides a unique view of the place of mistakes within a literary structure. Nabokov's flaws — as well as "flaws" — lead the reader to a greater understanding of his sense of language and his sense of that which exists beyond the limits of language.

A number of scholars have noted Nabokov's statements concerning the fact that his works exist in some complete form in his mind before he puts them on paper. Alexandrov: "he would write a work by putting down onto index cards random passages from various parts of the completed whole, which was fixed in its entirety in his mind" (*Otherworld* 30); Boyd: "It had always been a peculiarity of Nabokov's method of composition that he would envisage a novel in his mind complete from start to finish before writing it down" (*American Years* 643). It may seem ironic that this "complete" vision of the finished work could include flaws. However, Nabokov explains this sense of having the novel complete in his mind before writing it as having the *structure* complete in his mind, not every detail of the written work. He describes "the first real pang" of a work as "a rather complete vision of its structure in miniature" (*SO* 55). The initial vision is of the "structure" of the work; thus the process of composition is an effort to put words to that "complete" structural vision. Flaws are part of the complete structure, suggesting the presence of the higher levels.

One can see the technique of incorporating flaws into the complete structure on a few levels of *The Real Life of Sebastian Knight*. While the protagonist's fumbling along his own plotline is a fairly common device, this novel takes the idea a step further by having the narrator simultaneously fumbling along the writing of his text. The narrator's occasional inability to manage his paragraphs and chapters is a deceptive device which points toward higher levels of the narrative. That is, the reader is led to believe that the narrative is somehow spontaneously written at the time of V.'s quest. If V. seems incapable of controlling his narrative, however, it is only because the real author—Vladimir Nabokov—has not permitted him that power.

At the end of the second chapter, after another encounter which V. finds to be unrevealing in regard to Knight's real life, he complains that he is angry with himself for having disrupted the flow of his "second chapter" with a "useless pilgrimage" (21). Of course, anyone can revise a "second chapter" to remove such "useless" digressions. Even if we assume a fictional rush to publication (to counteract Mr. Goodman's book on Knight, for example), this at the very least shows amateurish planning. V. didn't need to write the chapter at all, we would think, if the "pilgrimage" had been truly "useless." In this sentence, V. also draws attention to the fact that it is raining. Rain, snow—and weather in general—often seem to be representative of authorial control.

But V.'s narrative includes all the possible wrong paths which he is led down by Nabokov. Nabokov is the one who makes it rain, and the textual weather carries V. right along with it. The deception is that the narrator is portrayed as spontaneously creating this chapter at the same time as he is shown to regret writing it down. We know, of course, that the narrative was not really written this way. Like the idea that Huck Finn wrote his own narrative, this knowledge adds irony to our perception of the narrator. Unlike with Huck, however, this irony diminishes our sense of the narrator's supposed insights.

4. The Metaphysics of Mistakes

Nabokov does not use quite the same technique in any of his other novels. He uses a similar device in *Despair*, but in that novel the narrator specifically does reread his text. In contrast, *Lolita* is not a spontaneously written or unedited text, although Humbert is pressed for time. One effect of this spontaneously created text is to show that V.'s creative process is almost antithetical to the work of memory. He and his text are continually moving forward, often unaware of the ever-receding nature of the past. V. seems unable to stop his own pen. Unlike the narrative of *Ada*, where more than one editorial hand is made visible within Van Veen's text, V. has no editorial help with his writing (at least no earthly editorial help). This emphasis on his lack of ability should make one aware of other structural levels at work.

An additional way in which V. lacks textual control is in his lack of control over the language. Edmund Wilson, after first reading *Sebastian Knight* in 1941, wrote to Nabokov, "I hope you will get somebody at Wellesley to read your proofs — because there are a few, though not many, mistakes in English" (*Nabokov-Wilson* 49). Nabokov responded with a letter containing the following comment, seemingly in agreement with Wilson: "You are quite right, quite right about the slips. There are many clumsy expressions and foreignish mannerisms that I noticed myself when reading the book again after five years had passed; but if I started correcting them I would rewrite the whole thing" (51). I don't believe that Nabokov truly felt any urge to rewrite this novel. The point he is indirectly making is that V.'s entire narrative is filled with clumsy English — clumsy English for a clumsy character. (One can find the same theme in *Pnin*, where, in contrast, outwardly awkward Pnin has thoughts in his native language that are perfectly articulate.) Wilson is "quite right" in his observation, but not quite right in believing this is a mistake on the part of Nabokov. To make the entire narrative read as smoothly as the prose of, say, Sebastian Knight, much of the novel would need to be revised. The mistakes and clumsy sentences, however, seem to be part of Nabokov's overall design.

Nabokov's response to Wilson's letter contains another hint that this is the case. Wilson wrote, "You tend to bend over backwards using *as* instead of *like* and sometimes use it incorrectly" (49). Nabokov wrote back, "I wrote it five years ago, in Paris, on the implement called *bidet* as a writing desk.... There is another fishy 'as' in that sentence" (51). Nabokov intentionally repeats what Wilson had so helpfully pointed out as a problem in his prose. He also makes clear that his usage is "fishy," not mistaken. The occasional use of fishy prose is another of Nabokov's metaphysical devices.

Edmund Wilson appears to have learned his mistake. In his next letter to Nabokov, he writes, "I don't believe a word you say about your book and am furious at having been hoaxed by it (though my opinion of it has rather gone up than otherwise)" (52). Wilson does not elaborate on this "hoax" in the letter, but there is a postscript to Nabokov's previous letter which begins "you just rang up" and mentions some other misconceptions which Wilson apparently had about the novel's structure. It is at least plausible that Nabokov explained to Wilson his tricks with seemingly insufficient English in their discussion over the telephone.

Michael Wood writes, "Mistakes — ones which are only mistakes and ones which are blunderings into insight — are absolutely central to *The Real Life of Sebastian Knight*" (50). He writes this in the context of V.'s encounters with luck and unexpected revelations, not taking this analysis of mistakes to the sentence level. Wood does recognize such mistakes, however, inserting a "sic" in his quotation of the following passage: "his mind was a turmoil of words and fancies, uncomplete fancies and insufficient words" (*RLSK* 48; Wood 30). Once again, I don't believe it is an accident that in a discussion of "insufficient words" V. incorrectly uses the word "uncomplete." The "mistakes" found in this work can be found not only in the odd plot twists, but in individual sentences, and even in a single word. Mistakes of all kinds are central to the novel.

Alexandrov recognizes a similar situation in *Invitation to a Beheading*. Cincinnatus's inability to use the language properly, he says, "may be read as a sign of the narrator's momentary entrapment in the dulling world of material concerns" (*Otherworld* 93). Language, especially when used incorrectly or awkwardly, becomes another form of mundane "entrapment." Like daily platitudes, dates, and the weather, language can become just another problematic object of the present. This is why the mistakes we see in *Sebastian Knight* tend to be associated with V., whereas Knight's prose is more often presented as transcending mere daily concerns. Language

4. The Metaphysics of Mistakes

does have the potential to transcend, but in the hands of V. it is unlikely to attain that potential. Alexandrov writes, "Narrative stumbling is thus like narrative forgetfulness in implying the existence of a higher consciousness that is the locus of the ideal version of the narrative, and that incorporates seeming imperfections into a larger artistic design" (*Otherworld* 93). V.'s entrapment in the trivial aspects of the world makes his situation similar to that of Cincinnatus. His "seeming imperfections," from wrongheaded plot turns to misused words, are part of the overall design.

However, Alexandrov's statement that this higher realm implies an "ideal version of the text" may be misleading. There is no "ideal version" where V.'s quest comes out fine and all the clichés function perfectly. Rather, this "higher consciousness" or higher structural level implies only the idea of an ideal version. This is similar to the conclusion of Nabokov's "The Art of Translation," where he states that he has come up with the "perfect" translation of a "perfect" line of Pushkin's poetry, but he chooses not to put those perfect words on the page. Actual words are unable to attain perfection. The great poetry of Koncheyev, in *The Gift*, is described as having "a unique perfection, bearing no resemblance to words and in no needs of words" (93). For Nabokov, that higher level is beyond the material of real words. A written text is necessarily "uncomplete"; an "ideal" text is necessarily unwritten. Nonetheless, the presence of mistakes suggests the possibility of perfection, even if such perfection is unattainable on this side. Even V.'s stumbling narrative can suggest the perfection of a successful quest; it can point toward a perfection that exists beyond the earthly terms of real words.

It is certainly an audacious device for a Russian writer's first novel in English to contain intentionally awkward and incorrect sentences. But Nabokov seems to have had ultimate faith in his readers: "I have the greatest readers any author has ever had" (*SO* 192). He may even have trusted his readers to appreciate purposeful errors. Edmund Wilson, however, might not have understood Nabokov's technique after all. Some of his later criticisms of Nabokov's English in the *Eugene Onegin* translation show that he still did not trust Nabokov's ability in this language. In that case, of course, Nabokov explicitly defended what Wilson believed to be faulty English, stating that the apparent errors which Wilson listed were in fact "the figments of his own ignorance" (256). Errors fit Nabokov's sense of a "complete" fictional structure, but they would simply be mistakes if found in his scholarship.

The Errors of "Pale Fire"

Nabokov incorporates imperfections into his fictional worlds so as to suggest the presence of a more perfect world. Thus the afterworld can be conceived as a realm of greater symmetry, of perfection that is unattainable on this side. While he intentionally incorporates flaws into his created worlds, this strategy may also be a means for accounting for unintentional flaws. Real human imperfections — errors by the real author — may thus have a metaphysical resonance. There is such a flaw in the poem "Pale Fire."

Though every line of the poem is in iambic pentameter, one must read with the accented voice of Nabokov's English rather than the American accent of John Shade for some lines to scan properly. The word "diamonds" must be read with three syllables in line nineteen. More noticeably, the word "Canadian" has only three syllables in the eighty-first line. In fact, the "-ian" or "-ium" ending is consistently a single syllable for Nabokov: "solarium" in line fifty-nine, "vulgarian" in line 125, "sanitarium" in line 199. There are more examples. Nabokov is apparently pronouncing the "i" as a "y." With this pronunciation the voice of Nabokov pushes through that of the American poet John Shade. (After one hears the recording of Nabokov reading his poetry, the sense of his voice overtaking that of Shade in these particular words is even more apparent.) There are other words which necessitate Nabokov's pronunciation to balance the pentameter: "glistening" as two syllables in line 261, "fiancé" as two syllables in line 386, "various" and "usual" as two syllables each in lines 416 and 425. These examples should suffice to show that Nabokov's pronunciation — rather than Shade's — is often necessary for the iambic pentameter to be consistent.

This is a flaw in both the poem and in the characterization of John Shade. In fact, it suggests that Nabokov never quite accurately heard the accent of American English. These foreignish pronunciations are not inten-

4. The Metaphysics of Mistakes

tional flaws that Shade has included in his poem to demonstrate the materiality of language. This mistake is Nabokov's, not Shade's, and it draws attention to the real author in a presumably unwanted way.

However, Nabokov's metaphysical sense of structure is not lessened by these non–American pronunciations. The structure of the book remains unchanged by mistakes (in contrast to "the mistake" made be Hermann in *Despair*: "my whole construction had been based upon just the impossibility of a blunder, and now it appeared that a blunder there had been" [203]). Kinbote points out the rhyme of one couplet — again/explain — which is inconsistent with American English, and says that while speaking, the American John Shade, would rhyme again/pen, not again/explain. Kinbote then points out, "The adjacent position of these rhymes is curious" (193). The previous couplet contained the rhyme then/pen. This is "curious" indeed. In fact, here we might catch Nabokov smirking behind the Kinbote mask: it is Nabokov's pronunciation which would rhyme "again" with "explain." Apparently Nabokov is aware that the American voice of John Shade occasionally gives way to his own. Thus, in a sense, his metaphysical tracks are covered: any error in the text can be attributed to the conjurer awkwardly intruding into his imagined world. I don't believe Nabokov recognized all the non–American pronunciations in his pentameters, but he did recognize the structural necessity of assigning all language which would not be consistent with an American poet to himself. The conjurer might not notice all of the fingerprints he leaves on his crystal land.

In his commentary, Kinbote suggests that Shade's poem might have gained an added ironic significance if there had been a line which did not scan correctly; he states that the section about "IPH ... would be quite Hudibrastic had its pedestrian verse been one foot shorter" (238). Thus he suggests that a flaw in the poetic structure — a "Hudibrastic" or mock-heroic moment — might have added to the overall meaning of the poem, especially in the lines where Shade writes of the institute which studies the hereafter. Such a seeming mistake would have demonstrated that narrative frames are never perfect vessels for metaphysical content.

Roger Salomon has discussed the importance of the "mock-heroic" mode for many of Nabokov's protagonists. Salomon demonstrates some ways in which "self-consciousness includes self-mockery" in Nabokov's art, both for these protagonists and for Nabokov himself. The inclusion of intentional flaws in a literary structure may also express this conscious self-mockery on many levels: "Nabokov's art ... reflects the persistance of the 'spiritual itch' at a time when epic gratifications are no longer possible." Thus the representation of a spiritual quest which contains its own mistakes is one means for building this limited epic potential into a literary structure, thereby reflecting the idea that "there is essentially only the self's heroic resolve to pursue glimmers" (189, 216). One may never permanently capture these metaphysical glimmers with perfect translations, perfect sentences or perfect structures. Rather, structures lead toward the highest possible level, toward the ideal of perfection, beyond the material truth of a book. In fact, it is often the gaps in an otherwise logical structure which are best able to convey that unfilled metaphysical frame of perfection.

Some of the mistakes of English in *Sebastian Knight* are intentional. Proffer notes some awkward sentences in *Lolita* and suggests that they are nothing more than mistakes: "Humbert's syntax is sometimes unintentionally shaky" (116). He doesn't quite say that Nabokov's syntax is shaky, only "Humbert's." In *Lolita* such awkward English could be better explained by the simple fact the Humbert is a non-native speaker. A cynic might even argue that the technique of having imperfections refer to the metaphysical possibility of perfection — in *Sebastian Knight* and *Pale Fire* — is just a con artist's trick to explain away such "shaky" English. To paraphrase a sentence of *Sebastian Knight,* Nabokov the conjurer certainly does cultivate the "con." Nonetheless, even if one considers this a less than honest conjuring trick, mistakes are accounted for in the metaphysical hierarchy of *Pale Fire.* The mind behind the masks is still a human one, even if it is at the top of Nabokov's creative hierarchy. The best mind is only a filter for the celestial essence: the original source cannot be perfectly translated into the terms of this world.

Regardless of the possible imperfections in the conjurer himself, the structural level of the real author — conjurer Nabokov — is the mediating presence between the celestial essence and the text. Of course, Shade is a conjurer as well, and, as Boyd says, one of the questions of the text is how closely we believe him to coincide with the top conjurer, the real author.

4. The Metaphysics of Mistakes

Boyd also suggests that the answer to this question might depend on how successful we believe Shade to be. Similarly, the success of Nabokov depends on how accurately he may have conveyed the celestial essence, how well he may have translated that initial sense of inspiration into earthly terms. Boyd writes:

> Shade, in acting as he does, in trying to understand death and the unknown forces beyond life by playing their own game, proves his aims close to those of *his* unseen maker, Nabokov, and then, on the last twist before the expanding spiral disappears from sight, Nabokov implies the hope that his own work in its turn may be somehow close to the aims of whatever mysterious forces lurk further beyond [*American Years* 455].

This is the top level of the creative hierarchy and the method by which the structure leads "beyond" the book. Some readers have found Nabokov's technique of self-reference to be bothersome. Andrew Field's primary argument is that Nabokov is narcissistic: "He is a hero of our time, the time of the culture of narcissism" (373).[1] Joyce Carol Oates wrote that Nabokov is too self-indulgent in his art: "Nabokov empties the world of everything except Nabokov" (107). Such arguments, however, overlook the mediating role of this level of the structure. If Nabokov fails to be humble, it is because he believes he is fairly successfully connecting with "whatever mysterious forces lurk further beyond." Boyd's phrase here is exactly correct: the forces remain unnamed and mysterious, though definitely present. Those errors of the text draw attention to the inability of language to perfectly encapsulate metaphysical truths.

Of course, a too-strong insistence on Nabokov's interest in errors might only make one sound like a lesser eccentric than the "librarian called Porlock" in "The Vane Sisters" who spent his final years "engaged in examining old books for miraculous misprints such as the substitution of *l* for the second *h* in the word 'hither'" (*Stories* 622). Nabokov often anticipates his readers, and may even provide parodies of some of his own techniques. Nonetheless, his literary vision includes "errors," and his sense of the inadequacy of language is tied to the idea that a higher ideal does exist. In regard to the mistakes in *Eugene Onegin*, Nabokov wrote that the "why and wherefore" is "beside the point"; for his own work, the why and wherefore may be the point.

Chapter 5

The Problem of Biography

Is there a Sebastian in the Text?

The answer to the question I have posed for the title of this section might seem to be both yes and no: there appear to be many Sebastians in *The Real Life of Sebastian Knight*. Here one might recall F. Scott Fitzgerald's thought: "There never was a good biography of a good novelist. There couldn't be. He is too many people, if he's any good" (177). The topic of biography — how one can know another's life and how one can express that knowledge in words — can show quite a bit about Nabokov's sense of "reality."

Perhaps the more important question is the one which V. asks more than once: "Who is speaking of Sebastian Knight?" (49, 50, 63). Many people speak of Knight in the novel — friends, family, lovers, secretaries, acquaintances. Many of these may seem to be nothing more than superfluous or suspect narratives added to V.'s own, each such narrative representing a wrong turn on his unsuccessful quest. Some of these characters show that they believe the knot of Knight can be easily untangled. Others give his "real life" varying levels of respect. The question is to what degree any version of Knight can claim authority.

Among the first narratives about Knight inset in V.'s text is one which Boyd says managed to "seep into" this novel from Nabokov's real life (*Russian Years* 188). In the autobiography Nabokov recalls revisiting the woman who was his French governess when he as a child, and finds her older, deaf and romanticizing the Russian past. In the novel, seemingly the same Mademoiselle — equally deaf and nostalgic — tells V. her (rather implausible) version

5. The Problem of Biography

of young Knight. Boyd is right that these two Mademoiselles are generally the same: there is a similar slap, a shared nostalgic "Ah!" However, the structural difference in the way these two scenes are narrated is very revealing. In the fictionalized version (that is, in the novel) Nabokov places Knight in the role of the intangible past, with V. representing the present. Here again, the single narrative voice of *Speak, Memory* is, in this novel, split between V. and Knight (just as it is in the uses of time: dates for V., timelessness for Knight, both for Nabokov's autobiographical voice). Knight here stands for that part of Nabokov which has become untouchable, unreachable, that which he calls in *Speak, Memory* "intangible property, unreal estate," two terms which specifically contrast the material of the imagination (and of the past) with that of the physical present, where there is, of course, tangible property, real estate (40).

Elsewhere, the events of Knight's past do not seem so closely based on Nabokov's own past, but the comparison of these two scenes shows an important aspect of Knight's role in the novel. His "real life" seems to have no conclusive evidence to prove its existence. There is evidence, but it is not clear what would constitute conclusiveness. There are no entirely reliable witnesses (and Knight's books are only presented in selections, made, of course, by V.). Mademoiselle appears, however innocently, to be maligning that life. She seems to turn Knight into a stock character of her own fantasy-past. The point is not that the past does not exist, but that it exists in myriad versions.

Other versions of that life are less innocent. Mr. Goodman's *The Tragedy of Sebastian Knight* may be the most notorious. Interestingly, though, Goodman's version of Knight's life is not the most notorious because it is less correct than other versions, such as that of Mademoiselle, or even, at times, V. Goodman's version is supposedly the worst because it represents the exact antithesis of Knight's sense of time. Goodman's version of Knight's life seems unable even to display a unique angle of reflection. Nicol writes, "Its type of biography, showing the artist as a child of his age, is rejected as a method of composition, for it provides a mirror of distortion rather than of perspective" ("Mirrors" 88). Goodman has not even attempted to attune himself to Knight's mind, the method prescribed by Nabokov for creating "plausible" biography (a method of which, to his inept credit, V. does seem vaguely aware). Goodman quite casually believes he can define Knight with the stereotypes of his time.

Goodman places every idea within his very narrow sense of a historical context, a method of thinking which subsumes all ideas to temporal stereotypes. Goodman's clichéd sense of time is directly connected to a clichéd sense of structure, with a predictable list of problems and potential problems of the "age," each separated by an ellipses. The list moves through economic problems, the possibility of war, social problems, and so on, all leading to the "structure of the universe" (115). Goodman is certainly an ancestor of John Ray, Jr.; both easily compile the standard societal problems to explain not only the text at hand, but the author of that text. The ellipses between each supposed problem of the "age" are V.'s ellipsis of Goodman's book. V. only allows us to catch brief glimpses of this book. These ellipses are ape-able gaps, easily filled in with the appropriate clichés. There is a right way and a wrong way to move from the topic of time to the topic of metaphysics and structure. Goodman's method is to theorize about this "age" by mentioning a few trendy topics, and then from those topics to make some grandiose claim about the "structure of the universe." Nabokov, Knight, and even V., know that structures which reflect metaphysical concepts — structures of "real life" — are not so facilely formulated.

It does not matter what Goodman's conclusions about the structure of the universe are: we need only know how easily he reached them. V. critiques Mr. Goodman by telling us that his "method is as simple as his philosophy." On a more intricate path, Nabokov's work also moves from the topic of time to some wider ideas about the connection between metaphysics and structures. Nabokov's method is also as simple or as complex as his philosophy, form not following function, but form in fact being the function itself: metaphysical content embodied in the complete structure.

The title of Mr. Goodman's book is more evidence of his clash with Knight over ideas of time: *The Tragedy of Sebastian Knight*. The idea of any fully lived life being defined as a "tragedy" is un–Nabokovian (and un–Knightian). Tragedy is a time-based idea, dependent on worldly terms and tangible property. Such an idea is reductive. In Nabokov's sense of trans-temporal metaphysics, with which Knight is in agreement, the tragic

5. The Problem of Biography

can never be the primary attribute of a full life. Real life encompasses and transcends the "tragic." An exception may be a life that is prevented from reaching fulfillment, such as the life of Dolores Haze. Leland de la Durantaye discusses this in his recent book (91–92). In essence, she has been deprived of her real life; that is the tragedy. For Knight, though, as for Nabokov, "tragedy" tends to be a reductive term.

The first book on Knight's bookshelf is *Hamlet*; the final book is *King Lear*—two plays that are commonly labeled as tragedies. At the start of one of his articles on Nabokov, without making mention of Knight's bookshelf, Appel offers the following quotation from William Butler Yeats: "They know that Hamlet and Lear are gay/ Gaiety transfiguring all that dread" (qtd. in "Portrait," 3). The label "tragedy," whether placed on "real life" or on a work of art, is only another attempt to enclose something into one's limited sense of a genre, like V.'s questing for detective clichés. Elsewhere Nabokov writes, "Shakespeare's dream-plays *Hamlet* or *Lear* cannot be called 'tragedies'" (*Gogol* 54–5). He says that the "prodigiously poetic background" of these works causes them to transcend such a reductive and generic label: "and by poetry I mean the mysteries of the irrational as perceived through rational words" (55). The term "tragedy" does not adequately encompass the mysteries inherent in poetry or in real life.

In Yeats' poem "Lapis Lazuli" Yeats also contrasts the sense of something beyond tragedy with the following more predictable lines, which could easily have been spoken by Goodman: "For everybody knows or else should know/ That if nothing drastic is done/ Aeroplane and Zeppelin will come out,/ Pitch like King Billy bomb balls in/ Until the town lie beaten flat" (294). The "Aeroplane" and the "Zeppelin" are the trendy threats of the present, which also concern Goodman. Yeats' "everybody" is the average man that is so central to Goodman's gloomy understanding of his era or "Goodman" himself: his name implies the mass opinion of good and bad, which includes the common opinion about impending doom. V. is sure to point out that Goodman's book has been well-received by the reviewers of the press (59). Yeats' wry line is excellent in pointing out the closed-mindedness and superficial confidence of mass pessimism: "everybody knows or else should know." Nabokov and Knight tend to be more positive.

Nabokov's Permanent Mystery

V. offers his description of Knight's sense of time and corresponding sense of the tragic, explaining that Knight did not consider contemporary calamities to be any more or less tragic than those of the past, even the distant past. He describes this idea by making a connection between space and time, stating that the distance of either does not make an even more tragic; both space and time are means for measuring existence, not excellent means for understanding real life (63–4).

Thus, with a slight imaginative step, the tragedy of years past should be no less poignant than the tragedy of today. Knight's sense of time does not allow the immediacy of an event to add to its degree of tragedy. V. states that for Sebastian the standard measurements of time were irrelevant, that the specific number assigned to the year was meaningless (63). Today's tragedy is no more or less tragic than an equivalent event of one hundred or one thousand years ago. Such a view is the exact opposite of Mr. Goodman's limited contextual view, where events increase in tragic importance the closer they come to one's temporal home.

This may seem a rather callous attitude, that the tragic scenes of the present day do not demand one's attention any more than those of distant history. It may seem more palatable as an approach to literature — the tragedies of *Hamlet* or *Lear* are no less tragic than the work of, say, Tennessee Williams or Arthur Miller. However, Knight's "year 1" (63) — the idea that an numerical understanding of the current time is meaningless, that all time can be considered as now: year 1 — is meant as an unchanging positive point, perhaps even a transcendent metaphysical point. It is not that tragedies are never significant, but that in the face of all potential tragedies, happiness is a quality of life which cannot be obliterated; he states that Knight would have been equally happy in any era — thereby refuting the idea that Knight is defined by his "time" — and compares Knight's particular kind of happiness to a child who is attending a pantomime but occasionally thinking about his scheduled dentist appointment for tomorrow (64). The pantomime may seem less real than the dentist, additionally so for that form of theatre's inherent silence, but the child's joy in this picture is no less real than its fear. Significantly, joy is portrayed as existing in the present, whereas fear — the dentist — is a foreboding sense of the future (like Yeats: "Aeroplane and Zeppelin *will* come out"; and

5. The Problem of Biography

Goodman: "the *next* super-great war" (115, my emphasis). Actual happiness, for Nabokov and Knight, is more real than forecasted doom.

Wood writes, "Before he wrote his first novel *Mary* (1925), Nabokov was working on but did not finish a novel called *Happiness [Schastie]*, and all his early stories turn on happiness and its loss: on loss as internal to happiness, not its end but its anticipated completion" (219). Once again, it is the anticipation which seems constantly to threaten happiness. As with other forms of Nabokovian timelessness and transcendence, it is some concrete reality which always threatens to bring joy back down to earth. In addition, Nabokov never portrays the sense of happiness as less real than the anticipation of its end. Happiness is never a one-dimensional emotion, and quite often it is the dominant one.

It is obvious in the novel that Goodman is meant to represent Knight's worst biographer. I want only to stress that it is specifically in theories about time that they most differ. Let me return to the more important structural question: is there a Sebastian in the text? And, again, the first step toward answering that question is another question: who is speaking of Sebastian Knight? I would argue that even the least successful speaker may achieve some degree of success. For Nabokov's epistemology, however, the word "refractor" would be more applicable than "speaker." Goodman is not Knight's worst biographer, rather he is his worst refractor. "The real for Nabokov is always refracted," writes Wood (31). He adds, however, "The real is not less real because it is refracted." The best perception of the "real" is nonetheless a refraction, and even the worst refractor may catch some glimpse of its source. Even the worst biographer may at times attain an interesting angle on the field of study. One might recall that the Invisible Man — from another book on Knight's shelf— attained invisibility through experiments designed "to lower the refractive index of a substance" (79–80). Here, too, the degree of refraction determines how thoroughly one may be perceived. Cincinnatus is condemned to death for being "opaque": "impervious to the rays of others" (*IB* 24). Opaque people, like Cincinnatus C. and Sebastian Knight, are difficult to perceive, thus difficult to put into biographies.

Not everything Goodman, the stereotypic refractor, says about Knight should be immediately discounted. We are, after all, only seeing

Nabokov's Permanent Mystery

Goodman's version of Knight through the frame of V. At one point Goodman writes that Knight had a tendency to act above the trivial concerns of everyday life, choosing instead to cultivate the aloofness of an artist, yet there was a "thorn" that prevented him from living in such a manner (61). V. immediately attacks this comment, stating that the very idea of this "thorn" is one of Goodman's fabrications. V. refuses to admit that Goodman might make even the most limited of successful insights. Nonetheless, a few pages further, V. uses the same word, writing that Knight may have preferred the most direct "ethical path," but that he always took "the thorniest aesthetic one" (80). Thus, the word "thorn" sneaks into V.'s own prose. His terms for describing Knight appear to have been tainted by Goodman's book.

The "thorn" of Knight's life does not appear to be completely invented after all. The difference is that Goodman feels that Knight's "thorn" was his inability to interact with the world — the "real" world rather than the fictional one. V., on the other hand, claims that it was the other world, the "aesthetic" one, which contained the thorn. Thus, Goodman suggests that Knight disregarded the difficulties of this side with an escape into aesthetics, whereas V. claims it was this side which was "easiest" for him, the aesthetic side presenting the difficulties, the "thorn." V.'s only defense against Goodman, it seems, is always to insist on the opposite. Perhaps Goodman is not so thoroughly bad after all. As readers, however, we do not have to choose one version over the other: none of the refracted Sebastians we find in this novel are exclusively incorrect. Mademoiselle, Knight's Cambridge friend, V. and even Goodman seem to have something to offer, some angle of light which the others might not be able to convey.[1]

Knight's book *The Prismatic Bezel* provides the key to this method of biography, as it describes a depiction of a landscape that is not a single painting, but rather a series of paintings showing different methods for depicting the landscape; the intended goal is to create a "harmonious fusion [which] will disclose the landscape as I intend you to see it" (93). This interaction of points of view is crucial to understanding Sebastian Knight's place in this novel. Nabokov's purpose is not to create endless subjective versions of a single picture, endlessly receding from the source, as Conrad Brenner wrote in his 1941 introduction to the novel: "the course taken by

5. The Problem of Biography

The Real Life of Sebastian Knight ... is the endless course away from the truth, the real: a book written to prove that there is no book here" (xiv). But this is not Borges' *Libro de Arena*, a book which conveys the sense of slipping through one's fingers like sand, a book written to prove the illusion of a book. One could say that this is, in contrast, a *Libro de Agua*, in which one finds the reflected likeness of Sebastian Knight: a "harmonious fusion" of inexact refractions.

There is a book here, although Sebastian Knight's real life, like any real life, may ultimately be intangible, something which one must finally accept as existing beyond all the many biographical refractions. The accumulation of landscapes is not an attempt to demonstrate the subjective nature of reality, as if "Thirteen Ways of Looking at a Blackbird" was written to prove the non-existence of blackbirds. The different depictions of Knight which are presented to us, fused into the entirety of this novel, should disclose — at the very least — a general Knightian landscape. This novel is not a fictional biography, such as the one Knight intended to write, but a series of word-pictures conveyed by a wide variety of characters. In Nabokov's view, "reality" is not subjective, but any given perspective of it necessarily is. Each adds an angle to the portrayal. Note also how differently the above sentence describing Knight's methodology would read if the final "as I intend you to see it" were omitted. The stress is on the artist's dominant hand, which begins to point to structural levels beyond Knight.

Stegner, in apparent agreement with Brenner, writes: "as we accompany the narrator on his search for knowledge both he and we learn less and less about its subject, until it becomes apparent, finally, that Sebastian's 'real life' will never be known" (63–4). This is another argument that there is no Sebastian in the text, though I don't know how one could argue that we learn "less and less" as the narrative proceeds. We certainly learn some facts about Knight's background, and his life, even having the chance to read frequent samples of his prose. However, the second part of Stegner's comment is correct: Knight's "real life" will never be known. This is more of a comment on Nabokov's sense of the nature of "real life" (thus the nature of biography) than a particular critique of the novel. The more information we receive about Knight's life, the more we should understand that his "real life" is not thoroughly fathomable. This would be true for any life, and it is an important concept which V. never grasps. Even the best text can only suggest a self.

Nabokov writes, in regard to a question about science's rational ability to "plumb the most profound mysteries of existence": "This appearance is very deceptive. It is a journalistic illusion. In point of fact, the greater one's science, the deeper the sense of mystery.... We shall never know the origin of life, or the meaning of life, or the nature of space and time, or the nature of nature, or the nature of thought" (SO 44–5). The further one explores the nature of "real life," Nabokov says, the greater one's sense of its mystery. The more we learn about Sebastian Knight, the more we should realize that his "real life" is not an object to be rationally analyzed. Learning that real life is ultimately a mystery is not the same as learning "less and less" about life. Therefore, to re-phrase Stegner's statement, as we accompany the narrator on his search for knowledge we learn more and more about its subject, until it becomes apparent that "real life" will never be completely known.

Reality, for Nabokov, is not an entirely subjective matter. Rather, it is a matter of precision. Brian Boyd explains, "This, in fact, is a key to Nabokov's work: not that nothing is real, as many readers idly suppose he says, but that it is only as the mind tries to peer past the generalization or the commonplace that things actually start to *become* real" (*American Years* 328). Jonathan Sisson makes a similar point, stressing the idea that Nabokov believes in the real, but "because of perceptual and mental limitations, one cannot arrive at a full comprehension": "Nabokov believes in a single, 'true,' ultimately uncomprehended reality" ("Cosmic Synchronization and Other Worlds" 16, 22). Life and reality are not entirely subjective, though they are entirely individualized. Precision and specificity are the qualities which can draw one closer to "reality."

Is There a Dolores in the Text?

Nabokov shows in *Sebastian Knight, Lolita,* and elsewhere that every biographical narrative is colored by the mind of the narrator. Therefore it is no surprise that each character, from Charlotte to Quilty to her husband

5. The Problem of Biography

Richard Schiller, seems to have a different version of Dolores. Miss Pratt, the headmistress of Beardsley School for girls, in her interview with Humbert, inadvertently makes this point by confusing their names in a number of comic ways, including "Dorothy Humbird" and "Dorothy Hummerson" (177–178). This is more than a mere comic interlude: it is a commentary on names. Pratt apparently does wish to discuss the Dolores of the dotted line, but she comes nowhere near that name. None of these names quite connects with the "real" Dolores. In her final name of the novel, of course, "Mrs. Richard F. Schiller," the original "Dolores Haze" is also nowhere to be seen. As Charlotte states in an earlier scene, "Little Lo, I'm afraid, does not enter the picture at all, at all" (83). The name "Dorothy Humbird" might cause a reader to recall the hummingbird which John Farlow hit during his shooting practice with Humbert: "not much of it could be retrieved for proof" (216). Lolita is lost among the many versions of her, and very little of her can be retrieved. There is not much "proof" of her life, not much conclusive evidence.

Humbert expresses his sense that Lolita beyond his control turns into a variety of wildly free "Lolitas"; he writes that the surrounding mountains, at a moment when he believes that Lolita has left him, seemed to be filled with "panting, scrambling, laughing, panting Lolitas who dissolved in their haze" (223–224). The unsolipsized Lolita is able to escape into her own name (even if that name — "haze" — is lower case in Humbert's view). Through the vast majority of the novel, however, the emphasis is on the narrator, the controller of names, and therefore we are rarely made aware that there is an original of Humbert's subspecies of Lolita.

The problem of the original of Dolores, or the real life of Lolita, is exemplified by the use of names in this novel. Humbert begins and ends his text with the name "Lolita," forming the definite frame of his sense of solipsism. The original little girl, however, is lost among the variety of names applied to her throughout the text. Leona Toker points out that "Lolita" is "the name used only by Humbert, with little or no sanction on Dolly's part" (*Nabokov* 206). Toker takes this as an argument for referring to Dolores Haze as "Dolly," in place of Humbert's "Lolita." I would argue, however, that the structural emphasis on the obsessive narrator provides evidence that we rarely catch glimpses of the original of Dolores (or Dolly or Lo or Carmencita). As shown on the first page of his text, Humbert is fully aware of the significance of names and the idea that different labels refer to different versions of the same girl. He explicitly tells us that his purpose is not to discuss the "Dolores" of the dotted line, but only the "Lolita" he had held in his arms. The child who we do see in this novel is primarily "Lolita," that is, primarily Humbert's chosen version of Dolores Haze. What she might have been named in another narrative, such as her own version of the story, is barely relevant.[2]

In Nabokov's screenplay, however, where Humbert's point of view cannot so thoroughly filter the girl, Lolita is able to assert her own name. Asked by a hotel manager what her initials are, she replies, "D.H. Dolores Haze." The stage direction then says, "Humbert has started to write his name on a register slip. He has got as far as 'Humbert Hu.' With great presence of mind he changes 'u' to 'a,' and adds 'ze'" (137).[3] The screenplay allows Lolita a brief autonomy over names that she doesn't have in the novel. In the novel, Lolita is hardly heard from except through Humbert's permission. Nonetheless, we do know that there is an original of Dolores which this narrator does not often respect.

One of the complications of the novel is that often Nabokov's metaphysics are nearly expressed by Humbert at the same time that they are unequivocally transgressed. For example, Humbert sees Lolita as the means of appeasing his lifelong obsession, as a fresh new version of his frustrated first love; he describes this connection between the two — his first love and Lolita — in a way that may coincide with Nabokov's ideal of timelessness. He simply conflates the two in his mind, but makes of it a metaphysical moment, as though time had "tapered to a palpitating point, and vanished" (39). This moment demonstrates Nabokov's thoughts about the transcendence of time as expressed in Humbert Humbert's worldview. Nabokov's metaphysical sense of transcendence (Sebastian Knight's "year one," *Speak, Memory*'s disbelief in "time") is specifically given to Humbert, though he is only able to express this sense through his intense illusions about Lolita. There is a sense of transcendence, though it is based on a very significant transgression.

Thus, through Humbert, we can see the misapplication of Nabokov's metaphysics — in his use of clichés, in his sense of time. Alexandrov has

5. The Problem of Biography

argued that Humbert's nympholepsy can often be seen as a misplaced sense of cosmic synchronization (*Otherworld* 162–163). In the biography, Boyd similarly writes,

> [H]is attractive urge to transcend the self decays at once into nothing more than its own foul parody, into the mere promotion of self.... We see him attempt to escape the trap of time, and hope for a moment that he may have found a way out for everyone; then we shudder, look again at the bars on his cage, and sigh with relief [*American Years* 228].

While I do not share that sense of "relief," I do believe that we should ultimately sense Humbert's misguided approach, not simply to some vague moral or ethical sense, but specifically to Nabokovian metaphysics.

What sets Humbert's sense of transcendence apart from Nabokov's is the fact that the moment of apparent transcendence comes at the expense of another individual, that it disregards the inviolability of another self. I am not speaking of Humbert's sexual violation of this girl, but of his inability to perceive her as a unique individual, rather than as a projection of his own mind. This, not sex, is what Nabokov means when he says that Humbert cannot see beyond the bars of his cage. When not enthralled by his pseudo-metaphysical moments of intense pedophilia, Humbert reduces Lolita to a few cultural clichés. Humbert disregards Lolita's original life, both in his aesthetics and his ethics: the two, for Nabokov, are never separable. V. makes a closely related mistake at the end of *Sebastian Knight*, and one might wonder whether those who accept V.'s final thoughts about his ability to partake of another's soul would also accept Humbert's similar thoughts. Can a soul be "solipsized"? Humbert says yes, V. says yes, Nabokov says no: this is a crucial difference. V. and Humbert both violate Nabokov's metaphysics: another's real life cannot be thoroughly inhabited.

Humbert also comes close to expressing Nabokov's thoughts concerning the ultimate impossibility of permanently grasping the celestial essence, the earthly presence of the otherworld. At one point, Humbert, seeing what he believes to be a nymphet in a distant window, seems to sense the "perfection" of unattainability; he states that there was a "fiery phantasm a perfection" which made his attraction also "perfect," specifically "because the vision was out of reach, with no possibility of attainment to spoil it" (264). This is very nearly Nabokov's sense of the celestial essence, or other world, or highest aesthetic and spiritual ideal. Only when beyond reach can perfection be appreciated. Had Humbert left it at this, his nympholepsy might have been a harmless, private infatuation, perhaps even a metaphor for Nabokovian art and metaphysics, like Nabokov's sense of the perfect translation untainted by real words. But rather than sustaining this appreciation of infinite perfections, Humbert feels the need to act: "grinding my teeth, I would crowd all the demons of my desire against the railing of a throbbing balcony...." At this point he begins to see the scene more clearly and "...Eve would revert to a rib, and there would be nothing in the window but an obese partly clad man reading a paper" (264). Here we have not the magician's, but the nympholept's doubts. The frustration of uncapturable essence leads Humbert only to the act of masturbation. Humbert's demonic desire takes off, and the seemingly transcendent vision reverts to the material world. The image of Eve reverting to a rib represents a reversal of Eden, a backwards movement whereby the human returns to the material and the male is left mateless. Humbert's nympholepsy denies real life to the original female. When one rudely grabs at perfection, one may find in one's hand nothing but disappointment — fat man reading a newspaper replaces one's "vision" of perfection.

While this passage seems to be an ultimate example of failed transcendence — the "great rosegray never-to-be-had" turning into an obese, partially naked man with a newspaper — it is equally important to note that Humbert's vision was a misperception from the start. There never was a nymphet in the window. That "throbbing balcony" represents Humbert's outward projection of his own hallucinations: nothing throbs in this scene except Humbert. Humbert, of course, continues to wish that arm had been a nymphet, that he could have kept his misperceived sense of perfection. It is as though John Shade had been nothing but disappointed that he and the lady in the magazine hadn't shared that vision of a white fountain. Humbert learns no lesson from this experience.

The same idea is presented earlier in the novel when Humbert describes "what looked like a nymphet in the act of undressing before a co-operative mirror." He states that "the vision" inspired him to "race with all speed toward my lone gratification." At that moment he states that this vision "transformed into the disgusting lamp-lit bare arm of a man in his

5. The Problem of Biography

underclothes reading a paper" (20). Apparently, for Humbert, there is something especially disturbing about the mental juxtaposition of newspapers and nymphets. Here, also, Humbert's illusion is destroyed by his need to act. While he almost appreciates Nabokov's epistemology of the unattainable essence — that the perfect quality cannot be captured — he quickly causes his own illusions to be destroyed, thereby finding himself unaccountably attracted to a "disgusting" man's bare arm. Once again, just as Humbert appears to be approaching Nabokovian metaphysics, he slips instead into his personal abyss.

These same nympholeptic illusions are responsible for the absence of the "real" Lolita from much of his text. While Humbert's thoughts about transcending time may remind us of Nabokov, these same thoughts show that the original of Lolita is thoroughly obscured. While Humbert insists that Lolita and his first love are one and the same child ("Everything they shared made one of them" [40]), his seemingly transcendent reverence for her completely obscures her original self. Still, his manipulative narrative strategy continually throws the reader off guard. Much of *Lolita*'s success lies in its ability to anticipate the readers' reactions. Humbert, too, lets the readers trip on the folds of his magic carpet. After stating that Annabel Leigh and Lolita are the same person, he adds, "I have no illusions, however." On the contrary, we should see that Humbert is full of illusions. Later Humbert bluntly states, "This book is about Lolita" (253). But Nabokov reminds us that the narrative is more honestly about the bars of Humbert's cage, that his view of the real Lolita is ever-obscured. Contrary to Humbert's own declaration, this book is almost entirely about Humbert.

Chapter 6

This Side

V. and the Sturdy Side

In 1937 Vladislav Khodasevich wrote,

> Peculiar to [Nabokov] is the realization, or perhaps only a deeply felt conviction, that the world of literary creativity, the true world of the artist, conjured through the action of images and devices out of apparent simulacra of the real world, consists in fact of a completely different material — so different that the passage from one world into the other, in whichever direction it is accomplished, is akin to death [98].

For Nabokov, Khodasevich is saying, the movement from the "real" world into a fictional world, or back again, is a type of death, a dying away from one world into another (regardless of how "realistic" that fictional world might seem). In part this is because the "material" from which fiction is composed is in fact "a completely different material." The area of creativity, the life of the imagination, exists on a completely different side than the "real" world.

As if to demonstrate Khodasevich's analysis, we have this portrayal of Sebastian Knight on the day of having finished a novel: he is collapsed on his floor with a number of completed pages placed on his desk. His position of complete collapse prompts the person who enters the room to wonder if he is dead. Knight replies that, no, he is not dead, "I have finished building a world and this is my Sabbath rest" (88). Here Knight (and Nabokov) makes it explicit that the novel is another "world" and that the return trip from this other world seems to be a form of death. The creative artist may continually die back and forth between the two sides. The return from the imagined world comes with the exhaustion of having created that world.

6. *This Side*

The "Sabbath" statement is significant as well. Not only does it call attention to the religious significance of the building of that fictional world, it also — at first — might seem to contradict an earlier statement made by Knight. Concerning what he called his "state of constant wakefulness" Knight states that his mind is constantly alert during the day, with no moments of rest (65). However, after returning from the other world, the world of fiction, he is enjoying a "Sabbath rest." The point seems to be that the side of constant wakefulness, of intense self-awareness, is the other side. Sebastian is fully aware of his Sabbath, even while resting. The return from that imaginative side is a return to time. Only on this side does Knight have his Sabbath, while perhaps some other timeless aspect of himself watches even as he has that Sabbath.

In fact, the return to time is an essential aspect of the return to this world, as shown in this image: "An abyss of blackness where all of a sudden a small greenish circle moves up: the luminous dial of a watch (Sebastian disapproved of watches in his riper years)" (137). Here the light of time acts as a guide, showing the direction back over the abyss. Knight, when closer to his own death ("in his riper years"), apparently, no longer believed in a device which was connected with only the less creative side, as if the side of non-fiction was a reminder of time, a reminder of mortality.

The physical presence of V. is also a means of connecting him to the material side of life, adding to the essential contrast between creative Knight and the more mundane V. The reader of *The Real Life of Sebastian Knight* has no idea what V. looks like. He is never described, either by himself or by any of the other characters. The closest he comes to a physical description of himself is in one sentence when Madame Lecerf sits next to him on a bench, and he states that "the bench was very short and I am rather — well — on the sturdy side" (169). All that we learn about his physical appearance is from an implied, unstated word: perhaps "overweight," or "fat," or to complete the structure of the sentence, "the bench was very short and I am rather large."

More importantly, the phrase he uses to describe himself—"on the sturdy side"—resonates significantly with some other passages in the novel. This phrase says more about V. than perhaps even he realizes. To begin an exploration of what "the sturdy side" might mean, we need only look to the next chapter, where V. quotes the following passage from Knight's novel *The Doubtful Asphodel*: "only one half of the notion of death can be said to really exist: *this* side of the question ... he was already on the other side, if he could see the beach receding; no, not quite — if he was still thinking" (175).

The issue of sides is here directly connected to the boundary between life and death. The living are only capable of knowing one "side," says Knight: the material side of life. In this image death is a receding from life, an image which complements the idea that this is the "sturdy side": death is a sort of floating or drifting into a less solid, less firmly knowable element. V. most certainly is on the "sturdy side," the immovable shore, as opposed to Knight, who is on the side less determined by earthly material, or what could be called the celestial side.

However, Knight's sentence, while beginning as a definitive statement about what we can (or cannot) know about death, changes directions and ends by raising doubts. The "he" of the sentence believes himself to be already deceased, as he sees the other side receding, but then there is a question of how thought can continue beyond that boundary, the question of whether or not one can know oneself to be dead. Significantly, the sentence changes directions exactly on the word "question," which seems to be intentionally used in place of the word I have used, boundary: part of the question may be whether there is any boundary at all.

Within this one sentence there are two structural similarities with the first-person narrative method of Nabokov's *The Eye*. After the narrator's apparent suicide in *The Eye*, he (Smurov) claims to have undergone two transformations: first, "it became clear that after death human thought lives on by momentum"; and second, "in respect to myself I was now an onlooker" (20, 27). The speaker in Knight's sentence also seems, as the sentence shifts, to be speaking of himself as "he," viewing his own departure, while wondering if — because of his continued ability to think — this was actually a departure at all. He too may carry thought over into death ("by momentum"), all the while watching himself do so ("now an onlooker"). These doubts and possibilities are all in keeping with the first part of the sentence: only the solid shore, from which this sentence itself departs, can be said to really exist, whereas the other side of the question,

6. *This Side*

the side of doubts, cannot be defined from here. The sentence begins with an apparent line of logic, only to curve into uncertainty. In regard to the nature of this "other side," no final conclusions are offered.

Shores, sides and the creative process are combined in a description of Knight's struggle with words; this process is "the bridging of the abyss" between one's creative thoughts and earthly words, and it comes with a "feeling that the right words are awaiting you on the opposite bank in the misty distance." Bare, unworded thought — original thought — strives for those words while still "on this side of the abyss" (81–2). The art of composition involves an interaction between the celestial side of inspiration and the sturdy side of the written word. (Kinbote describes Shade while writing: "he followed the images wording themselves in his mind" (*PF* 89).) The fight to find the right words, for Knight, the struggle to write fiction, involves crossing to another shore, leaving this solid side to battle over a misty abyss. No wonder, then, that Knight seems dead after crossing back to this side. No wonder, either, that V. prefers to remain "on the sturdy side."

Boyd refers to V. as Knight's "rather colorless half brother" (*Russian Years* 499). At one point, V. recalls a girl in a boat with sixteen-year-old Knight; she is "at the helm," but V. cannot make out — or recall — any details about her, not even a color: she is a "mere outline, a white shape not filled in with color by the artist" (136). V. too is a "mere outline," colorless as far as descriptions go. This is so despite his being on this side of the abyss, that is, on the describable side. The "artist" chooses not to fill in those colors for us.

There are times when V. takes his colorlessness to extremes. Susan Fromberg points out that the narrator of this novel is only called by name once (429). At a chance meeting in Paris, Knight casually says hello and calls him V. (69). At other times V. goes out of the way to avoid mentioning his own name. In one introduction he encounters Mr. Silbermann, who states his name and puts out his hand; V. writes that he shook the man's hand and "named myself" (125). At another time he tells us that he introduced himself, but does not quote the introduction (148). Other omissions are more conspicuous. In one exchange, after Helene Grinstein directly asks him what his name is, he replaces the gap of his answer, where his name should be, with an ellipsis (134). This avoidance can become comic, as in the following introduction where he misquotes himself, "My name is so-and-so" (140). Thus, in the entirety of the novel he is called "so-and-so" as often as he is called V. The name so-and-so might even be said to have precedence over the name V., because so-and-so is the only name which he calls himself. No name, no description: apparently the purpose is to obscure the presence of the narrator from the novel.

However, V.'s personality pervades the narrative as much as — and often more than — the personality of the supposed biographee. Named or not, the narrator's personality remains inseparable from the text. Though only an outline, he is at the helm. In one paragraph the incompletely named narrator points out his own absence, letting us know that he has been careful to keep himself—his personal interests and problems—out of the book. He tells us that he is not going to tell us about his business concerns. He insists that he is dedicated to the pursuit of Knight's life story and that he happily keeps his own problems out of the narrative (139). This is similar to Nabokov's telling his class that they will not learn of Saavedra's maimed hand from him (*LDQ* 6). Why mention the maimed hand except to arouse interest in the biography of the man with that hand? V. too is teasing the reader with an apparently superfluous paragraph alluding to just how interesting his own life is. All of these suggestive phrases in that paragraph are intended to pique our curiosity: just who is this interesting V.? He clearly has the urge to take over this ostensible biography of his half-brother, though we can feel him overtly asserting his supposed objectivity. (Wood is correct to write that Kinbote is a "hysterical descendant" of V. [43].) The paragraph begins ("The reader may have noticed ...") by making sure the reader does indeed notice the idea that, as he says, he has not put much of himself in the book. This paragraph is a parody of selflessness.

V.'s is a boisterous absence, a loud outline. Nowhere in the narrative is he not present. The only physical detail we know of him is that he is large, but he is large in more ways than one. V.'s is an obtrusive pose of objectivity. Soon after the quoted passage where the girl is described as an outline, there is a description of a "V-shaped flight of migrating cranes" (137). On this level of the novel's structure, all of *Sebastian Knight* is, in fact, a "V-shaped flight." Though he may remain achromatic, his personality colors the entire text.

John Irwin has written a detailed analysis of the significance of the "V shape." A very brief summary of this analysis is that this shape "represents the physical basis of the functioning of human intelligence" (141). This is due to a number of human physiological traits, including the path in which light rays enter the eyes, the natural V shape of the opposable thumb, and the shape of a variety of human tools, including the hinge. It is perfectly consistent with Nabokov's narrator that, according to Irwin's analysis, V. would be further connected to the physical and material level of the narrative. V. represents the sturdier side of the structure, while the structure as a whole develops the contrast between V.'s sturdy side and Knight's less tangible, more imaginative side.

Thus, V.'s apparent physical description of himself—"on the sturdy side"—has more significance as a metaphysical statement than as a bodily depiction. It turns out to be a much more specific statement about himself than the relatively meaningless detail that he is large.

Gradus and Idiotic Death

Another Nabokovian character who is entirely on the sturdy side — as opposed to the celestial side — is perhaps his most specific representative of death: Gradus of *Pale Fire*. While Nabokov believes that the celestial essence is always manifest in this world to those who are able to perceive particularities, he often portrays death as a mindless disregard of this celestial presence. General ideas are a form of death and, conversely, death is represented as simple mindlessness: "idiotic death toddled by our side" (*SM* 245). He also makes an obvious analogy with sleep: "in absolute darkness ... my mind would melt in a travesty of the death struggle" (109). To all appearances from this side, Nabokov says, death is the melting of the mind in "absolute darkness."

Michael Wood writes, "Death in his work is almost always seen as a rough interruption, a violent discourtesy, a surprise" (203). As examples he then gives Lolita and Humbert (not Charlotte, for some reason, whose surprise death would provide much better support for his argument), Adam

Nabokov's Permanent Mystery

Krug of *Bend Sinister*, "Cincinattus" [sic] of *Invitation to a Beheading* and Luzhin of "*The Defence*" [sic]. All of these "rough interruptions," however, come at the conclusion of their respective novels. Structurally, they are no surprise at all. With these deaths Nabokov would almost seem to agree with Hemingway, who writes, "All stories, if continued far enough, end in death, and he is no true-story teller who would keep that from you" (122). Nabokov, in contrast, believes death is only the physical finish, and not the end of the essence of real life. Even Humbert writes, "every limit presupposes something beyond it" (283).

Nabokov does sometimes portray the randomness of death, as Wood states; sometimes he will surprise the reader by abruptly announcing a character's death at the end of a paragraph, as with Humbert's first love Annabel Leigh and with Sebastian Knight's mother (*Lolita* 13; *RLSK* 8). But this is another means of stressing death's apparent mindlessness, even its ineptness. Equally as often he represents death as merely the most predictable finish. Though sometimes unpredictable, death is not really a surprise. It is the most mundane occurrence imaginable. Death is the ultimate cliché. It requires no imagination to believe in mortality.

Nabokov could not say, with Walt Whitman, "No array of terms can say how much I am at peace about God and about death" (66). Death, for Nabokov, is an insult, even a shameful secret. Nonetheless, in *Pale Fire* John Shade explains his experience of "playful death" when he was eleven years old in terms which are remarkably similar to those of Whitman. Shade writes, "I felt distributed through space and time;/ One foot upon a mountaintop ...One ear in Italy, one eye in Spain" (l.147–151). Whitman writes, "Space and Time! now I see it is true, what I guess'd at.../ My ties and ballasts leave me, my elbows rest in sea-gaps,/ I skirt sierras, my palms cover continents" (48).[1] Both poets seem to be describing their sense of transcending "space and time." However, while they seem to be transcending their physical selves, they are only expanding their sense of physical space, not transcending it at all. Their respective beings now seem to be the size of continents and mountaintops. Shade considers this to be a foreshadowing of death; Whitman sees this larger sense of self as a means for exploring the multiple visions which surround him.

Shade concludes by saying that the amazement of this experience has

6. This Side

stayed with him along with "the shame" (l.166). Similarly, in *Speak, Memory* Nabokov describes the dead relatives he sees in his dreams as characterized by shame: "They sit apart, frowning at the floor, as if death were a dark taint, a shameful family secret" (50).[2] Neither Shade or Nabokov share Whitman's proclaimed sense of peace about death or, for that matter, about space and time. (Whitman's celebratory "Space and Time!" becomes Shade's lowercased "space and time.") There are times, on this side, when one ponders death and feels only shame at one's own powerlessness. One is thus confronted with the logical dominance of death.

The idea of traveling to that other side, through suicide, does cross Nabokov's mind. He writes of his attempts to find his way out of "the prison of time" only to find that it is "without exits": "Short of suicide, I have tried everything" (*SM* 20). Here Nabokov touches on an idea which Kinbote takes further. In his "simple and sober description of a spiritual situation" Kinbote discusses the temptation of suicide. He argues that a firm belief in an afterlife should provide one with a sense of optimistic expectancy, and he questions if anything should prevent one from immediately exploring the other side: "no wonder one weighs on one's palm with a dreamy smile the compact firearm ... no wonder one peers over the parapet into an inviting abyss" (147). For Kinbote, a pistol represents a potential key to the afterlife, an invitation to a suicide. Scholars have debated whether to accept Nabokov's statement in a 1967 interview that "Kinbote committed suicide ... after putting the last touches to his edition of the poem" (*SO* 74). Regardless of one's decision to accept this extratextual evidence of suicide, within *Pale Fire* he certainly expresses his possible reasons for taking his own life. Kinbote, with his perverse version of looking-glass logic, suggests that those of firmest faith should be most susceptible to suicide. Those with the most clearly defined idea of the beyond should be most wishful of quickly getting there.

Kinbote's "inviting abyss" is the opposite of Shade's "inadmissable abyss" (l.179), as Boyd points out (*American Years* 446). These are two possible reactions to a discontent with death in life: to fight its foul presence, as Shade does, or to hasten its inevitable approach, as Kinbote suggests. As expressed in *Speak, Memory*, the latter approach is the only one which Nabokov refuses to attempt.

Nabokov's Permanent Mystery

That same abyss is present in the first sentence of the autobiography, though it is in no way inviting. The abyss is simply darkness, unpeopled by any popular myths or established religion. No definable God resides over Nabokov's sense of the afterlife. He states that he is only able to find "the faintest of personal glimmers in the impersonal darkness on both sides of my life" (20). Shade and Nabokov both seem much less capable than Whitman of a complete sense of transcendence over death: "And as to you Death, and you bitter hug of mortality, it is idle to try to alarm me.../ I recline by the sills of the exquisite flexible doors,/ And mark the outlet, and mark the relief and escape" (66). Though a number of scholars have discussed the presence of ghosts in Nabokov's fiction, and their ability to influence this side, death's door is never quite so exquisite or flexible for Nabokov. Fyodor says the door of mortality reveals nothing of the other side ("death in itself is in no way connected with the topography of the hereafter, for a door is merely the exit from the house and not a part of its surroundings" (*Gift* 309); V. remains isolated outside the wrong door in the hospital where Knight has already died. At best, as in the concluding scenes of *Sebastian Knight* and *Lolita*, the door is only half shut, allowing for some celestial interaction. Despite the title of his final novel, dying is never so "fun" in his art.

When contemplating the abyss, Nabokov often finds only darkness. Shade calls it "inadmissable"; Nabokov says there are "no exits." However, this idea of absolute darkness is also "inadmissable" because Nabokov refuses to accept it. The possibility that death has the last word is one which is inadmissable in Nabokov's metaphysics.

Nabokov believes that logic leads to the problem of death: none of the five senses is capable of perceiving an afterlife. In *Pale Fire* the pure physicality of death is illustrated through the character of Gradus. As the plot of *Pale Fire* progresses, Gradus — the embodiment of death — comes closer "in space and time" and gradually becomes more of a physical presence; his facial features become more apparent, including "a wart on the chin" (186). As the physical fact of death approaches, space and time seem to intensify: one cannot transcend the wart on death's chin, let alone become the size of a continent. Gradus is directly connected to time, that means for measuring life on this side. In much the same way that V. structures his

6. *This Side*

chapters, a section on Gradus often begins with the precise account of his whereabouts in terms of time.

To increase our sense of the physical presence of Gradus, we then learn that he is suffering from a disturbingly vivid bout with indigestion: "a scalding torrent of indigestion" (280). Few things are less spiritual than diarrhea. The significance of the name "Gradus" is complex in *Pale Fire*, but in *Look at the Harlequins!* one of the meanings is succinctly expressed: "death is silly, death is degrading" (240). That this dyspeptic individual should make contact with us all is indeed degrading. Death's progress is a mindless pursuit. This is the source of Shade's "shame." Gradus is entirely a material presence: "Spiritually he did not exist" (187–191). There is no real life of Gradus; there is nothing original about the approach of death.

The sense of death as an ultimately unavoidable material presence, Nabokov suggests, is the rational view. When contemplated on a logical, material level death is a disturbing physical presence. The indigestion of death will eventually get to everyone. In fact, this is the only rational reaction one can have to death, the only logical observation one can make: one cannot rationally verify anything on the other side of that door. One cannot get beyond Gradus's face. For Nabokov, however, death is not merely a material occurrence. Material objects are not necessarily the most "real." This is why V. is unable to attain the "real life" of Sebastian Knight through his external, "scientific" quest. This is also a reason for Nabokov's biographical critique of Chernyshevski, the 19th-century Russian materialist, in *The Gift*. In that novel the real life of Fyodor is found more in his poetry and his imagined talks with the poet Koncheyev than in his "real" Berlin surroundings. Those imagined talks are a higher order of reality: "a real conversation would be only disillusioning" (343). Only the life of the mind, the world of imagination, can approach perfection. Nabokov's belief in something beyond, his sense of the celestial essence, depends on what he calls "irrational and divine standards" (*LL* 373). The irrational standards of the imagination permit one to move beyond material reality. Nabokov builds this metaphysical concept into his literary structures. Thus it is only in those moments when they lapse into logic that Nabokov's characters are disturbed by the idea of death. That magic melody that V. hears from Knight's bookshelf has nothing to do with logic; Humbert's concluding pages move beyond his "real" world, past or present. That inspirational shiver a person receives from a striking artistic moment has no rational explanation. That death exists is a rational, logical belief; that there are higher, more "divine" standards is not.

Consistent with his idea that the plot of the story is not where one can find the ultimate meaning of a story — rather it is in "the secret points, the subliminal co-ordinates": "These are the nerves of the novel"— Nabokov does not place a great amount of emphasis on death (*Lolita* 316). That is, death is not where one should search for meaning. Conclusions are often not-so-conclusive in Nabokov's work.

In many of his works, Nabokov creates endings that suggest something beyond the final words of the text. This, too, creates a sense of inconclusiveness. These endings point toward a next level, beyond the book. Examples include the ending of *Pnin*, pointing to further adventures for the main character; the ending of that grammar book in *Speak, Memory*, pointing to the future possibilities contained in the language; the ending of *Glory*, with Martin following a path characterized by — the final two words of the novel —"mysterious windings" (205). These endings act as arrows to a beyond, to an intangible next level beyond the book. Even the interviews of *Strong Opinions* end by pointing toward something else; this final interview, supposedly conducted by a "docile anonym," ends with the words "Let us now turn —" (207).

Often, Nabokov likes to create a tone of remoteness at the end, rather than a mere ending. *Pale Fire*'s index ends with the idea of distance. He describes the final paragraph of *Lolita*, where Humbert refers to himself and Quilty only by initials, also as a distancing effect, creating "remoteness of tone": "I am glad I managed to achieve this remoteness of tone at the end" (*SO* 73). Some of these suggestions beyond the book, these unworded continuations, demonstrate very clearly that Nabokov uses this technique to add another dimension to his works. *The Gift* ends with the idea that "the shadows of my world extend beyond the skyline of the page" (366). The final words of *Invitation to a Beheading* most directly connect these inconclusive conclusions to a metaphysical technique, as Cincinnatus heads in a direction where he will find souls more compatible with his own. One should also recall the ending of "The Art of Translation," with that essay

6. This Side

pointing toward a final idea of perfection. That — perfection — may be the place beyond the page.

Each of these methods for creating a conclusion which does not conclude — false endings, structures leading beyond the book, creating a tone of remoteness — works to lead the reader to look for levels beyond mere plot. Each suggests that the apparent ending is not the end at all. That is another way in which Nabokov builds his metaphysical ideals into his literary structures.

Kinbote concludes his commentary with the idea that Gradus awaits us all, but that is still not the last word of the novel: the index is yet to come. One might read this as Nabokov's response to Hemingway's statement that death is the true end of every story. Plot is never the point, and a lack of logic is necessary for one to perceive the ever-peripheral presence of the celestial essence.

One cannot perceive the live source of the celestial essence by studying the start and finish of any given life: the time before birth and after death yield no secrets. All one can see at the start and finish of life is the most obvious plot, the "two eternities of darkness" (*SM* 19). Shade speaks of "Infinite foretime and/ Infinite aftertime" (l.122–123). Real life, Nabokov believes, gleams through between these two points, in the daily details. Thus Shade's fifty-one-line, detailed explication of his method of shaving is not at all trivial (l.887–938). The appreciation of such seeming trifles is the greatest method for appreciating "real life."

Shade also reaches the conclusion that life is about the perception of patterns; he states that he is able to discover: "some kind/ of correlated pattern in the game" (l.811–813). But Nabokov's poet doesn't quite reach the highest level of Nabokovian metaphysics because he is always a little too logical (that is, unless we consider him to be the author of poem and commentary, which is an entirely different topic, already much discussed by scholars of Nabokov). He is on the proper path, but doesn't seem to realize — at least in the poem "Pale Fire"— that the perception of "patterns" is an irrational act.

For Nabokov, however, the ending is never so definite. The place where a reader might expect an ending is precisely where Nabokov offers questions.

Nabokov's Permanent Mystery

Line 1000 of "Pale Fire," the unwritten final line of the poem, provides another Nabokovian commentary on conclusions, one which — like the final moment of *Sebastian Knight*— draws attention to the materiality of the written word. Kinbote tells us that this line "remained to be written ... and would have completed the symmetry of the structure" (15). In his note to that line he fills in the words (292). However, the line should not be considered a fill-in-the-blank with an obvious answer. Shade left the line unwritten so as to incorporate the theme of the first line into the structure of the poem: line one-thousand is the shadow of line one. Kinbote almost gets this right, as he makes this comment on the line: "our shadows still walk without us" (15). Though this is how the line should be read, as the unwritten shadow of line one, Kinbote, of course, can't help supplying the words rather than respecting that shadow. In regard to one of Pushkin's fragments, Nabokov writes, "There is nothing more futile, and more tempting, than filling such gaps as left here.... [It] is automatically supplied by the ear" (*EO*, vol. 3 350). Shade's last line can also be supplied automatically by the ear, but should not be filled in as though this were some sort of puzzle. Elsewhere Nabokov says that "'lane' is the last word of Shade's poem" (*SO* 73). Thus death — with the rhyme "slain"— does not have the last word of the poem. This reflected final line is another of Nabokov's unworded suggestions of the other world.

As far as his reputation as an American poet, Shade suggests his reputation is slightly behind that of Robert Frost (l.425–426). Frost writes in "The Figure a Poem Makes" that one purpose of his poetry is to create "a momentary stay against confusion" (440). Shade similarly seems to be trying to contain his sense of "confusion" or of metaphysical doubt through his poetry, saying that he understands his life "only through my art" (l.972). One might view Shade's poem as a Frost-like frame, a very momentary stay against confusion. *Pale Fire* as a whole, however, when one includes Kinbote, could be a comment on the inevitable return to confusion. For Nabokov, the frame of a well-structured poem is too fragile to make much of a stay against the real life forces of confusion. Boyd writes, "Shade's poem, with its highly formal verse pattern and Parthenon-like elegance of its architecture, subjects powerful emotions to deliberate control. Kinbote's commentary yields to the lurch of his obsessions" (*American Years* 435).

6. *This Side*

The iambic pentameter of Shade's poem stands in complete contrast to the uncontrolled imagination of Kinbote. *Pale Fire*, poem and commentary, is a trampoline against confusion: an ecstatic skyward bounce, a playful embrasure of chaos. Nabokov writes: "The material of this world ... is chaos, and to this chaos the author says 'go!'" (*LL* 2). Poetry such as that of Shade or Frost can only offer the most temporary of stays against chaos, while other authors — such as Nabokov or Whitman — might find inspiration in the chaos itself.

Kinbote mentions — though not by name — Frost's "Stopping by Woods on a Snowy Evening." He specifically appreciates the finish of the poem, the final two lines, noting that they are "identical" and that the repetition creates a metaphysical resonance: "one personal and physical, and the other metaphysical and universal" (203–204). Frost's final two lines are "identical," as Kinbote states: "And miles to go before I sleep,/ And miles to go before I sleep" (Frost 225). He thus suggests that one should interpret two identical lines in such a way that the significance resonates, rather than repeats. In the first line, he says, the meaning is "physical"; in the second, "metaphysical." This is closely related to what I said about Shade's reflected lines, 1 and 1000: the first is a material, written line; the second resonates beyond the material words on the page. There is a suggestion here that Nabokov is using a technique similar to the one in Frost's poem, perhaps, as he does with Whitman, specifically having Shade respond to a prominent American poet. Kinbote, however, despite an astute reading of Frost's lines, ends his note by overlooking any possible connection to Shade's poem: "Shade could never make *his* snowflakes settle that way." The irony, of course, is that Kinbote points us toward the relevant poem by Robert Frost, but then not only misses the point but makes a negative comment about Shade's talent.

Admittedly, though, this reflection of line 1000 is a relatively simple structural trick. In the ending of "The Art of Translation," Nabokov does not supply the "perfect" words of the perfect translation, so the reader is left with only an abstract idea of translated perfection. Here, of course, in Shade's one thousandth line, any good reader could supply the unwritten words. John Shade tends to be a little too rational. In his rational pursuit for the meaning of life and death he has finished with a very rational reflection.

Nabokov, of course, will make sure that *Pale Fire*—the novel—is much more than rational.

Nabokov's structures must be perceived in their entirety in order to be appreciated. One must see how far the highest level leads away from the dominance of Gradus, how far this attempt to strive for the highest creative level leads away from the lowest material level. One must also appreciate the position of the real author in this hierarchy. The real author is the highest possible level on *this* side, and through imagination and creativity can connect somehow with the ultimate mystery of the other side. Nabokov firmly believes that the source of his art exists in some sense of the beyond. The live source of inspiration is the highest level of all his structures and of his sense of "real life."

Some have recognized the presence of this beyond, but misread its significance. William Carroll, for example, writes:

> The "mind behind the mirror" is the presence felt by virtually all of Nabokov's protagonists, and their search for or flight from this mind forms a central movement in the novels. Whether that mind is described as "God" (by Kinbote) or, much more frequently, as an evil demon, its powers remain oppressive [100].

The first sentence is correct; the second is entirely wrong. The recognition of and movement toward this higher power is not oppressive at all. For Cincinnatus, Fyodor, Krug, Knight, Shade and many of Nabokov's other protagonists the presence of this higher mind brings a sense of relief, even a sense of bliss. The highest mind is the primary source for artistic inspiration. Kinbote does not think of "God" as evil: *this* side is oppressive to him. He sees suicide as a step toward that higher mind, thus a possible relief. One's way of thinking, not the potential for otherworldly influence, is often oppressive to Nabokov's characters. Very few of these characters view the mind behind the mask as "an evil demon," and those characters who do are incorrect.

Nabokov tells us that this "mind" is his own, that his is the controlling mind beyond these fictional worlds. In none of his works does he take the role of an "evil demon," as Carroll states. If one detects an excessive amount of authorial *schadenfreude* in such worlds as that of *Laughter in the Dark*, for example, it is because Nabokov often creates worlds which invert his own values (like Zembla). That a young girl might torment a blind man

6. This Side

has nothing to do with Nabokov's sense of the otherworld. Similarly, Humbert's sense of nymphets as demonic is a reflection of his own obsessed (Carroll might say "oppressed") mind, *not* a true otherworldly influence in the Nabokovian sense. In addition, Nabokov's madmen are most often, Lear-like, capable of perceiving their own madness, suggesting that there is always a level of mind above that of the purely oppressed. The "mind" of the other side is saner than any mind on this one; the highest mind is capable of making ultimate sense out of the chaos of real life. Boyd writes, "Perhaps from the other side of life any death, no matter how seemingly pointless, may become the center of a glittering web of meaning" (*American Years* 455).

Carroll may have misread Nabokov's sense of the other side because there are a great number of oppressed minds in those fictional worlds. In Nabokov's metaphysics, however, the appreciation of details — which equals the perception of the celestial essence — is capable of alleviating the oppression. Artistic appreciation is a method of thinking which can bring one closer to Nabokov's sense of a more benevolent beyond. The "evil demons" are exorcised as one moves up on the aesthetic structure. Gradus, the lowest level, has the most oppressive way of thinking: "He worshiped general ideas ... [s]cientists, writers, mathematicians, crystallographers and so forth, were no better than kings or priests: they all held an unfair share of power of which others were cheated" (152). Death is a generality. Gradus thinks that precise thoughts are "diabolical." One can only imagine the ignorant disdain Gradus might have for the power of the conjurer, the emblem Nabokov so often uses for the creator of artistic worlds. If he were familiar with such a creator, conjurers would surely be added to his list; in fact, it might replace the general "and so forth" at the end of the list: "writers, mathematicians, crystallographers and conjurers." Those are among the people who the generality of death disdains the most.

Chapter 7

The Otherworldly Role of Water

Water plays a greater role in Nabokov's personal lexicon than has previously been recognized. Sinks, drips, drinks, and even ice and snow may have a metaphysical importance in Nabokov's art. Puddles and rainstorms reflect a deep, perhaps transcendent meaning. Water, in a variety of forms, consistently represents the possibility of transcendent communication for Nabokov. He consistently presents water as the means by which one may connect with the other side.

In *Glory* Martin Edelweiss lies in his "hot and uncomfortable" bed while contemplating death and the existence of ghosts. As he does so, he momentarily senses death approaching, only to discover that the presence he felt was nothing but water:

> He imagined how he himself would be dying some day, and felt as if the ceiling were coming down on him slowly and inexorably. Something began to drum rapidly in the darker part of the room, and his heart missed a beat. But it was merely water that had been spilled on the washstand and was now dripping onto the linoleum [92].

Martin's fearful anticipation of death is replaced by water. In this image, water seems to be an appeasing sign sent from the other side, indirectly telling Edelweiss that his fear is unfounded. Water is also connected to his doubts about ghosts, suggesting that their presence is possible.

Water is used the same way in *The Gift*. As Alexander Yakovlevich Chernyshevski lies dying, the sound of water represents the illusion of nothingness, the limited vision of those who see nothing beyond. He says to Fyodor, "Of course there is nothing afterwards.... There is nothing. It is as clear as the fact that it is raining." Chernyshevski's certainty of nothingness, however, as the next paragraph shows, is a misinterpretation of

7. The Otherworldly Role of Water

the facts: "And meanwhile outside the spring sun was playing on the roof tiles, the sky was dreamy and cloudless, the tenant upstairs was watering the flowers on the edge of the balcony, and the water trickled down with a drumming sound." Needless to say, Nabokov never had much sympathy for the finite conclusions of existentialists. A few pages further on, Fyodor speaks the better lesson of this deceptive dripping, "Definition is always finite, but I keep straining for the faraway; I search beyond the barricades (of words, of senses, of the world) for infinity" (329). Though Chernyshevsky never gets the message, the reader (and Fyodor) see that the water in the above scene demonstrates the presence of more outside than the firm believers in nothingness are capable of perceiving, that perhaps there may even be a "dreamy and cloudless" spring day somewhere beyond one's limited perception.

One may look at these passages from *Glory* and *The Gift* on their own terms, and perceive the relevance of water without the need for other texts. Each image is capable of standing for itself, to some degree. However, Nabokov's use of water is consistent, and one can better appreciate the metaphysical role of water in Nabokov's lexicon by looking at examples throughout his body of work.

The story "Ultima Thule" provides another example. In responding (somewhat) to questions about an afterlife and that question to which Nabokov himself only responds in his own terms—"does God exist?"—the character Falter, who "stands *outside* our world, in the true reality," significantly juxtaposes a statement about revealed "essence" with a request for water: "I certainly cannot doubt that, as you put it, 'essence has been revealed to me.' Some water please" (*Stories* 512). Falter refuses to elaborate on the nature of this "essence," and instead there is a reference which is best understood within the personal terms of Nabokovian metaphysics. He, too, knows more than he can say in words, though perhaps some water might help. Water, for Nabokov, is the sign of communicated essence and the means by which that communication can be made.

In *Ada*, the telephone is replaced by the "dorophone," a communication device which literally runs on water: "All the toilets and waterpipes in the house had been suddenly seized with borborygmic convulsions. This always signified, and introduced, a long-distance call" (260). The proper protocol for answering the dorophone is to say, "*A l'eau!*" This is, obviously, a bilingual pun on the English "Hello," and the French for "by water." It is also a pun on Nabokov's sense of communication by water.

Water as a means of communication takes on additional significance in this novel when Lucette commits suicide by drowning. After the drowning, the possibility of water acting as a means of communication with the other side — truly "long distance" communication — is further developed. Here is a mistyped word corrected by one of Van's editors: "Although Lucette had never died before — no, *dived* before, Violet — from such a height ... she went with hardly a splash through the wave that humped to welcome her" (493). (Some "mistakes" remain in this novel also.) Although it is the site of suicide, water does not symbolize a permanent end. Boyd discusses "the messages Lucette seems to send from her watery grave" (*American Years* 560). Rather than discuss the details of this communication in *Ada* or elsewhere, I only want to stress that Nabokov often uses water as the means of interaction between the two sides. Water thus becomes an aspect of the novel's structure, as a means for communicating between levels.

In *The Real Life of Sebastian Knight*, V. says to the painter Roy Carswell, in regard to Knight, that any person is capable of looking into water. Carswell responds by saying that Knight was especially skilled at doing so (118). Knight was particularly able to understand the other side of mortal life, the celestial side, Carswell seems to be saying. Like Falter, he is using Nabokov's language, making a statement which might not mean as much when read alone. The context is Nabokov's metaphysical imagery. Water could represent the means by which Knight can communicate with this side and the means by which he can make himself known within V.'s text.

While any depiction is limited in its ability to portray "real life," the one painting of Knight described in the novel, by Carswell, seems to be the only undisputed portrayal, combining some sadness with his twinkling eyes, clearly portraying the color of his eyes and hair (117). Nonetheless, this is not a strictly realistic painting; rather, the portrayal seems as though it is a reflection of Knight in water. One must look into the watery reflection to see the "receding" body of Knight. Once again, it seems that water can convey an idea from the other side.

There are plenty more examples of Nabokov using water in this way:

7. The Otherworldly Role of Water

the icicles of "The Vane Sisters," Krug's puddle in *Bend Sinister*, and perhaps the puddle — the authorial watermark — at the end of the fourth chapter of *Pnin*. Shade's daughter Hazel commits suicide by drowning; Humbert contemplates drowning Charlotte and later vividly recalls the word "waterproof." The aspiring artist Victor Wind "places various objects in turn — an apple, a pencil, a chess pawn, a comb — behind a glass of water and peered through it at each studiously" (*Pnin* 98–9). Water is a means for looking through to the other side, an emblem for interaction with an other realm.

Thus, with an additional understanding of Nabokov's private iconography, Carswell's painting earns further credibility as the most insightful image of Knight, though it tells us nothing about what V. would consider Knight's "real life," nothing of his loves, travels, friends, problems. Carswell says that he was trying to make sure that he avoided "story-telling" (118). Nabokov, too, resists telling the "story" of Knight, suggesting that "real life" is more than a story, more than a plot. (In his lecture on *Anna Karenin*, Nabokov makes clear that one must understand the plot, but that plot alone is not enough. A novel should be appreciated "on a higher level than plot" (*LRL* 144).) But V. is unsatisfied with this artistic rendering, almost childishly declaring that he needs to know more, that he needs to know all, that his sense of Knight cannot remain "incomplete": "it's a scientific necessity." (V. suddenly seems to have learned the proper form of the word "incomplete.") He stated this same wish for a "scientific" approach earlier (63), as if Knight were a dissectible specimen. This assertion of a "scientific" method gets to the heart of V.'s ideas about an objective rendering: he demands that Knight's past can treated as something tangible.

The last line of this chapter, however, profoundly finalizes the painter's debate with V. (referring to V.'s quest for Knight's last love); there he says that he would wager his painting against the possibility of V. finding her (118). It is precisely his painting, his artistic depiction of Knight, that he will bet against V.'s "scientific necessity": the painter is willing to place the validity of his version against that of the would-be biographer. Carswell's metaphoric portrayal — a receding image reflected in a pool of water — is more likely to capture the essence of Knight's real life than is V.'s insistently "scientific" quest.

Nabokov's Permanent Mystery

Alexandrov follows some significant raindrops in *Lolita* (*Otherworld* 178–181). His discussion of water imagery fits perfectly into this analysis of Nabokov's use of water as the means of transcendent communication. He argues that "the series of rain and water images can be interpreted as hints that Charlotte's spirit is a constituent element of Humbert's fate" (181). Charlotte, like most of Nabokov's ghosts, is characterized by water. As in the conclusion of *Sebastian Knight*, a watery ghost can make its presence known through a restless dream: "for some minutes I miserably dozed, and Charlotte was a mermaid in a greenish tank" (132). Nabokov often uses water as the image for movement back and forth from the other side to the earthly side. This is not to say that every rainfall in *Lolita* is a sign from Charlotte. This is only to say that if one reads on the highest level of Nabokov's literary structure, one should see that this novel is, among other things, a ghost story.

Nabokovian characters tend not to disappear after death. Correspondingly, true Nabokovian teleology extends the structure of a text beyond its apparent conclusion. The highest structural level is camouflaged — sometimes by its own obviousness — throughout the text. This suspicious spinster, for example, having stopped to question Lolita outside of her house, could be a disguised ghost: "The odious spinster ... stood leaning on her slim umbrella (the sleet had just stopped, a cold wet sun had sidled out).... 'And where is your mother, my dear?'" (180). Alexandrov provides other examples of "meteorological and water imagery" which, he argues, could convey the presence of "Charlotte's occult presence after she dies" (*Otherworld* 181). I would only like to stress the consistency of Nabokov's imagery regarding transcendent communication and the fact that this highest level of the literary structure is an indefinite realm which a reader cannot unequivocally claim as "real." No ghost is objectively presented in this text, but one should recognize that the possibility (I would say probability) of ghosts is part of this novel.

The point is not to hunt down all the possible clues to Charlotte's ghost, as many have done with the clues to Quilty; the point is only to recognize that hers is a presence in the text which exists beyond Humbert's conscious perception. Humbert himself doesn't know why he so strongly insists on the power of water, as he combines in his mind Charlotte's after-

7. The Otherworldly Role of Water

life with the means of her death: "your eternal heaven among an eternal alchemy of asphalt and rubber and metal and stone — but thank God, not water, not water!" (88). He says this in response to his own decision not to drown Charlotte, but Humbert does not realize that one need not die by water — like Lucette — in order to communicate by water — like Sebastian. Water is the means of travel between this side and the other side, between the material world and the "world" of the celestial essence. Humbert further demonstrates his ignorance of Nabokov's use of water in the screenplay, calling it "the anonymous fluid" (174). Obviously he sees no potential for transcendent communication in a fluid he considers to be "anonymous." On the other side, identities may not be so fluid — as I will discuss in chapter ten — and water may not be so anonymous.

Many readers have noticed that during his final scene with Lolita Humbert recalls Charlotte saying the word "waterproof," referring to his watch. No one that I know of, however, has noticed that after the death of Quilty, Humbert writes, "I ... consulted my wrist watch. The crystal was gone but it ticked" (304). One would assume that his watch, without the crystal, would no longer be waterproof. We might recall that Sebastian Knight, "in his riper years," also loses faith in watches. Humbert's time has not yet stopped, but it is now susceptible to water, that medium of the afterworld. In Nabokov's terminology, Humbert has traveled closer to the timelessness of the other side.

Nonetheless, Humbert portrays himself as almost completely unaware of the potentially transcendent presences which surround him. He tells us that he has reread his own text, but one gets the sense that he has not been able to do so at leisure because his time is running out. Upon rereading, he is only able to state, "At this or that twist of it I feel my slippery self eluding me, gliding into deeper and darker waters than I care to probe" (308). That is, he doesn't want to read the implications of his own text too closely. One reason Humbert doesn't wish to read too closely, he says, is because he senses that the deepest waters are separating himself from himself. In this he is correct: Humbert is separated from Humbert through the mirror-medium of water, dissociated from himself in the act of imaginative writing. He senses this, but does not want to confront the fact, probably because this movement entails his own death: first, figuratively, through the creative process; then, literally, as this creative effort leads to his actual end. Humbert does not consciously want to probe this possibility.

We the readers can peruse the text, rereading to eliminate the dominance of linear time, as Nabokov wishes us to do. We can transcend Humbert's sense of time, and in that way we can see the creative level which stands above the narrator. When Humbert says that he wishes to avoid the deepest "waters" of himself, he is unintentionally telling us, in Nabokov's terms, that he wants to avoid a complete separation from his material self. He does not care to probe those signs from the other side. Humbert's best attempts at transcendence are weighed down by his own physical self. For Nabokov, however, the celestial essence is ever-present, regardless of what any particular narrator might believe.

Another sign that one is in the highest region of Nabokov's literary structures, the level of greatest imagination, is the presence of Lewis Carroll. Carroll represents the imaginative other side, whereas water represents the means of communication from that side. In one sentence from *Lolita*, we can see the connection between water and wonderland as a "breeze from wonderland" seems to italicize Humbert's thoughts "as if the surface reflecting them were wrinkled by the phantasm of that breeze" (131). Wood writes of this passage: "thoughts turn physically into words and are mirrored in something like water" (103). Thoughts from wonderland turn into words through the medium of water: this is the process of Nabokovian transcendent communication. The celestial essence is not actually contained in any words, but it may be glimpsed or intuited through certain signs such as water. Wood also shows that this passage draws attention to the physical nature of words on the page by referring to Humbert's "thoughts" as italicized. Words exist entirely on the material side; however, when they are sent through water, they are capable of conveying something — perhaps transmitting messages — from the other side.

Chapter 8

Nabokov's Originals

The novel which Nabokov was planning for publication at the time of his death in 1977 was entitled *The Original of Laura*. A few months before his death, he described this as a "not quite finished manuscript" and wrote, "I must have gone through it some fifty times" (*SL* 562). Now that the incomplete manuscript of this novel has been published, we are able to see that work in progress. It is much less complete than he suggested, and many of its main themes remain incomplete. In fact, the meaning of that title — the significance of an "original" — is not entirely clear from the published *Laura*, but the concept becomes more clear in a number of Nabokov's other works.

A passage in *The Eye* gives some idea of Nabokov's sense of an "original." The idea of an "original" obscured among various versions is here conveyed by the narrator of that novel:

> I could already count three versions of Smurov, while the original remained unknown. This occurs in scientific classification. Long ago, Linnaeus described a common species of butterfly, adding the laconic note, "*in pratis Westmanniae.*" Time passes, and in the laudable pursuit of accuracy, new investigators name the various southern and Alpine races of this species, so that soon there is not a spot left in Europe where one finds the nominal race and not a local subspecies. Where is the type, the model, the original? [53–4].

The narrator here is searching for the "original" of Smurov. His metaphor of investigation suggests that — like a butterfly reclassified into a series of subspecies — the concept of an original source does exist, though the source itself may appear to be long lost. The narrator resolves this comparison with hope for recapturing the past: "Then, at last, a grave entomologist discusses in a detailed paper the whole complex of named races and accepts as the representative of the typical one the almost 200-year-old, faded Scandinavian specimen collected by Linnaeus; and this identification sets everything right."

Nabokov's Permanent Mystery

The narrator of *The Eye* is certainly related to V., and sounds almost the same as he talks of "this quest of mine for the real Smurov" (89). And although V. does consider his an equally scientific quest, he may be less sensitive to the subspecies, the multiple versions which come down from the original. The narrator of *The Eye* is wary of all reflected images: "I resolved to dig up the true Smurov, being already aware that his image was influenced by the climatic conditions prevailing in various souls—that within a cold soul he assumed one aspect but in a glowing one had a different coloration." This narrator understands the need to "dig up," through the weight of various accumulated versions of a self, from the glowing to the cold, the "true," the "original": the "real life." V. does not seem as aware of the need to search further back, through the detritus of definitions, in order to rediscover the original, seeming to believe rather that he can piece Knight together through a collection of his subspecies. Former friends, lovers and acquaintances: V. does not see that these are only hot and cold souls, variously tempered versions, and not direct connections through which one comes into contact with another's "true" self. Perhaps we, however, can see through V. and assert the existence of an original.

This comparison between the "quest" of *The Eye* and that of *Sebastian Knight* becomes even more interesting when one considers that in *The Eye* it is finally revealed that the narrator *is* Smurov, that the narrator's search had actually been for his own "real life." The being who had apparently been watching himself after death, quoted earlier, was in fact the I—the "eye"—watching Smurov, two parts of a split self. This could be further evidence that V. and Knight are two parts of a single self, as Page Stegner argues. This could also explain why they are "half"-brothers, and why there are so many other "halves" throughout the novel: the celestial and the material represent two halves of one person. V.'s quest through the places of Knight's past may represent a quest for his own identity. This is an interesting possibility, but it does not provide a solution as to how one might perceive the original of Knight. Structurally, this idea suggests that V. and Knight may be synthesized on some higher level. However, I see it as another intriguingly deceptive solution to the novel, perhaps further obscuring the real life of Sebastian Knight.

Obscurity is an important theme in the novel, and this theme suggests

8. Nabokov's Originals

that an original can be obscured in a number of ways. Throughout the novel, beginning in the first paragraph, the word "obscure" can be found, most often applied to words and personalities. In the first paragraph there is a Russian lady who wishes her name to be withheld due to an "obscure reason." By the end of the meandering paragraph, full of obscure lines of V.'s randomly associative logic, he reveals her name. However, her identity is no less obscure once her name is known. We still have no idea who Olga Olegovna Orlova is, and we never do, despite having a definite knowledge of her name. The additional words — the full, alliterative name — seem to be only further steps away from the original, like the label of a subspecies. Equally, the name "Sebastian Knight" does nothing to help us attain his identity.[1] A name may be a version of an original, like another narrative, which only succeeds in further obscuring the source. Therefore, we need to look at some other ways in which a "gleam" of real life can shine through the obscurity of words.

The idea of a poet's talent gleaming through the obscurity of his poetry can be taken as a clue to the way in which an original self can be sensed, especially when that talent is described as "real" talent: real talent as a sign of real life. (We might recall here that Nabokov defines poetry as "the mysteries of the irrational as perceived through rational words" (*Gogol* 55). Words can only convey — not contain — these mysteries.) Something of the real life of Alexis Pan can be seen gleaming (we are told) through the many ineffective words of his poetry (26). V. also uses an image of light to describe Knight's sense of his mother, saying that Knight may not have recalled her clearly, but "probably" sensed her as "a soft radiance in the background of his life" (16). This "soft radiance" is the opposite of obscurity; it is the definite presence of a self. Definite, though not entirely definable: had Knight tried to attach a narrative to this sense, a plot full of dates and events, a biography of his mother, the "soft radiance" would most likely have been obscured or lost, rather than enhanced. Thus V. uses the words "probably" and "in a way" to temper any certainty about that self. Had he attempted to bring that soft radiance to the foreground, he would have destroyed its delicacy.

In addition to metaphors of light, V. makes other comments which are clues as to how Nabokov believes a "real life" can be perceived. Some of these clues come as comparisons between real life and the appreciation of a melody. He describes Knight's growing sense of self-awareness as a sense that "the rhythm of his inner being" was much greater than the rhythm he encountered within others (64). He specifically criticizes Mr. Goodman for being "out of tune" with Knight throughout his book (18). Rather than a seemingly clichéd phrase, to be "out of tune" is a specific accusation, an epistemological critique (probably, as often, unbeknownst to V.). A sense of the inner rhythm of an individual is one way in which to appreciate the original.

V. explains his written efforts to convey Knight's life involve trying to recreate the "rhythmical interlacements," as opposed to creating a standard chronological structure (135). Often, though, V.'s attempts to re-enact the interlacements of a life only result in a dissonant biography. The perception of an original rhythm — a sense of another's real life — is not something one can hunt down. One cannot arrange a scientific quest for a celestial tune. This concept of a melodic reality to an original life makes those who might wish to attain a true knowledge of that life little more than passive receptors. One can, however, easily make oneself incapable of perceiving the melody. Mr. Goodman is "out of tune" because his preconceived thoughts prevent the mystic music of Knight from entering his head. He is an unsuccessful receptor, unable to tune into Knight because his mind is filled with the static of clichés. Only an unobstructed mind can sense the real life music coming from the other side. Complete respect for the original does not even allow one to place a label or a name on the melody.

At one point, V. does appear to have a brief appreciation for the rhythm of Knight. He looks at Knight's books and notices one shelf that is neater than the others and seems to convey some suggestive music. After listing the fifteen books, he writes, "The melody gave a small gasp and faded" (39). Perhaps this melody is a "gasp" of Knight, "gasp" being a word which usually describes something human rather than musical. The books appear to have no "musical" interconnection beyond the fact that V. believes they all belonged to Knight. In this moment — a passing paragraph which might seem insignificant to the reader as well as to V. — V. seems to have had a completely unplanned sense of Knight, "a vague musical phrase" which comes to him from somewhere outside of his quest. He

8. Nabokov's Originals

does not study the shelf in an attempt to deduce some implied harmony. The music, of course, does not break into an overture; rather, it is a simple yet intimate hint as to where Knight's real life could be discovered. The proper response might have been to read those books, or at least to understand that here quite possibly was a source of Knight's passion. (Any one of them could be quite interesting in regard to either Knight or this novel, as Susan Fromberg has shown with *Dr. Jekyll and Mr. Hyde*.) Perhaps this quickly fading melody is a hint that V. should pay more attention to the relevant texts than continuing to pursue his ineffectual quest. (Nicol argues that V. should — and does — come to know Knight better through his "increasingly sharp interest in Sebastian's works" ["Mirrors" 88].) Perhaps Knight has sent an intuitive rhythm to V. through these books, a fleeting harmonic sense of his real life.

The idea of comprehending another's real life by becoming attuned to its individual rhythm must be kept in mind to appreciate the comedy of the exchange between V. and Madame Lecerf, when she heads for the radio and V. exclaims, apparently terrified, that she must stay away from it (156). The reason V. would react so frantically to the possibility of music, practically panicking, and apparently frightening the bull-dog, can only be understood within the full context of music in this novel. Music has an epistemological role in regard to the knowledge of another life. If the radio is playing, it will ruin the atmosphere in which one is attempting to sense the melody of Knight. Here, at least, V.'s instinct seems correct: the radio is a "horror of horrors" for being an impersonal source of sound. When played in the background, this sound is a disruptive force. Only with the radio tuned off can one hope to hear the fading melody of a past personality.[2]

The radio, it would seem, this intrusive music, is another way in which to obscure the original. Words, names, radios and narratives are all agents of obscurity. Only if one strives to be purely in tune can one sense the "soft radiance" in the background, or the "vague musical phrase" contained in the belongings of one's bookshelf. The essence of the other side is delicate, and easily lost. The original of a real life seems only able to express itself to a listener who is firmly in tune, because the original comes from a source which is easily obscured by the material of this world.

The idea that there *is* an objective reality — a "real life" — which is not perceived by less sensitive souls is also conveyed by some of the animal analogies in the book. A few of these analogies help to illustrate by analogy the theme of limited perception (often accompanied by the topic of evolution). For example, Knight writes of his own inability to fit into his surroundings, saying that he was something like "a colour-blind chameleon" (65). Thus Knight, similar to Nabokov as he describes himself during his Cambridge years, is unable to appreciate his immediate surroundings because his real self cannot adapt to that atmosphere. Neither of them are willing to relinquish their Russian-ness; therefore, they each live more in the mind than in England. With a related analogy, V. writes that discussing Knight's books with Nina Rechnoy would be equivalent to "discussing sundials with a bat" (172). Whether or not V. is correct in his assessment of Nina's character, his analogy claims that she has a physiological inability to perceive the value of those books, which certainly implies an inability to perceive a crucial part of Knight's real life. There is a hint that V. may be wrong, however, because he once again focuses on the significance of time: a discussion of sundials — or any other time-keeping device — with Knight would prove equally futile. Of course, the point is not that a bat cannot tell time, but that it is incapable of sensing light. In this case, V.'s analogy may not be apt, but once again there is the implication that certain people are incapable of appreciating certain objective facts, like time or light or books. This reflects on the idea that there is a hierarchy of biographical sensitivity presented in this novel: those with better perception tend to be more attuned to "real life."

Knight further stresses the significance of sensitive perception, stating that one who does not notice the distinct lip of one's cab driver is in fact a "monomaniac" (107). The failure of the average person to notice such details leads Knight to wonder if he is the only sighted person living among the blind or the only sane person among the mad. He specifically states that he feels this way when he notices a girl's "slight, very slight limp" (107). Knight knows that real life is in those details which common perception often overlooks. This "monomaniac" is actually the ordinary person, a practical person, one with the common, everyday view of his or her surroundings. Knight and Nabokov, in contrast, share the extra-ordinary sense of perception.

8. Nabokov's Originals

In *Speak, Memory* there is a "sturdy Swiss hiker" who, we are told, carries "Camus in his rucksack." When queried, this hiker says that he has not seen any butterflies on the path "where, a moment before, you and I had been delighting in swarms of them" (129). The carrying of Camus in one's rucksack is, apparently, another sign of blindness: the existentialist is blind to butterflies. (This narrative moment may also contain a nod to imagination: it does not seem reasonable that Nabokov or his companion could know what was contained inside of that rucksack. Only the imagination could plausibly ascertain that hiker's reading material, based on his lack of perception.) The sturdy Swiss hiker's reply — "None" — says nothing about his surroundings, but everything about his state of mind, his view of the world.

Knight is in agreement with Nabokov regarding this topic: reality is in the details, but no detailed description can convey an all-encompassing reality. A girl's slight limp is an aspect of reality to which many would be blind, just as some are blind to books, bats are blind to sundials, and Swiss hikers who are too far on the "sturdy" side are blind to butterflies. The ordinary view of one's surroundings tends toward the cliché by missing the details. Habitual perception disregards distinct lips and limps.

There is a hierarchy of perception. Those who are incapable of appreciating the surrounding details may be monomaniacs, existentialists or madmen, but at the very least they are blind to something real. Implicitly, some will be impervious to the presence of another's real life. The original is an objective existence which will remain out of reach to most, and when within reach it will always be subjectively perceived and therefore cannot be captured. The subjective perception of a real life is attainable only by those who are attuned (those without radios or Camus, those who see butterflies). Elsewhere Nabokov suggests that the "original" of a species is something that cannot be attained, although it is a "definite" presence that can be "perceived":

> the original of a being, nonexistent in our reality but unique and definite in concept, that recurs ad infinitum in the mirror of nature, creating countless reflections; each one of them perceived by our intelligence, reflected in that selfsame glass and acquiring its reality solely within it [*Butterflies* 216].

The original of an individual's "real life" is also something that can only be perceived in mirror-like reflections, but those reflections contain a doubtless "reality." Even for those few who are attuned, the real life of another human being is perceived as if in a passing musical phrase, not in the phrase placed on the page. To re-phrase Nabokov's translation of Tyutchev: a biography once written is untrue.[3]

In *Invitation to a Beheading* Cincinnatus feels that, with sufficient time, he could have created a verbal structure for his essence: "Oh, if only I had known that I was yet to remain here for such a long time ... my soul would have surrounded itself with a structure of words" (205). The struggle with language, he feels, is a struggle to form a structure which can express the original of one's soul: "surely there must be an original of the clumsy copy" (93). V.'s clumsy quest, Cincinnatus' clumsy copy: both suggest the distant existence of an original. Cincinnatus, however, understands the elusive nature of the celestial essence and the difficulty of capturing an original in words: "I am making one last effort — and I think I have caught my prey ... but it is only a fleeting apparition of my prey!" (94). V.'s prey — Sebastian Knight — also remains out of reach. Like the butterfly of light, like the irrational perception of true poetry, the original always slips from captivity in language.

Thus Nabokov's concept of an "original" can be applied to biography, autobiography, translation, memory, as well as to the higher levels of perception which are necessary for sensing real life. Aesthetic sensitivity is a metaphysical trait. The contrast with V.'s clumsy quest — the contrast between V.'s mind and that of Knight — conveys the idea of a hierarchy which leads in the direction of the original, the live source.

Chapter 9

The Metaphysics of the Zig-Zag

Those of Nabokov's characters who are linear thinkers tend to have restricted worldviews, sometimes dangerously restricted. These characters may have a certain degree of mad imagination, but ultimately their constrained worldview is self-destructive (or worse). Nabokov creates a great number of characters who attempt to fit the surrounding world into their limited visions, usually by refusing to see those elements of real life which might work against their pre-defined concepts — Humbert with his sexual obsession, Kinbote with his royal one, Hermann of *Despair* who plots a murder on the basis of his delusions, Luzhin of *The Defense* whose sense of the world is ultimately restricted to the grid lines of a chessboard. Goodman is an inept biographer, forcing all the world into his stereotypic ideas about an "era." Even V. is closely connected with a quest for a linear solution to the problems of "real life" — hence, the clichés, the dates, the desire for a successful "scientific" quest. Like many of Nabokov's characters, V. is unable to see beyond the immediate present, beyond the cramped quarters of a narrow personality. For Nabokov, any dedication to a straight line is a self-debilitating monomania: the multi-dimensional zig-zag is the only real path to transcendence.

Nabokov develops his metaphysics of the zig-zag over the course of his earliest novels. In *King, Queen, Knave*, Martha thinks, "Life should proceed according to plan, straight and strict, without freakish twists and wiggles" (10). This need for life to be "straight and strict" later prompts her to plot the murder of her husband. Ellen Pifer points out that this mode of thinking is a denial of the "real": "The unexpected, the unusual — hence unique and real — is to Martha an aberration" (30). Martha's straight-line

Nabokov's Permanent Mystery

philosophy for attaining one's desired ends with the swiftest possible means is contrasted to Franz, whose scattered imagination leaves him almost unable to function. Here is Franz as a sales clerk in a sporting-goods department:

> He remembered forever his first customer, a stout old man who asked for a ball. A ball. At once this ball went off bouncing in his imagination, multiplying and scattering, and Franz's head become the playground for all the balls in the store, small, medium, and large — yellow leather ones with stitched sections, fluffy white ones bearing the violet signature of their maker, little black ones hard as stone, extra-light orange-and-blue ones of vacational size, balls of rubber, celluloid, wood, ivory, and they all rolled off in different directions leaving behind a single sphere shining in the middle of his mind when the customer added placidly: "I need a ball for my dog" [78–79].

The sentence scatters off with all those possible balls, whereas the style of Martha's strict statement allows no room for twisting or wiggling. Logic seems to be the manner of a simpler mind. (In *Transparent Things* we are informed that "real life *was* ridiculous" [63].) Admittedly, Franz's fertile imagination renders him incapable of carrying out this easiest of tasks, but an incapacitating sense of the world's wide variety appears to be a higher, and certainly more likeable, quality for a character to possess than the purely functional calculation which is willing to eliminate an individual. (And Franz does, with a little help, make the sale.)

In addition, Franz's scattered imagination seems to resolve itself in a kind of Platonic ideal of ball-ness — "a single sphere shining in the middle of his mind" — as though his detailed conception gives him a greater appreciation for the nature of the object itself. At some level, Franz can comprehend something like the original of a ball, before the single sphere bounces off into all of its multiple subspecies. Each type of ball derived from that single shining sphere is analogous to each narrative derived from that single shining Knight, Sebastian — each version of his life composed by various characters. The zig-zag pattern is the only path back toward the original.

In *The Eye*, Nabokov further explores the theme of the multi-dimensional zig-zag as a higher ideal. Here the narrator discusses "basic law[s]," an extension of Martha's idea of the straight line, and makes a philosophical statement which is far beyond anything Franz would have been able to articulate:

9. The Metaphysics of the Zig-Zag

> It is silly to seek a basic law, even sillier to find it. Some mean-spirited little man decides that the whole course of humanity can be explained in terms of insidiously revolving signs of the zodiac or as the struggle between an empty and a stuffed belly.... Luckily no such laws exist: a toothache will cost a battle, a drizzle cancel an insurrection [27–28].

Smurov knows that any straight line of logic imposed on the world, whether it is silly or insidious, will necessarily be reductive. A toothache or a drizzle can undermine any all-encompassing philosophy. He goes on to contrast the lines of logic coming from those reductive philosophers to "the wavering nature of life." Life itself, he says, comes in the structure of a zig-zag: "A mysterious thing, this branching structure of life: one senses in every past instant a parting of ways, a 'thus' and an 'otherwise,' with innumerable dazzling zig-zags bifurcating and trifurcating against the dark background of the past." The zig-zag, for Nabokov, is not a plain back-and-forth pattern, but a dazzling trifurcation, a pattern of unpredictable wiggles.[1]

Nabokov's metaphysical zig-zag is much more than the knight's move of chess. This is not the ordinary zig-zag, but one which branches and bounces in multiple directions, one which could hardly be contained by the regulated lines of a chess board. This, not the straight line, says Smurov, with Nabokov in agreement, is the true pattern of real life. Franz's imaginative conception of the great variety of balls becomes a statement about the very nature of life itself. Despite pseudo-philosophic attempts to render everything into a one-dimensional definition, a basic law, real life insistently zig-zags away in innumerable dazzling directions, some of which may even extend into intangible dimensions beyond the merely real.

Keeping in mind Nabokov's structural hierarchy, it should be clear that these zig-zags are not merely plot twists. In fact, in regard to plot, Nabokov as often as not finds the expected plot twist to be just another type of cliché, and reverses the expectation. This technique is explained by Rex in *Laughter in the Dark*:

> "A certain man," said Rex, as he turned around the corner with Margot, "once lost a diamond cuff-link in the wide blue sea, and twenty years later, on the exact day, a Friday apparently, he was eating a large fish — but there was no diamond inside. That's what I like about coincidence" [135].

Nabokov is as interested in the absence of patterns as he is in the patterns themselves. Thus a too-predictable plot "twist" is another type of straight line, a supposed surprise which only follows the basic law of plot surprises. As always, for Nabokov, plot is never the place for a full structural development of a philosophic concept. In order to reinvigorate the zig-zag and bring a narrative back toward the unpredictability of real life one must perform a sort of double twist, continually being certain — as Rex in the above quote — to turn "around the corner." But purely playing a game of predictability on the level of plot, like the characters in Poe's "Purloined Letter," is not zig-zag enough for Nabokov. (Though, of course, Poe's story may, as John Irwin has shown, be self-reflective *ad infinitum*, thus a profound comment on predictability.)

The topic of unpredictable plots is also present in Nabokov's short story "The Passenger," where a writer tells a story which is obviously designed to reveal a murderer sharing a compartment of a train with the writer himself. Structurally, the "surprise" coincidence is set up for the conclusion, but the person turns out not to be the murderer after all, only an average passenger. The writer's point is that the predictable conclusion does not occur, that "Life" does not fit the "frame of a short story": "how nicely all that would have fitted into the frame of my night journey, the frame of a short story. Yet, it would appear that the plan of the Author, the plan of Life, was in this case, as in all others, a hundred times nicer" (*Stories* 187). Again the concept of the "frame," for Nabokov, seems to represent standard material structures: the zig-zag travels beyond the frame. Real life exists outside of the boundaries of the expected structure.

The potential triple twist, however, is suggested by the critic who sits listening. In what one might call the trifurcating structural move of the story (Nabokov's story, rather than that of "the writer"), the critic remarks, "I am well aware that you like to produce an impression of inexpectancy by means of the most natural denouement; but don't get carried away by your own method." A simple backlash reaction to a predictable plot is apparently not intricate enough to attain the proper metaphysics of the zig-zag. The critic states that the double plot twist might be predictably unpredictable, that the truly unpredictable technique might be to return to the single twist, though the writer believed he was reacting to the predictability of unpredictable plots in the first place. This story shows the *ad absurdum* quality of solely relying on this structural level of zig-zags.

9. The Metaphysics of the Zig-Zag

The full metaphysical implications of the multi-dimensional zig-zag must come with higher structural levels than plot.

Boyd writes that in *Glory*, Nabokov's fifth novel, he was able to incorporate what I have termed the metaphysics of the zig-zag into the structure of the novel: "*Glory* is the first Nabokov novel shaped to match the lack of structure in an individual life" (*Russian Years* 357–358). With this novel, Boyd writes, Nabokov "began to recoil from the neatness and implicit determinism" of his previous plots to focus more on "the doodles of impulse, the zigzags of chance." This interest in the implications of the zig-zag was not sudden. The major development in *Glory* is that now the zig-zag theme is literally built into the novel. Now the structure matches the metaphysics. Rather than only contemplating zig-zags, the reader is now able to experience them. The primary structural development — the way in which Nabokov works zig-zags into the novel on a higher level than the plot — is in the non-linear transitions, not only between scenes, but within paragraphs and even within single sentences. Boyd writes that in this novel the "transitions reflect the unique pattern of Martin's mind" (Martin Edelweiss, the protagonist). The structural zig-zags in this novel convey the zig-zags of an imaginative mind, one which often strays from the real world into its private fantasies.

This particular structural technique — the use of imaginatively non-linear transitions to reflect the workings of an individual's mind — is one which Nabokov develops to embody greater metaphysical concepts in *Speak, Memory*. Alexandrov writes that in Nabokov's autobiography "the theme of timelessness is reflected in the unmarked transition between contiguous sentences referring to experiences on different continents" (*Otherworld* 41). That is, Nabokov's famous "magic carpet" metaphor, with which he declares his disbelief in time, is built into the structure of the autobiography through the use of unmarked, seemingly magical transitions. In this book the structural zig-zags represent more than the simple workings of an imaginative mind, but of an imaginative mind that is capable of transcending space and time. Alexandrov further explicates a scene in which Nabokov describes himself chasing a butterfly "near the family estate" and "without any warning or transition, at the end of the second sentence Nabokov shifts from the flora of his pre–Revolutionary boyhood in northern Russia to an herb, a flower and a tree from the American West" (40). He continues: "the nature of the transition between the two sentences captures the collapse of time the author experienced." Foster also argues that the structure of *Speak, Memory* reflects a "sense of life's essential sinuosity" (191). Franz's imaginatively scattered concept of a ball has become — by the time of *Speak, Memory*—a transcendent metaphysical twist in the narrative line.

Nabokov's metaphysics of the zig-zag is also crucial to *The Real Life of Sebastian Knight*. The contrast between the zig-zag and the straight line is essential to the structure, and thus the metaphysical concepts, of this novel. Similar to *Speak, Memory*, the zig-zag moves beyond plot to transcend time, but with a different structural technique. Because the detective quest, the straight-line search for a novelistic solution, is not the way in which to find "real life," Sebastian Knight is closely associated with the zig-zags of the novel. Knight wrote five books, and V. describes his method of composition as a series of "curves and gaps and zigzags" (82). These "gaps" are not only his way of writing, but also his way of "thinking" (33). V. does not attempt to edit the frustrated clichés out of his text, or the other failed directions of his "quest," because he senses that these many odd turns and "gaps" are somehow able to convey the very nature of Knight.

At one point V. wonders if Knight would have discovered in it the "Knightian twist" which would have made up for the multiple errors of a "blundering biographer" (156). Thus an apparently "blundering biographer" might best be able to write a book that contains the essential "Knightian" twists and wiggles and gaps of Knight's — and all — real life. The idea that the shape of real life is best understood as a zig-zag is something that Martin learns in *Glory*: "It was then that Martin understood for the first time that human life flowed in zig-zags..." (8–9). The zigzag structure of that novel is also a theme of the novel. It is also a technique the Nabokov develops as he strives to create literary structures that convey this sense of real life.

As I have discussed in the section concerning V.'s linear use of dates, Knight's sense of dates is less predictable. As V. explains it, the date of Knight's death somehow conforms to his personality, as though the date of death is only an additional twist or wiggle, and certainly not the final

9. The Metaphysics of the Zig-Zag

one. He explains, in a passage spaced by suspension dots, that the date — 1936 — seems to reflect something of Knight, as though the date is a reflection of his name in water (181). Here the definite date dissolves into an imaginative reading. The dots represent V.'s thoughts flowing, or attempting to flow, into those of Knight. In another context Nabokov writes that "suspension dots" are used in Russian obituaries, and may represent departed words: "Leonid Ivanovich Shigaev is dead.... The suspension dots, customary in Russian obituaries, must represent the footprints of words that have departed on tiptoe, in reverent single file, leaving their tracks on the marble..." (dots in the original) ("In Memory of L.I. Shigaev," *Stories* 364). V. uses the style of a Russian obituary to report the date of his brother's death, but he also attempts to recapture Knight's words, to place them on the page. He tries to follow those tracks on the marble and capture the departed prose. Knight would apparently prefer to apply an imaginative reading, a sinuosity which reveals the illusion of seeming solidity which surrounds dates: even a date can be made into something more than a mere measurement, more than a convenient frame. V. is correct in stating that Knight would stress the sinuous dissolubility of any linear measurement of time. Real life resists the linear.

In fact, Nabokov's multi-dimensional zig-zag is such a powerful force that one might even twist into eternity. The potential transcendence of the zig-zag is present at the start of the final chapter of *Sebastian Knight*, in a sentence which connects weather, water, zig-zags and the possibility of transcendent communication; there we see drops of rain trickling down the train window, taking a "zig-zag" path (190). The zig-zag quality of the novel might make the presence of Knight seem as dubious as these raindrops. However, knowing that Nabokov associates the zig-zag (twists and wiggles, sinuosity, trifurcating structures, meanderings) more closely with "real life" than a straight line, we should see — as apparently V. does not — that this detail of the weather could be a sign from Knight. If this initial zig-zag hint is not enough, moments later the same weather seems a bit more insistent that we (and V.) see its potential source, referring to it as "ghost-like" (190–191). Sisson writes, "V. may indeed be with Sebastian in the form of the ghost-like snowflake" ("*Knight*" 635). The zig-zag of that snowflake might be further evidence of this presence as, of course, is

Nabokov's Permanent Mystery

Nabokov's consistent use of water as a means for transcendent communication.

Of course, this suggestion may also be rejected by a reader. As with the suggestion of an otherworldly presence in our real lives, no objective or scientific proof is possible. Some may feel certainty; others may just as certainly feel doubt. No reader can be sure that this snowflake is Knight: the theme is permanent mystery. Nonetheless, Nabokov does develop this zig-zag theme to develop his sense of "real life," showing that a life might extend beyond any mundane or expected frame, beyond any limited definition.

The essence of the zig-zag may even be able to carry a character beyond the book. Just as the unnamed writer in "The Passenger" found that "Life" does not fit "the frame" of a short story, just as those disintegrating frames of Nabokov's mother were not needed for her to retain her memories, Nabokov creates some characters, like Knight, whose lives seem to slip beyond the standard frame of the novel. There is a "real life" which no frame can contain, and some Nabokovian characters display that divine spark. *Pnin* will provide my final fictional example of Nabokov's metaphysics of the zig-zag.

At the end of the fourth chapter of *Pnin* there is an image which none of the characters of the novel witness: "Presently all were asleep. It was a pity nobody saw the display in the empty street, where the auroral breeze wrinkled a large luminous puddle, making of the telephone wires reflected in it illegible lines of black zigzags" (109). The pattern of the straight line — here represented by telephone wires — is again contrasted to the zig-zag. Connolly writes, "This enigmatic image perhaps resonates with the image of the oblong puddle with which *Bend Sinister* begins and ends, described by Nabokov as evoking the writer's link to the character of Krug" ("Pnin" 203). Here we have another example of Nabokov's water imagery: the zig-zag is the view through water, the emblem of communication with the other side (like, perhaps, the above snowflake). The zig-zag lines may be "illegible" because of the impossibility of translating transcendent communication into the material terms of this side. Thus, within the Nabokovian lexicon, there is also an implicit contrast between modes of communication here: the telephone wires of earthly communication and

9. The Metaphysics of the Zig-Zag

the metaphysical zig-zags of liquid, water. There is more water imagery in *Pnin*, such as the protagonist's epiphanic encounter with his sink. The connection Connolly makes with the puddle of *Bend Sinister* further suggests that this zig-zag should be associated with Nabokov's transcendent ideals.

In the conclusion of the novel, Pnin is able to transcend "the frame" of his book: "I watched them [Pnin and his dog] recede in the frame of the roadway ... free at last." The straight-line narrator, in contrast, is left behind with "a British breakfast of depressing kidney and fish." Some have read the ending differently, arguing that this surreptitious narrator has after all seized Pnin's position at the university. However, the final page shows that Pnin survives beyond the book—"where there was simply no saying what miracle might happen"—and that the narrator's shallow victory leaves him with very little. As in *Sebastian Knight*, the two patterns—the straight line and the zig-zag—represent two different possibilities in the plot of the novel, and two contrasting types of mind. Pnin, despite his hardships, is associated with Nabokov's ideals, while the narrator is left behind with the ironic reward of a British breakfast. Pnin moves beyond his book, as we know, accompanied by his little white dog, to land a comfortable job in *Pale Fire*. Perhaps Nabokov derived this idea of fictional compensation elsewhere: he says that one of Tolstoy's characters "is finally given a soft job with a big salary for services rendered to the author" (*LRL* 198). Judging by his telltale Hawaiian shirt in *Pale Fire*, the same may be true for Pnin.

No one who insists on a straight line will be satisfied, Nabokov suggests. Even Tolstoy seems to have been tricked by the temptations of a linear quest. Nabokov writes: "Most Russian writers have been tremendously interested in Truth's exact whereabouts and essential properties.... Tolstoy marched straight at it, head bent and fists clenched, and found the place where the cross had once stood, or found—the image of his own self" (*LRL* 141). Even the cross, it seems, zig-zags out of the straight path of Tolstoy. Real life will not stand still. A straight line can match the shape of a personality, but it is a shape which severely limits one's possibilities, restricting one into "the image" of one's own self, the bars of one's cage. Essential "Truth" cannot be stalked, even for a determined Tolstoy.

Nabokov's Permanent Mystery

The zig-zag is an aspect of Nabokov's structures which could easily be confused with plain game playing, simple manipulation of the reader, but Nabokov's zig-zags — his twists and wiggles and meanderings — have a metaphysical and structural purpose. The multi-dimensional zig-zag is a metaphysical ideal. With this concept Nabokov is able to match his metaphysics with his aesthetics, his beliefs with his literary structures.

Chapter 10

The Authorial Role

One way in which Nabokov draws some attention to himself in *The Real Life of Sebastian Knight* is by naming the novel within the text. Concerning Mr. Silbermann, V. writes that if he ever should read *The Real Life of Sebastian Knight*, he would like to thank him for his help (131–132). In this passage V. directly draws attention to his authorship while using the name of the book which we hold in our hands. The same title, however, has a different significance for the narrator than it does for the real author.

For V. this title is probably a reaction to the title of Mr. Goodman's popular book, *The Tragedy of Sebastian Knight*. His choice of title could be a marketing technique or at least an attempt to sway the common perception of his half-brother's real life: asserting that his version is the "real" one. Knight's life was not a tragedy, V. says with his title: here is the truth, here is the real life. We can also see in the above quote that V. claims to be offering his writing without revision (as noted earlier, as if this were a spontaneously created text), so that his choice of title came before the book was finished. The title, then, shows his certainty in his quest: he *will* attain that real life and successfully convey it with this book. However, as Shlomith Rimmon points out, the first paragraph of the text disrupts the biographical expectations set up by the title: "the title ... suggests Sebastian's preeminence, but the very first paragraph reverses this impression with seven pronouns relating to the narrator ('I,' 'my,' 'me') and only two mentions of Sebastian" (124). Thus V.'s title may suggest his confidence in his biographical quest, but the text that he writes draws undo attention toward himself.

Nabokov's title, in contrast, is implicitly interrogating the very nature of biography. What does it mean to claim to convey one's "real life" in a text? How much or how little of an author's "real life" can be deduced from the content of their fictional works? Bodenheimer describes the title of her book, *The Real Life of Mary Ann Evans*, with an explanation that could be applied to Nabokov's title: "my title plays with the dubious promises of the biographical situation: the yearning to know which sends readers and writers on biographical quests, and the impossibility of knowing anything that is not somebody's fiction of the self..." (xiv). This is a good explanation of Nabokov's *The Real Life of Sebastian Knight*, but not of V.'s *The Real Life of Sebastian Knight*. It is a good explanation; only the word "impossibility" is too strong for Nabokov's sense of how one can know another's life: there are less tangible ways in which one can know another's life.

With his title, Nabokov is clearly criticizing a mind such as V.'s that believes any individual's "real life" can be so easily and confidently confined to a page. At the same time, something of Sebastian Knight *is* conveyed from the page. This, too, is reflected in Nabokov's title; as Clare tells Knight, the purpose of a title is to "convey the colour of the book,—not its subject" (70). This sounds quite a bit like Carswell's method of painting his portrait of Knight. The "colour" of this fictional author created by Nabokov—Sebastian Knight—is conveyed by the book (otherwise the book would be either a dismal failure or a purposeless puzzle). Nabokov's title tells us that from this book we should get a sense of Knight.

Perhaps more importantly, in regard to the overall structure, the use of matching titles draws attention to the fictionality of the work. By now it has often been argued that Nabokov's self-referentiality is not a closed system, a game which continually reflects upon itself to the neglect of the "real" world, but rather this is a technique for drawing attention to his role as the author, the creative agent; self-referentiality and artifice point outside of the text. Foster: "This tendency, at once self-reflexive and metaphysical, hints at an authorial realm outside the fiction so as to convey, by analogy, the sense of another world beyond our own" (15). Making one more aware of the fact of holding a book, a created object, should make one more aware of the presence of a creative agent, drawing one's attention outside of the book, to a level of appreciation for the created nature of this created world, rather than into an abyss of fictionality.

The structure of the novel leads to the name of Nabokov. V. writes, in regard to Knight, that he "fail[s] to name" another author who is so "baffling"; specifically, he finds the author "baffling" because V. is a reader

10. The Authorial Role

who would like to "see the real man behind the author" (112). (The word which V. repeats — "baffling" — is perfect in this context as it specifically suggests the impossibility of receiving a satisfying answer, a solution to the riddle of Knight's art.) On one level (V.'s) this "real man behind the author" is Sebastian Knight behind his fictional works, as presented in the text. On the next level (Knight's), the "real man" is Vladimir Nabokov behind Sebastian Knight, the real man behind his fictional author. On one higher level the same phrase resonates into the meaning of the real Vladimir Nabokov behind the authorial name of Vladimir Nabokov on the book's cover: if we desire some biographical insights into the real Nabokov from the book we are destined to be baffled.

The connection between Nabokov and "Nabokov" is not relevant to the metaphysical scheme of his literary structures. It is, nonetheless, an interesting topic, the complex ways in which Nabokov mixes biography into his fictional worlds. Tammi has written that "such effects are puzzling for the analyst, and previous critics have sometimes commented on them with a note of fascination bordering on awe" (35). V. says he "fail[s] *to name*" any author so baffling. This is more significant than saying he "does not know" any such author: the only biographical point we can determine with certainty *is* the name, which suggests the existence of the "real man." Ultimately the intermingling of biographical details and fiction does little more than point to the name and suggest a presence behind it. The name, however, like the name of Olga Olegovna Orlova, reveals nothing.

Nabokov's sense of the authorial role in a literary work, or the author's relation to the fiction, can be understood — and complicated — by looking at the ways in which he discusses this topic in his lectures. At times, he is adamant that one should not confuse the fictional narrator and the real author. His lecture on Proust's *The Walk by Swann's Place* includes this emphasis on a strict division between author and narrator: "One thing should be firmly impressed upon your minds: the work is not an autobiography; the narrator is not Proust the person.... Let us not, therefore, go into the author's life. It is of no importance in the present case...." He then equivocates to some degree by telling his students that "the narrator and the author do resemble each other in various ways and move in much the same environment" (*LL* 208). Here he insists on the idea that the narrator is

Nabokov's Permanent Mystery

not "the person," and that the author's real life should not be of any concern to the reader. However, we cannot take the above precaution at face value. One must keep in mind that Nabokov wrote these lectures for an undergraduate survey course. He is not necessarily speaking down to his audience, but he is focusing on the fundamentals. The above statement about Proust's fiction is aimed at eliminating the basic mistake of considering a narrator and an author to be one and the same. In the same lecture, Nabokov steps away from that adamant position, allowing some leeway by stating instead, "the narrator is not quite Proust" (210).

In fact, Nabokov's lectures often include biographical tidbits which seem aimed at arousing the students' collective curiosity about the "real" writer, rather than at persuading them to ignore the actual person. For example, lecturing on *Don Quixote*: "We are interested in books, not people. Of Saavedra's maimed hand you will learn not from me" (*LDQ* 5–6). Of course, most of the students probably do learn of that maimed hand from Nabokov's comment. The many questions this detail would provoke are quite obvious (how? where? was it his writing hand?), but assumedly the lecturer Nabokov would squelch such questions. The end result, it would seem, would be to raise the students' interest in biography, while insisting on the fiction as a separate entity.

Nabokov most often introduced biographical facts into his lectures with a disclaimer: "As you know by now, I am not one to go heavily for the human interest stuff when speaking of books.... *But* books have their destiny ... and sometimes the destinies of authors follow those of their books," and details of Stevenson's death follow, or "I hate tampering with the precious lives of great writers ... *but* this I must say," and Nabokov's thoughts on Tolstoy's brain follow (*LL* 204, *LRL* 138, emphasis added in each). Despite his overt statements to the contrary, these class lectures actually create a greater tension than Nabokov admits between biographical facts and fictional facts, or what he calls "the fiction of facts [and] the facts of fiction," a choice of words which clearly indicates an interaction between the real author and the author's fictional world (*LDQ* 1).

Another conceivable level of literary structure, the "real" author's relation to the author within the fiction, Tolstoy's relation to "Tolstoy," is for Nabokov entirely a question of biography, and is therefore all but irrelevant

10. The Authorial Role

to the study of fiction. That is, the way in which an author chooses to fit the fiction is what matters, not how this fictional deity differs out in the "real" world. Thus, Nabokov can insist on his own presence within his fictional works and say at the same time, in that same lecture on Tolstoy, "no biographer will ever catch a glimpse of my private life" (*LRL* 138). He is interested in studying the self-portraits, not in detailing the ways in which an author may have beautified or distorted this or that fact.

The largest introductory section of Nabokov's huge translation of Aleksandr Pushkin's *Eugene Onegin* is entitled "The Structure of 'Eugene Onegin.'" One of the primary topics which Nabokov discusses in this section is Pushkin's relation to his fictional work, a relation which Nabokov describes on a number of levels. He goes into some detail in discussing the structural "components" of (as he capitalizes) "Pushkin's Participation" (vol. 1, 19). Here, unlike in the undergraduate lecture on Proust, we have Nabokov's full development of his ideas about an author's possible relation to the text. Nabokov states that it is Pushkin's own voice which one hears in the first-person narrator of *Onegin*. Without qualifying the word "real" with quotes, Nabokov says Pushkin makes "allusions to real circumstances and real people" (19). Nabokov allows only a slight acknowledgment of a possible difference between Pushkin the real author and Pushkin the narrator. He says the narrator is in fact a "stylized Pushkin" and that his allusions to actual events and people are "more exactly, stylized autobiographizations" (19). The word "stylized" acknowledges the fact that a narrative voice is necessarily a controlled portrait, but also suggests that Pushkin is trying not to differentiate between his narrative voice and his "real" voice. Nabokov is stating that the "real" Pushkin is, as closely as can be possible, the Pushkin of the text and, at this point, is acting as the narrator.

The real author's role, however, becomes further complicated in Nabokov's analysis of the poem's developing structure. In his analysis of stanzas XLV–XLVII, Nabokov notes an interesting structural effect: "Up to this stanza Pushkin had been haunting the canto but not actually appearing in it as a person in the novel. Pushkin's voice had been heard and his presence felt, as he floated in and out of the stanzas in a ghostly atmosphere of recollection and nostalgia" (25). Pushkin's relation to the beginning of his work had been a sort of "haunting," a presence which could not quite be pinned down. At this earlier point Pushkin was "an incorporeal participant" (23). Although yet to descend into the text at this point, the ghost-like Pushkin still has some level of divine power within his fictional world.

In these next stanzas, however, Nabokov states that Pushkin changes his relation to the text and takes on fictional flesh, becomes corporeal within his own work: "Henceforth Pushkin will be a full-fledged character, and he and Onegin will actually appear as two persons" (25). Here, then, is a significant point: Nabokov believes an author can transport himself intact into his own fiction. This is not an autobiographical technique, but an example of Pushkin himself participating in his own fiction. According to Nabokov's analysis, this "stylized" Pushkin is the author, narrator and a main character. He sees no need to differentiate the various narrative roles from the "real" Pushkin; on the contrary, he wants to make clear that Pushkin himself takes on each of these roles. Pushkin moves from a narrative haunting of the text to setting foot in his own fiction. Thus, an author's relation to the text can cover a great range within even a single work. In Nabokov's own novels, the authorial role represents the top level of the visible structure.

Barabtarlo describes this sense of the authorial role in *Sebastian Knight*: "Sebastian is absent, so is V. Their maker is present, filling every cell and fiber of the text, imperceptible and incomprehensible by the characters" ("Narrative Stance" 75). Nabokov in his lectures often refers to authors as various types of gods — "In connection with *Bleak House* we are concerned with one of those authors who are so to speak not supreme deities, diffuse and aloof, but puttering, amiable, sympathetic demigods, who descend into their books under various disguises" (*LL* 97). Tolstoy's deific role, in contrast, is distant: "in those great chapters that are his masterpieces the author is invisible so that he attains that dispassionate ideal of authors which Flaubert so violently demanded of a writer: to be invisible, and to be everywhere as God in His universe is" (*LRL* 143). An author's relation to the written work can range from that of a supreme and invisible deity to that of a puttering demigod. It is not accidental that Nabokov suggests a level of divinity for any role an author might choose. To appreciate a literary structure, according to Nabokov, one must know precisely what kind of god the author has chosen to be.

10. The Authorial Role

Thus, the hierarchy leads from V. and his clichés, through the sinuous character of Knight, and through the unseen real author Nabokov (the god of his created literary), toward some higher creative ideal. The highest level of Nabokov's sense of literary structure, and of "real life," is the ultimate mystery. As Barabtarlo writes, the "maker" fills "every cell and fiber of the text." Krug, the father and philosopher of *Bend Sinister*, describes his son in a similar way:

> a little creature, formed in some mysterious fashion (even more mysterious to us than it had been to the very first thinkers in their pale olive groves) by the fusion of two mysteries, or rather two sets of a trillion mysteries each ... the whole suffused with consciousness, which is the only real thing in the world and the greatest mystery of all [188].

As one moves up the Nabokovian literary structure, one moves toward higher levels of consciousness, toward ever greater mystery, and that mystery is "the only real thing." Recognition of the real author is a recognition of a higher creative source, someone above the text, and is therefore a quick step to the highest level of the structure.

Chapter 11

The Indivisible Pearl

The highest level of Vladimir Nabokov's literary structures is the level for which no term is adequate, as I have discussed in the introduction. Any term meant to convey Nabokov's metaphysical sense — even his own, celestial essence, here-and-there-after, *potustoronnost'* — will be limited. This is a level which cannot be completely defined. Therefore, my purpose will be to show some of the ways in which he builds this unwordable concept into the literary structure, while not attempting to offer an explication of that essence.

One of the primary techniques Nabokov uses to build his metaphysical sense into his novels is by refusing to provide a real conclusion. For example, in ending *The Real Life of Sebastian Knight*, within the structural terms of the ending of preceding pages, the conclusion is not possible. V. had been presenting his text as a spontaneous creation. The text represents unrevised writing, jotted into V.'s notebook as he proceeds on his quest. In this sense, the text is the quest. However, the text also represents a return which matches V.'s many other returns in the novel, as I have discussed previously. The final pages show V. supposedly returning not only to the location of his half-brother's death, but to the time of that death. The possibility of a spontaneously created text cannot logically coexist with the return to an event. A return in time, of course, can only occur mentally, not as part of a physical quest. V. is borne back ceaselessly into the past while seeming to believe that the quest is proceeding toward his half-brother's "real life." These two aspects of the novel's structure could be read as incompatible or contradictory.

However, presenting a conclusion which is not possible on realistic terms is one technique which Nabokov uses in order to avoid closure to

11. The Indivisible Pearl

his literary structures. The apparent end tends to be only the next step. To look for a solution to the text in the final few pages would be to bring the structural significance right back down to the plot. Thus Nabokov creates a conclusion which rests on questionable grounds and which can in many ways be separated from the rest of the text. (Boyd has noted that Nabokov creates a "fantasy epilogue" in *Despair* (*Russian Years* 388).) We have seen that Humbert Humbert's final pages may also be read as an act of his imagination. Barbara Wyllie makes the interesting argument that the actual finale of the narrative — Humbert's true emotional peak — comes at the end of chapter thirty, as he contemplates a neon sign and recalls the word "shadowgraphs" (163–167). She writes, "[I]t is the shadowgraph scene, with its depth of revelation and insight, which provides the narrative's pivotal cathartic moment. Quilty's murder is thus reduced to a hollow act serving merely to conclude the charade that is Humbert Humbert's revenge scenario" (167). Thus, the "real" ending is more subtle and more evocative than that standard "revenge scenario." The art of the conclusion, as carried out by Nabokov, is often one final creative move, making the overall structure less predictable than the average reader might expect.

There are many suggestions that the final pages of *Sebastian Knight* are meant to be read as V.'s dream, including the fact that he falls asleep, says that he had a bad dream, and upon apparently awakening begins to narrate past events with a much greater sense of immediacy. This is the structural shift which Nabokov uses to set up the unreality of the concluding pages — sleep, dream, awaken to convey past events with an immediacy not found elsewhere in the narrative. V. says, however, that part of him remains in the dream (188). We should question whether V. has really awakened, or whether he has only awakened to some other level of reality, which question reminds one of Knight talking about "his dreams, and the dreams in his dreams, and the dreams in the dreams of his dreams" (157). V. even says directly that the compartment of his train was like one of his dreams (190). As in the deepest of sleeps, time has become unclear for the dozing narrator. V. does not wake up, but on some level of his mind he is aware that sleep has taken him over. The fact that he is sleeping and yet still seems to be the narrator says that we have moved to another level of the narrative.

There is something of an alternate ending previous to this moment. Before slipping into the dream sequence of the final two chapters, V. makes some comments about Knight's last book. Then he concludes with the idea that he might decide to translate that book into Russian (180). This could be read as the real end of his quest, and here we can see another hint of "The Art of Translation." V.'s thought that he might translate Knight's final book into Russian is a much more appropriate tribute to Knight than the claim that he can inhabit his soul. The desire to translate may be a sign of respect for the original. This is, however, only a thought of translation, not an attempt to put that final work into new words, which may be even more of a tribute to Knight and his work, perhaps suggesting that V. has discovered a more appropriate way to understand Knight and his life. Rosemarie Bodenheimer accurately states that V. "discovers in the shimmering velleities of Knight's prose his most suggestive autobiographical glimpses" (xiii). On one level of the novel, V.'s quest ends here, with the final two chapters going on to other levels of "reality."

With an example of what I call Nabokov's deceptive transcendence, this dream involves the thought of one last spiritual communion with his dying brother. Through the "half-opened door" of a hospital room, V. senses the presence of his half-brother and feels assured that he is learning more than he had ever known about Knight merely by listening to his breathing (201). V. learns, of course, that he had been listening to the breathing of the wrong man, that Knight had died the day before. V. then determines that the moment of understanding he has had through the half-open door is nonetheless still valid. He feels he has gained an insight despite the mistake; he says that the minutes he spent listening to the wrong man breathe changed his life just as much as if it had been Knight dying on the other side of that door (202).

It is significant that V. is led to the wrong room due to a spelling error. Rather than having been sent to the room of Sebastian Knight, V. was sent to the room of a Mr. Kegan. Nabokov again draws attention to the materiality of language — the limitations of language — by intentionally playing with "mistakes." Here there is a contrast between an alphabetical flaw and V.'s sense of revelation. He feels as if he has transcended the material flaw and found some sort of spiritual insight. The lesson may be that

11. The Indivisible Pearl

language, just as any material, is left behind in the transcendent moment. At the same time, it is precisely the misspelling which seems to have provoked the moment.

There is a similar spelling flaw which provokes a semi-transcendent moment in *Pale Fire*. John Shade believes that he and a "Mrs. Z." have shared a vision of a "white fountain" across "the border" between life and death (59–61). Both have experienced near-fatal moments and, according to a magazine article which Shade reads, both have glimpsed a similar sign on the other side. Shade initially believes that this shared vision marks an objective proof of the concrete existence of the other world. He describes their fountain as if it were empirical evidence of an other world, saying that the evidence is "substantial as a tooth,/ And almost vulgar in its robust truth!" (l.765–766). This is one point in the poem where Shade and Nabokov do not coincide. Nabokov would consider this tooth-strong truth — this shared white fountain — to be a sure sign not of the other side, but of a *poshlust* mind. This vulgar vision (not "almost") shows the same naive need for "scientific" proof of life after death that V. shows. It is naive because it is unaware of the inconclusive nature of the celestial essence, the here-and-there-after. Here, in his desperate need for some answers about the other side, Shade seems to be susceptible to clichés. With a momentary lack of taste, or lack of discretion, Shade is able to overlook the accumulated clichés which Mrs. Z. clumps together with the white fountain — those oft-used elements of the standard afterlife, including angels, stained glass, and soft music (l.752–754).

The objective proof, of course, turns out to be a typo. Whenever one clings to tangible proof of the celestial essence, in Nabokov's work, that "proof" is destined to change. In these two cases the material was false from the start, yet Shade and V. seem to attain some insight from the revelation of the mistake. This is the method of deceptive transcendence. It is almost as though Shade and V. have been tricked by a material flaw into a moment of firm faith. From this experience Shade learns to appreciate "the game" and, perhaps more importantly, learns that he should not try to place a label on that game (as the philosophers of I.P.H. seem so intent on doing), not to make his search a search for an answer.

Shade has come to understand, "No sound,/ No furtive light came from their involute/ Abode, but there they were, aloof and mute" (l. 814–818). Nabokov's sense of the other world is not quite so mute or lightless, but Shade has learned one important lesson of Nabokovian metaphysics: not to attach words to his sense of the celestial essence. This does not mean he should quit writing poetry, any more than Nabokov should have quit writing due to the non-verbal quality of this essence. It only means that he is aware that no words can perfectly contain that essence.

Nonetheless, words can continuously strive to come closer to that essence. Fyodor mocks that very idea, that commonplace, that words are inadequate:

> The oft repeated complaints of poets that, alas, no words are available, that words are pale corpses, that words are incapable of expressing our thingummy-bob feelings (and to prove it a torrent of trochaic hexameters is set loose) seemed to him just as senseless as the staid conviction ... that yonder mountain has never been climbed... [*Gift* 154].

He then refers to a man who "cheerfully scrambles to the top" of that mountain. Here, then, is an optimistic view of the theme: words may seem inadequate or limited, but that appearance may only exist because no one has yet reached adequacy. No one has yet climbed to that mountaintop. Nonetheless, that mountaintop is still there. The poet must keep striving.

Words are material, definitions are reductive, and conclusions are inessential. Shade has learned that mistakes are part of the pattern, but that is not necessarily a pessimistic lesson. In keeping with this sense, he half-stammers to his wife his understated lesson of potential transcendence, saying that he might be able to find his way "to some — to some — 'Yes, dear?' Faint hope" (l. 833–834). This "faint hope" is everything, but he has learned not to pin greater words to it. Fyodor's confidence that one day that mountain will be climbed is related to Shade's "faint hope"; the difference is in the characters. Fyodor is younger, somewhat naïve, and ambitious; Shade is older, no longer naïve, and has learned of some of the limitations and hardships of life. Shade has learned a bit more about just how deceptive one's sense of transcendence can be, just how tantalizingly out of reach that mountaintop always seems to be.

Transcendence cannot be sustained. The moment which sees beyond the material world toward the source of the other side is always brought

11. The Indivisible Pearl

back to the material, and is then surrounded by doubts. Recall that in regard to time — one measuring tool of the material side — Wood pointed out that the transcendent moment is accompanied by an "imminent and inevitable return" (84). A perfect example of the imminent return from a transcendent moment is Cincinnatus' glimpse of "something real" in *Invitation to a Beheading*. He looks into his mother's eyes and "just for an instant, an instant — but it was as if something real, unquestionable (in this world, where everything was subject to question), had passed through, as if a corner of this horrible life had curled up, and there was a glimpse of the lining" (136). Cincinnatus has glimpsed the "lining" of life, a celestial element which cannot be expressed (though there are many attempts: "ultimate," "secure," "horror," "pity"). He states that he is also able to see this "spark" within himself. This is not a moment of deceptive transcendence, like that of Shade or V. No trick led him to this vision. Cincinnatus is having a pure view of something beyond his "horrible" life. This is a moment in which he sees the source, and for that moment the vision is "unquestionable," beyond doubt, beyond the reach of words.

For one brief moment, his mother's gaze is the conduit of a celestial sparkle, of something "unquestionable." Leona Toker writes, "What is here revealed to Cincinnatus is not transcendent reality but the possibility of authentic relationships in 'this world'" (*Nabokov* 79). For Nabokov, however, the potential for transcending "reality" is ever present — though often overlooked — in this world. Perhaps that spark represents the source of "authentic relationships," as Toker states, but in Cincinnatus's inauthentic world an authentic relationship could be a transcendent experience. Cincinnatus has glimpsed a higher realm. Because it cannot be put into words, we learn as much from his reaction to this "spark" as from any of the attempts to describe it: his "soul" is "leaping for joy." The moment passes, and immediately this quick vision of the lining of life transforms into "the lining of her pocket": inexpressible epiphanies inevitably return to the material of this side. Here, even a transcendent sense of the maternal returns to mere material.

This transcendent moment is closely related to that brief melody which V. senses from Knight's bookshelf. Both express a non-material sense of an original self. The lining of life, the original: these words represent the same concept. Any glimpse one may gain of an original self would be equally as fleeting as Cincinnatus' glimpse of the lining of life, equally as fleeting as that momentarily harmonious "gasp" of Knight's books. Fromberg says that one of the books of Knight's shelf—*The Anglo-Persian Dictionary*—does not belong to Knight at all, an idea which might throw V.'s entire sense of melody into question. If Fromberg is correct, and the evidence is that Clare once took a class in which she might have used such a book (*RLSK* 80), the possibility of doubt is present in the "sequence." Once that melody has faded, and one studies the books, the material conduit of that melody, one may find many reasons to doubt that the melody meant anything, or that it even existed. But the moment of the melody remains unquestionable, even if everything in the world is subject to question. The original melody comes from some source beyond the books. This is essential to Nabokov's metaphysics.

The material does not contain the essence. Just as Cincinnatus' transcendent moment is reduced to his mother fumbling through the lining of her pocket, V.'s moment with the brief melody might be brought back to a book which did not even belong to Knight. Thus the moment of the melody might be another example of deceptive transcendence. "Deception," for Nabokov, is not a derogatory term. In this case it only reflects the unpredictability with which the celestial essence chooses the material through which it will express itself. Once again, real life is in the twists: the transcendent moment is no less real for having been sparked by an unpredictable source.

Nabokov describes *Invitation to a Beheading* as "a violin in a void" (7). When visualizing this image, one must be careful not to visualize only the wooden instrument suspended in a void. The material is not the essence. The success of the violin exists in its sound: the music of the instrument is the intangible element contained in the void, filling the void. ("Dead is the mandible, alive the song," writes John Shade [l.244].) Thus, with the analogy of the violin to the novel, Nabokov is saying that the novel can contain a celestial element, but the material is merely the transmitter. V.'s style of scientific analysis will never lead to the real music that he seeks. (One might recall Nabokov's translation of Pushkin's poem "Mozart and Salieri," where Salieri says, "Stunning the sounds/ I cut up

11. The Indivisible Pearl

music like a corpse; I tested/ the laws of harmony by mathematics.") It is clear that one should not pluck out the pages of a novel and attempt to test them for their essence. One might even be taking the wrong approach by interrogating every word. The celestial aspect of a novel is no more contained in the material of its pages than the celestial essence of an individual is contained in the flesh.

Cincinnatus dreams of stripping himself beyond material, down to the original: "I am taking off layer after layer, until at last ... through the process of gradual divestment I reach the final, indivisible, firm, radiant point, and this point says: I am! like a pearl ring embedded in a shark's gory fat" (90). This is an image of the unencumbered soul, the original, the real life of Cincinnatus. This is the celestial essence condensed. That this "pearl" is an emblem of the soul is made clearer in the following passage from Nabokov's analysis of *The Song of Igor's Campaign*: "The image of the soul dropping out like a pearl occurs in religious works as late as the seventeenth century" (124–125). The lines he is analyzing are, "you let your pearly soul drop/ out of your brave body/ through your golden gorget" (l.608–610). "Gorget" is Nabokov's translation of a protective covering over the area above the chest bone, below the throat, which in "Russian traditional belief" is the "point of exit of the soul." That Cincinnatus' pearly soul is described as embedded in "a shark's gory fat" further conveys the grotesque nature of the material world which surrounds him (the nightmare/ *poshlust* world of this particular novel). The indivisible point of the soul—the pearl—is able to transcend even the least artistic constructs and prisons.

A useful contrast can be made between this Cincinnatus *sans* physical self and H.G. Wells' Invisible Man (again, from one of the books on Knight's shelf).[1] In an earlier scene, famous among Nabokov scholars, Cincinnatus removes all of his physical features, starting with his clothes and ending with his arms: "He took off the linen trousers and shirt. He took off his head like a toupee, took off his collarbones like shoulder straps, took off his rib cage like a hauberk. He took off his hips and his legs, he took off his arms like gauntlets and threw them in a corner" (32). After removing his physical self, Cincinnatus "simply reveled in the coolness." Wells' Invisible Man uses the same word—"revel"—to describe his newfound invisibility, saying that he wanted to "generally revel in my extraordinary advantage" (93). Both the Invisible Man and Cincinnatus stress that their unique situations make them cold: Cincinnatus, "It will be cold getting out of my warm body"; Invisible Man, "I had not reckoned that, transparent or not, I was still amenable to the weather and all its consequences.... And so, shivering, scared, and sniffing with the first intimations of a cold..." (Nabokov, *IB* 26; Wells 94). Those are the points of similarity between the two, but the difference between them is more essential to each of their states. The Invisible Man suffers from cold precisely because of his physicality. His ability to go unseen ultimately makes his material self much more of a burden than it would normally have been. Invisibility only emphasizes his physical nature, whereas Cincinnatus' experience is a transcendence of materiality, a metaphysical statement that the truest self is not encumbered by one's physical nature. His cold is caused by the bare exposure he senses from removing all material layers, the cold of a purely exposed soul. This soul is the internal pearl which remains untouched by material.

There is the same contrast between a valuable gem and the everyday material world in *Sebastian Knight*: "I know that the common pebble you find in your fist after having thrust your arm shoulder deep into water, where a jewel seemed to gleam on pale sand, is really the coveted gem though it looks like a pebble as it dries in the sun of everyday" (188). One glimpses a jewel through the water, but after grasping that "gem" it turns to a pebble. This too is an image of "faint hope": one needs to believe the initial vision, that there was a "coveted gem," though it cannot be dried out and kept for "everyday." This pebble is a soul-less pearl, a gem with its soul extracted. The tantalizing nature of the transcendent gem tempts one to capture it, but one can only capture the material.

Violins, books, rocks: one can hold these, but the celestial essence cannot be scientifically extracted. There is always the return to the material, to the less-than-celestial. The same idea is expressed in *The Invisible Man*: "Great and strange ideas transcending experience often have less effect upon men and women than smaller, more tangible considerations" (43). This, too, expresses the sovereignty of tangible platitudes and the impossibility of sustained transcendence. When the moment passes, one is left

11. The Indivisible Pearl

with only the memory and perhaps a tangible reminder — a pocket book, a pebble, misspelled words, someone else's *Anglo-Persian Dictionary*. The sense in the soul is all one has to verify that the experience of the internal pearl — the glimpse of the lining of life, the melodic moment conveyed by a bookshelf— was something real.

Chapter 12

Merging Souls, Inviolate Lives: Nabokov's Problematic Beyond

One of Nabokov's main concerns in regard to the afterlife is the question of identity. What happens to the individual self—the personality—after death? There seems to be a great fear, expressed in various ways in his art, that the self will not survive into the afterlife, that all identities will merge together after death. Ultimately, Nabokov does not attempt to provide an answer about this feared merger. That, nonetheless, is one of his primary fears. This theme centers around the topic of how one can define the soul.

In the concluding pages of *Sebastian Knight*, the vulnerable moment of return from transcendence comes when V. feels the greatest need to resolve the questions which have plagued his quest. This is when he discovers that his sense of transcendence has been prompted by a mistake, a deception. He cannot, like Shade, express the mildly sublime confidence of a "faint hope." His continual quest for material will never get him to the pearl of the matter: in the end, he once again attaches words to his experience. In fact—and here I am in disagreement with many readers—his conclusion, in the terms of Nabokovian metaphysics, is simply wrong. Despite the futility of his quest, V. claims that the mistaken moment has taught him a deep though fully expressible lesson. Therefore, V.'s final declaration—though it is the final paragraph of the novel—is not Nabokov's conclusion.

V. concludes with the idea that the afterlife "may be the full ability of consciously living in any chosen soul"; he goes on to say that these inhabitable souls are "unconscious of their interchangeable burden" (202–203).

12. Merging Souls, Inviolate Lives

From this theory of the soul, he then concludes, quite conveniently when one considers all the errors of his quest, that he *is* Sebastian Knight. Apparently, he has somehow discovered those "undulations" that had eluded him throughout the novel.

Even more significantly, V.'s desperate need for a conclusion, even in the backward path of his dreams, has led him to make a final statement which contradicts Nabokov's beliefs. Rowe points out that Nabokov "frequently leads the reader to subtly unjustified conclusions" ("Honesty" 171). V.'s overt statement, starting with "namely," goes against Nabokov's refusal to name metaphysical names. Nabokov's metaphysical beliefs are beyond words; V.'s conclusion is quite easily put into words.

The idea that one can usurp another's soul is shown to be an insipid proposition in a number of Nabokov's novels. In *Despair*, deluded Hermann says of his victim Felix, "Ah, if I had known him for years of intimacy, I might even have found it amusing to take up new quarters in the soul I had inherited. I would have known every cranny in it; all the corridors of its past; I could have enjoyed the use of all its accommodations" (176). Hermann has no respect for the original of Felix's soul. No soul can be taken up like a lodging. Specifically, we can see that Hermann's concept of adopting another's soul is false in regard to his sense of that soul's "past": "I would have known ... all the corridors of its past." Hermann uses the word "its," not "his," as though the "soul" and the "past" were both material entities, rather than intangible qualities of the mind. The past is never as easily accessible as Hermann suggests, at least not in Nabokov's view, especially not someone else's past. V. is not as bluntly intrusive as Hermann, but his final philosophy is the same: other people's souls can be co-opted at will.

In *Bend Sinister* we can find Nabokov attacking the same idea in a more political manner. Toad the tyrant declares:

> Your groping individualities will become interchangeable and, instead of crouching in the prison cell of an illegal ego, the naked soul will be in contact with that of every other man in this land; nay, more: each of you will be able to make his abode in the elastic inner self of any other citizen, and to flutter from one to another, until you know not whether you are Peter or John, so closely locked will you be in the embrace of the State [97].

This concept, of course, this declaration of co-dependence, flies in the face of all hierarchies and is antithetical to Nabokov's beliefs. Though the above statement obviously can be read as a satiric attack on communism, or on any other form of government which believes in its complete ability to subvert individuality, Nabokov's point is not only political. V. is as wrong to say that "any soul may be yours" as The Toad is to declare that the "ego" has been made "illegal." Though V.'s thoughts may seem less dangerous than the idea that every soul will be "locked ... in the embrace of the State," he nonetheless has the same concept of the human soul. His epistemology is equivalent to that of the tyrant, based on a belief that any other soul can be fully taken over.

"Naked soul" is a key term in The Toad's above quote. The term "naked soul" could refer to the soul untouched by material, just as "the pearl" is used in *Invitation to a Beheading*. The "naked soul," in Nabokov's terms, not those of the tyrant, is the original self—bodiless, without appended narratives, timeless. Nabokov puns on this term in *Invitation to a Beheading*: "Rodion had cornflower-blue eyes and, as always, his splendid red beard. This attractive Russian countenance was turned upwards toward Cincinnatus, who stepped on it with his naked sole—that is, his double stepped on it, while Cincinnatus himself had already descended from the chair" (29).[1] The "naked soul"/ "naked sole" is the free, internal aspect of Cincinnatus which can act as he wishes, here stepping on the jailer's face.[2] Rodion cannot move into Cincinnatus' soul, as he wishes. The "double" is the secret self, that which reflects one's most private personal desires and one's greatest imagination.[3] This is the part of the person which contains that otherworldly essence, and as always this essence places it beyond the reach of words: "'Citizens, there is among us a —' Here followed a strange, almost forgotten word" (32). The essence of Cincinnatus cannot be named, let alone co-opted by his antagonists.

V. would have us believe (along with Hermann and The Toad) that he could place himself inside the naked soul of his half-brother, and then, perhaps, in The Toad's terms, "flutter" off to another one. However, in Nabokov's worlds souls can merge in theory only. Pierre, the professional executioner, claims that "the structure of Cincinnatus' soul is as well known to me as the structure of his neck" (175). The idea of knowing a soul is mocked by making it seem as easy as knowing a neck. In addition, for Pierre, Hermann, and The Toad, inhabiting another's soul is associated with murder.

12. Merging Souls, Inviolate Lives

Can there be a more benevolent method of inhabiting another's soul? Fyodor of *The Gift* suggests that there is, that one may settle into another person as one would settle into a comfortable chair:

> He tried as he did everywhere and always to imagine the inner, transparent motion of this or that other person. He would carefully seat himself inside the interlocutor as in an armchair, so that the other's elbows would serve as armrests for him, and his soul would fit snugly into the other's soul ... and for a minute he would actually become Alexander Chernyshevski, or Lyubov Markovna, or Vasiliev [35–36].

Among the key words in this passage are "imagine" — imagination is the only real tool one can use to enter into another's soul — and "for a minute" — such an understanding can only be momentary. Fyodor is not usurping the souls of his interlocutors; he is not striving to eliminate their individual egos. Perhaps if V. added that phrase — "for a minute" — to his grand statement that he is Sebastian Knight, then his claim might be more palatable.

Even for Fyodor, however, with his poetic and sensitive attempts at understanding the souls of others, there is something crude about the suggestion that he knows these souls: "He ... would sometimes immerse himself with a thrill of curiosity and revulsion into the vast bowels of Vasiliev..." (36). Yes, if the soul of another is inhabitable, the bowels must be even easier to enter. Finally, Fyodor seems a bit voyeuristic with his self-proclaimed ability to move from soul to soul: "when Fyodor moved over into Mme. Chernyshevski ... he marveled at many things, as a prim traveler might marvel at the customs in a distant land...." Somehow none of the characters who claim the power to enter into souls ever fear that their own souls may be equally accessible. In fact, whether they are tyrants or poets, they tend to have rather large egos and inflated ideas about their own skills.

The most important scholar to have seen this same merging of souls as a prominent aspect of Nabokov's metaphysics is Leona Toker. She has a different interpretation about Nabokov's sense of the exclusivity of the soul, writing,

> Nabokov seems to imagine the contact with the Beyond not as negation but as incipient merger, a carnivalistic removal of partitions. The individual world loses its hermetic separateness, and the individual identity moves not toward nothingness but toward a dissolution in something infinitely greater than itself. Such moments of divestment are the essence of mystical experience, yet the loss of identity is also associated with death [6–7].[4]

Nabokov's Permanent Mystery

Clearly, Nabokov is interested in the question of merger and identity, but ultimately he did not try to define what "contact with the Beyond" entailed. Certainly on *this* side souls are not as adaptable as hats, not so easily exchanged. V., Hermann, and The Toad are incorrect, even disrespectful of the sanctity of another's soul.

In regard to "the Beyond," Toker seems to set up only two possibilities at this point of her argument: loss of identity or nothing. She says that Nabokov conveys his metaphysics "not as negation," "not toward nothingness." Nothingness is certainly not a part of Nabokov's metaphysical sense. However, a "carnivalistic removal of partitions" is not the only other option, and the ever-hierarchical Nabokov does not seem like one who would hope for the carnivalesque in an afterlife. As I have argued, Nabokov associates death — the going to the other side — with the creative process, and Toker is correct to state that this involves a threat to one's identity. It is wrong, however, to state that this is his definition of "the Beyond." Nabokov does not define "the Beyond," and does not provide clues to some secret system which he senses there. Still, it is quite possible that a massive merging of souls would only make for a rather cramped atmosphere, an uncomfortable otherworld.

More specifically, let us look at how this topic works in *Pnin*. Toker writes that in this novel "both the protagonist and the narrator are cancelled out: each dissolves in the image of the nonexistent other" (*Nabokov* 26). She states that the narrator expresses this "very serious anxiety" (7) in the following passage: "Man exists only insofar as he is separated from his surroundings. The cranium is a space-traveler's helmet. Stay inside or you perish. Death is divestment, death is communion" (*Pnin* 20). She seems to suggest that the narrator speaks the final truth of this novel. However, as I discussed earlier, the conclusion reinforces the individual identities of each character (unique Pnin and the surreptitious narrator) through an integral contrast in the narrative line (the multi-dimensional zig-zag and the straight line). There is no question that *Pnin* is another novel in which the topic of distinct identities and the possibilities of merging souls is interrogated. Nabokov is certainly concerned with this question. However, whereas this narrator states that "death is divestment," Cincinnatus earlier showed that divestment is *not* death, but a reduction of one's physical existence

12. Merging Souls, Inviolate Lives

down to an essential self. Divestment, for Cincinnatus, is the exact opposite of a loss of identity. In fact, it might be the individual's final defense against an intrusive and corrupt world.

Pnin, too, maintains his identity. No merger has taken place. He has not been "cancelled out." In fact, Pnin himself expresses a horrific sense of this definition of "the Beyond" as a locale where all souls merge into one. In regard to Liza's "impure, dry, sordid, infantile soul" Pnin thinks, "If people are reunited in Heaven (I don't believe it, but suppose), then how shall I stop it from creeping upon me, over me, that shriveled, helpless, lame thing, her soul? But this is the earth, and I am, curiously enough, alive, and there is something in me and in life —" (58). Here Pnin's thought breaks off, precisely at that point in which he appears to be on the verge of placing a label on that "something in me and in life." This definitive "something," the equivalent of Cincinnatus' pearl-like soul and the "something real" he sees in Cecelia C.'s eyes, is once again exactly that which cannot be placed into a systematic description of "The Beyond."

Toker writes, "*Pnin* is characteristic of Nabokov's major fiction in that its highly self-referential narrative points to something beyond itself..." (*Nabokov* 34). That is correct, but she continues this sentence, "...to human experience rendered universal by the cancellation of the discrete identities of the characters." It would have been better to have left that sentence, as Nabokov leaves his metaphysics, with only "something beyond itself." Sisson emphasizes that in the poem "Fame" Nabokov refrains from taking his metaphysical sense beyond just such a phrase — "something else, something else, something else": "The bliss that Nabokov finds in art, especially when these combinations disrupt ordinary vision to the extent of stimulating a sense of cosmic synchronization, seems to spring from a revelation of a mysterious 'something else'" ("Cosmic Synchronization and 'Something Else'" 174–175).[5] Cincinnatus repeats a similar phrase: "I repeat: there is something I know, there is something I know, there is something ..." (95).[6] Nabokov does not define his sense of the other side, but nonetheless I think he would shudder to find that it contained a system similar to that of The Toad.

One can easily imagine Knight expressing a horror comparable to that of Pnin at the thought of V. clamoring into his soul. In fact Knight mocked this possibility of "the cancellation of ... discrete identities" in one of his books, *The Prismatic Bezel*. In this novel, the reader discovers that all of the apparently distinct lodgers in a boarding house are connected to each other in a ridiculously coincidental way, but also a way that mocks the possibility of interchangeable souls. Knight's novel reveals that each member of the boarding house — the novelist, the art student, the colonel, the violinist, and so on — are all related, either by marriage or by blood — a brother, a father, a fiancé, another brother, and so on — and the "gradual melting process" goes on until all individual traits are eliminated (91). This is the dissolution of identity *ad absurdum*. But if one accepts the afterlife as a dissolution of identity, how else would it dissolve except *ad absurdum*? Certainly all the souls must tumble together until, amidst the confusion, all identifying characteristics are "quietly wiped out" (91).

Again, V. states in his conclusion that the beyond "may be" a place where souls can be inhabited, even, apparently, the souls of those who do not desire to be inhabited: souls in this hereafter are "interchangeable." This is part of V.'s final dream. It is not, as I said, a theory of tyranny, although the same idea is tyrannical when applied by The Toad. Rather, this is the would-be biographer's final fantasy. There may be some truth to the possibility of the merging of souls in the hereafter, but V. should have remained with the "may be." As a question or a conjecture, the theory cannot be disputed. As an assertion or a theological system, characters like Pnin are correct to express their disgust.

The final pages are separable from the rest of the text because they represent V.'s dream, his impossible return through time to the moment when he learns of Knight's death. Priscilla Meyer writes that V. "is rewarded by spiritual union with Sebastian" (45). However, this only seems to be V.'s wish: we do not see Sebastian participating in this wish. Meyer also discusses the "possibility of communion with the spirit world ... in the novel," arguing that "Sebastian's spirit does aid V." (50, 52). One can accept this "possibility" in the novel without accepting V.'s theory of merging souls at the end. That is, the question of Sebastian's influence on the text (or of any Nabokovian ghost on any other text) could be taken as further evidence that identities do not dissipate after death.

Nabokov does not set out the merging of all souls in the hereafter as

12. Merging Souls, Inviolate Lives

his metaphysical system. In fact, there is even a glimpse of the illegal ego sneaking into V.'s final assertion. He states that the hereafter involves "consciously" living in another soul, and yet all souls are "unconscious" of this ability. What V. actually wants is for his soul to be conscious and all the others, especially that of Knight, to be unconscious — inert, unchanging, and easily accessible. Ultimately, this final theory is really only a childish fantasy, one more attempt to reduce real life to a straight line. One senses that the real life of Sebastian Knight has once again slipped beyond V.'s clumsy grasp, zig-zagged right past him, and slipped beyond this concluding theory which, because of its placement in the text, could easily be misread as Nabokov's own. Gennady Barabtarlo has a similar sense of V.'s concluding paragraph: "The reader is made to feel as one who, after carefully inching one's hand into the folds of the net in the hope of finding and nipping a long-hunted rare insect, triumphantly grabs one's own left thumb — and wakes up" (*Aerial* 214).[7] The indivisible pearl-point of a self cannot be transfixed by a text or violated by a biographer; the celestial essence — the essential component of every individual — cannot be cancelled.

Humbert Humbert is another supreme believer in the malleability of souls, especially that of his favorite nymphet, Lolita. Much has been discussed concerning Humbert's sense of solipsism, but the topic of solipsism can also be directly connected to the problem of adaptable souls. Humbert firmly believes in his ability to inhabit Lolita's real life, beginning by obliterating her real name on the first page. Lolita, however, makes an opposing comment on this metaphysical question. Humbert overhears her saying to one little friend, "You know, what's so dreadful about dying is that you are entirely on your own" (284). Thus her instinctive sense of individual inviolability extends to a metaphysical sense of eternal solitude. Her seemingly casual statement places her in opposition to such diverse characters as V., the narrator of *Pnin*, The Toad and Humbert. For Lolita, it seems, the fear is not that some other soul will intrude upon her own, but that any type of authentic connection with another person appears to be impossible. In this sense, Lolita remains untouched by Humbert, regardless of how deeply he disrespects the sanctity of her soul. The real life of Dolores Haze escapes Humbert's grasp as surely as Knight's escapes that of V. No

Nabokov's Permanent Mystery

one is ever solipsized: solitude is too strong. Boyd writes that Nabokov's art represents "an incessant effort to find a way out of the goodly prison of consciousness" (*Russian Years* 36). Perhaps, Lolita suggests, it would be better if souls could come into contact, if the solitude of consciousness could be overcome.

Structurally, Nabokov's novels are often like those open-ended sentences ("There is among us a —"; "there is something in me and in life —"). This is the way in which "The Art of Translation" concludes, suggesting a perfect eternal something without threatening the essence of that something by putting it into words. Within V.'s dream he listens through a half-closed door and feels that he has gained some insight, that this sense of what he believes to be his half-brother's breathing is a sign from the other side. V. has not passed through that door. Though he may have truly sensed something on the other side, he is still only able to fully experience *this* side.

There is no systematic metaphysical conclusion we can draw from Nabokov's work, other than the firm but ultimately inexpressible knowledge that there is something. There is another side, and the door, after all, is only half-closed: we can catch glimpses. With this larger view of the overall structure of *Sebastian Knight*, one can make a connection to the failed clichés of the first level, the plot, where the doors did not quite close correctly. The doors of this novel are inconclusive, unpredictable — the pneumatic door does not slam as easily as it would have in a clichéd story, the "well-oiled" swing of a predictable plot twist does not work out. Nabokov builds this same sense into the entire literary structure by creating a novel which cannot be concluded, a supposed detective novel that ends with the assertion of permanent mystery.

In his autobiography Nabokov describes the aftermath of having created one of his first poems as having lost his previously secure sense of self; he looks into a mirror and has the "shocking sensation of finding the mere dregs of my usual self, odds and ends of an evaporated identity which it took my reason quite an effort to gather together again in the glass" (*SM* 227). One's daily identity evaporates in the effort of inspired creation, necessitating a mirror to help one reassemble one's self upon return. There is, to say the least, in Nabokov's art a problematic interaction between

12. Merging Souls, Inviolate Lives

autonomy and creativity.[8] The inviolability of the self is often called into question. While some — Andrew Field, Joyce Carol Oates — have thought of Nabokov as among the most narcissistic of writers, in truth he is not confident in the security of the self.[9] Identities are threatened; characters continually claim the right to co-opt or merge with the souls of other characters.

The idea of death as a form of dissolution is also central to the unfinished *The Original of Laura*. In this novel, Philip Wild undertakes the exercise of eliminating himself by eliminating thought: "to think away thought" (243). He refers to this as "delicious dissolution": "Dissolution, in fact, is a marvelously apt term here...." As he discusses this "mysterious technique," however, he is unquestioningly present — assertively present — in the text (245). In fact, his character comes into view even more clearly through his discussion of the attempts to dissolve himself. Perhaps the final point here comes in the novel that Nabokov wrote before *Laura*: "The I of the book/ Cannot die in the book" (*LATH* 239).

Ultimately, Nabokov raises the problem of merging souls — raises it often — without offering a solution to that problem. Nonetheless, when one follows the philosophy of The Toad or of Hermann, when one sympathizes with the heartfelt convictions of Pnin or Cincinnatus, I believe that Nabokov's hopes lie more with the latter. There is no definitive solution to Nabokov's beyond, and perhaps every identity eventually evaporates there. John Shade, however, seems to speak for Nabokov, offering the closest one can get to a final word on the issue, when he says that he will refuse the afterlife if it does not keep those traits that are so important to life on this side: "the passion and the pain," "this good ink, this rhyme," "the trail of silver slime/ Snails leave on flagstones" (l.525–536). One's personal work — one's "passion," one's "rhyme" — may amount to little more than the trail of slime left behind by a snail. Nonetheless, the poet wishes to cling to that slime, to those seemingly insignificant details which combine to create "mortal life." One can only hope that shuffling off that mortal coil, that snail's shell, does not entail losing one's small self.

Chapter 13

The Teleological Potential of Words

One reason why words seem unable to express the celestial sense is that the "real" is more complex than language. For Nabokov, "real life" is more completely detailed than any language could hope to be. Foster explains what he calls Nabokov's "asymptotic approach" to descriptions in *Speak, Memory*: "the steadily increasing detail implies an asymptotic approach to an ideally full but unrealizable description" (188). The "increasing detail" brings one closer and closer to closure, but never finishes off a complete description of real life. There are never enough details. Using Foster's term, I would add that Nabokov's is also an asymptotic approach to language and to real life.

Those who are hyper-aware may have a greater sense of "reality," but this is in no way a practical skill. We looked at the way Franz was a less-than-efficient salesman as his mind branched off into all of the possibilities contained in the word "ball." Similarly, Sebastian Knight describes his "state of constant wakefulness" as an uncontrollable number of associated thoughts prompted by simple, everyday events. He states that this constant complexity of thought is "utterly useless for practical application" and that it renders him incompetent, unable to deal with the common occurrence that provoked such thoughts (65). Here Knight is talking about his uniquely intense sense of perception, not directly relating this idea to language. However, the logical continuance of this idea would connect Knight to Borges' character Funes, who was even more paralyzed by his acute perception. Funes' intense perception demands an impossibly precise use of words: "Not only did it disturb him to think that the generic symbol *dog* would contain so many disparate individuals of diverse sizes and diverse

13. The Teleological Potential of Words

forms; it bothered him that the dog of three-fourteen (viewed in profile) would have the same name as the dog of three-fifteen (viewed from the front)" (130).[1] As in *Transparent Things*, Funes is also able to visualize the complete history of every object. This is an infinitely asymptotic approach to perception and language. While such perception may be a trait of cosmic synchronization (as discussed by Sisson and Alexandrov), it can be — for both Funes and Knight, as well as Franz — incapacitating. One must filter one's world in order to function. (Funes requires an entire day to reconstruct in his mind an entire day.) On a linguistic level, however, Nabokov may see this infinite variety as a sign of celestial influence. Heightened perception is a sign of celestial insight. As one attains higher levels of perception, one also attains a higher appreciation for the limitations of language.

The perfectly celestial word is one which cannot be written; the concept of such a word, however, within Nabokov's metaphysics, is enough to assure the abstract existence of the word and therefore of the signified object. If we can conceive of the perfect word, the immaculate translation, then we can believe in its existence. This is the highest level of the literary structure, the level which grades into mysterious meanings beyond the book. The inadequacy of language is, of course, a common modernist concern, but for Nabokov this very inadequacy implies the abstract possibility of adequacy. The idea that language cannot encapsulate the celestial sense only reinforces the unearthly nature of that sense.

At the end of the eighteenth chapter of *Sebastian Knight*, there is a moment which directly connects to this concept of the perfect metaphysical word. The final disruption of reality in this novel also centers around the use of words. Within his dream, V. describes his sense of receiving some sort of transcendent message, some answer to all his questions about the meaning of life and death; he says that there were words of extraordinary import, striving to "solve" these ultimate questions, but the words had no apparent meaning once he woke up (188). However, taking this sense of celestial insight and putting it into words is akin to translating the perfect lines of a poem into a new language. The solution remains elusive. V. is unable to convey this resolute phrase upon awakening, stating that the meaningless words that were left in his head were an incoherent new version of that extraordinarily meaningful phrase. Here Nabokov raises the suggestion that literary art may be the process of translating the celestial, translating the other side into the terms of this one. Alexandrov writes that this moment demonstrates "Nabokov's sense that the otherworld is fundamentally unknowable in earthly terms" (*Otherworld* 150). I would add that this demonstrates Nabokov's sense that the celestial essence is fundamentally knowable, although it cannot be placed in earthly terms. It is knowable, but not permanently knowable, as uncapturable as the butterfly of light. Simply because the essence of the gem cannot be captured does not mean that it is non-existent.

Similarly, Nabokov's many mirrors may suggest to some that he is a nihilist, that those mirrors deflect all attempts at achieving an absolute sense of reality. Those mirrors, however, do reflect something definite, something real, even if that real something remains permanently elusive. Lucy Maddox finds *Sebastian Knight* to be a "failure," writing, "We do, ultimately, hold a dead book in our hands." The reason for her conclusion may be a misreading of mirrors:

> Perhaps Nabokov intended for us to finish his book with the same haunting suspicion that V. has on finishing Sebastian's book [*The Doubtful Asphodel*]; that is, if Nabokov's book mirrors Sebastian's book which in turn mirrors the way life itself teases those who believe in an absolute solution that can be systematically sought out, then Nabokov has succeeded — but it is a Pyrrhic victory [49].

But the understanding that truth is elusive is not a "Pyrrhic victory": it is one step closer to the truth. For Nabokov, no system will sustain that metaphysical knowledge, no words can capture the ever-elusive truth. That may be frustrating for some readers, but it is essential for understanding the art of Nabokov.

From the start of the final chapter of *Sebastian Knight*, earthly words don't seem to be working quite right. V. tries to recall the name of the hospital where his brother is dying; he cannot remember the name of the "sanitorium" [sic], wondering what "on earth" that name could be. He mentally grapples with the letter M, then loses the word in the rushing rhythm of the train (190). Once again, in the midst of a paragraph about insufficient words, there seems to be one which is misspelled; earlier it had been spelled two different ways: "sanitarium" and "sanatorium" (119, 184).

13. The Teleological Potential of Words

Such mistakes suggest the presence of a realm above words (or perhaps, with this particular example, a sloppy proofreader). In this scene the word, "on earth," doesn't quite come to him.

V. seems to be grasping for the right word from the other side, as if seeing the word through a mist, but unable to make it appear (193). The dominance of time adds pressure to the dominance of this material concern for words, as V. feels time running out for his half-brother. He tries desperately to fill the verbal frame in his mind. That there is a verbal frame assures him that there is also a word which will fit that frame. This device of vacant verbal frames is one that Nabokov uses elsewhere.

In *Speak, Memory*, Nabokov struggles to recall the name of an almost-forgotten dog ("a female fox terrier with bells on her collar and a most waggly behind"). First he writes, "I cannot recall the dog's name...." Two pages later, as if perfectly filling the frame of an absent thought, he writes, "I try again to recall the name of Colette's dog — and, triumphantly ... over the glossy evening sands of the past ... here it comes, here it comes ... Floss, Floss, Floss!" (*SM* 150–152). The word arrives like an obedient terrier. Of course, Nabokov could have revised his writing and included the dog's name from the outset of the scene. Instead, he has created a structure which highlights the difficulties of memory and the pure satisfaction of verbal re-discovery. The recovery of the word is also a triumph over time.[2]

In such a structure we can see the possibility for attaining the perfect word. V. also feels a need to exclaim his discovery: "St. Damier!" (196). Although V. needs the name of that hospital for a very specific reason, Nabokov's structure stresses the mental process of satisfying a verbal frame which has been emptied by faulty memory. In all of these scenes we see (and share) the process of perfect verbal closure. Such scenes represent an earthly version of the discovery of that unspeakable celestial word. The ultimate discovery of the all-encompassing celestial answer is conceivable because the process of that verbal rediscovery would parallel the process of recalling a lost word — like the forgotten name of a dog or a hospital. Our attempts to duplicate that process from this side, filling in that spiritual sense with the word "God" or "Otherworld" or "Celestial Essence," are always unsuccessful, incomplete.

Nabokov's Permanent Mystery

Some of the select among Nabokov's characters are given the words to express this same sense of the metaphysical limitations of language. As quoted earlier, Fyodor of *The Gift* states, "Definition is always finite," that his poetic endeavor is to "search beyond the barricades ... of words" (329). Fyodor knows that striving for infinity involves a reach beyond words. To place a name on the celestial essence is to make finite that which is infinite, to place pins into the butterfly of light. For Fyodor, as for Nabokov, the impossibility of this process does not mean that one stops striving. Paradoxically, writing is one means of striving for that something beyond words. The creative process can bring one into closer association with the infinite and, I would argue, Nabokov believes it even allows one to make occasional contact with the celestial source itself. The celestial shiver of inspiration is a sure sign of that contact.

Nabokov's description in *Speak, Memory* of his English grammar book is a clear example of the way in which this metaphysical idea of language relates to the literary structure of a work. In the following passage this principal is reduced to its most basic elements. The grammar book begins with the simplest words: "the compiler was handicapped by having to employ—for the initial lessons, at least—words of not more than three letters" (79–80). At this stage of the structure, the students must rely on their imagination to bring these three-lettered words up to the level of plot: "my imagination somehow managed to obtain the necessary data." This is the most basic level of language and structure. However, the lowest level is necessary for the overall structure to attain its full potential.

The hierarchy of the grammar book's structure is, of course, based on a development of the level of language. Gradually the language becomes "real": "and at the very end ... a real, sensible story unfolded its adult sentences ('One day Ted said to Ann: Let us—')...." The story unfolds butterfly-like, as the language has reached an "adult" stage. As Nabokov presents the end of the grammar book, consistent with his teleological sense of literary structure, even this book resists closure: "One day Ted said to Ann: Let us—" The words "let us" lead to potentially infinite possibilities of language. At this point the language has fully come to life. ("A language is a live physical thing," he writes in *Sebastian Knight* [82].) Nabokov then concludes his description of this grammar book with a

13. The Teleological Potential of Words

thought about where the full-fledged language might lead: "that promised land where, at last, words are meant to mean what they mean" (*SM* 80–81). This might remind one of the finale of *Pnin*, where Pnin is free "at last" and is off to lands "where there was simply no saying what miracle might happen." There is simply no saying what miracle might happen after a student has learned a language. The language may even bring one to some surprise "promised land."

At the same time, however, there is a hint of language's limitations in this final statement. Nabokov writes that in this promised land of full-fledged language "words are meant to mean what they mean." He significantly does not say that in this magic land "words mean what they mean." Rather, his focus is on the intention of the student-cum-artist: in the promised land words must be intended. Or perhaps the words could be "meant" to mean what they mean by some higher power. Either way, the phrase places some subtle emphasis on intentionality. The creative agent is essential to Nabokov's conception of the teleological potential of language. That, perhaps, is the "magic": when used to their utmost teleological potential, words are the work of a will towards infinity, as Fyodor stated. The grammar book is a Baedecker to the beyond. The structure of the grammar book shows that in the linguistic promised land words are intended to achieve their fullest expression, their highest evolutionary potential.

Chapter 14

Not Quilty: The Problem of Persecution Mania

I have discussed Humbert's newfound appreciation for the real life of Lolita in the end of his narrative. Although Humbert is surely among the most manipulative of narrators, this understanding shows that he has moved beyond the idea that he can solipsize Dolores Haze, even if that understanding is only in his imagination. Imagination, for Nabokov, often represents a higher realm. It is no less of an understanding if it occurs through art rather than taking place in the real world.

The second key scene to the conclusion is the one in which Humbert shoots Quilty. Not only am I going to argue that this scene is also a product of Humbert's imagination, I am going to argue that there is no objectively "real" Quilty anywhere in the text. What seems to be Quilty is most often a projection of Humbert's mind. Many readers do not notice that Quilty is only directly present in the murder scene. Nowhere else in the novel is he unquestionably portrayed. I do not mean to argue that there is no Quilty, but that every appearance and seeming appearance of Quilty is filtered through Humbert's paranoid mind. Once again, I am not attempting to provide a new solution to this novel; rather, my intention is to complicate things further, to add to the mystery.

Before looking at the scene in which Quilty is killed, or "killed," we need to examine some of the evidence in the novel. First, Humbert's direct testimony is equivocal. He calls himself a "murderer," yet says elsewhere, "If I ever commit serious murder ... Mark the 'if'" (9, 47). We could conclude from this that his murder was not a "serious" one. (It is, in fact, a very comic scene in the book, in both movies, and perhaps most of all in Nabokov's reading of the chapter.) He also states, "Emphatically, no killers

14. Not Quilty: The Problem of Persecution Mania

are we. Poets never kill," and tells us at another point, "I am no poet. I am only a very conscientious recorder" (88, 72). He may be "conscientious," in his own way, but he is not clear. Humbert is the accused criminal who tries on the telltale glove one day only to find it too tight, then puts it on for a perfect fit the next. His own direct testimony (before the murder scene itself) seems to do nothing more than muddle the picture. The single thing we do know about Humbert's attitude toward this "murder" is that he never for a moment appears repentant.

John Ray, Jr., however, provides more useful information, or rather lack of information: he never mentions the murder. Ray writes of "the fatal summer of 1947" and believes that if Humbert had received appropriate counseling "there would have been no disaster" (5). The year 1947, however, was when Humbert first took Lolita on the road after Charlotte's death, *not* the year of the supposed murder, which was 1952. That summer was fatal for Charlotte, disastrous for Lolita, but not relevant at all to Clare Quilty. This is why Ray uses the word "disaster," though one can sense Nabokov's manipulative hand here. Ray seems to be the type who would not refrain from directly naming the crime. In regard to himself at the time of writing, Humbert says that he has "an altogether different mess on my conscience" (169). His situation is a mess and a disaster, but not a serious murder.

All of this evidence comes in addition to the dates, which in themselves should be enough to prove that the time of the murder coincides with the time that Humbert spent writing *Lolita*. He says that he spent the fifty-six days of writing "in the psychopathic ward for observation, and then in this well-heated, albeit tombal seclusion" (308). Nowhere does he specifically state that he is in jail for murder. Ray again prevaricates on this question, stating that Humbert wrote this text "in legal captivity" (3). Wood observes that this phrase suggests "a zoo rather than a prison" (108). Indeed, as in his conspicuously using the term "disaster" rather than "murder," the term "legal captivity" seems precisely phrased to suggest that Humbert is not in a prison at all. (Humbert's "well-heated ... seclusion" could also suggest a zoo.) Wood goes on to connect this idea of the zoo to Nabokov's comment about the ape who is only able to draw the bars of his own cage. In fact, rather than arguing that Humbert is in an asylum rather than a prison, one could make the argument that Humbert's state of captivity is a metaphor for his state of mind while writing the novel.

Without question, however, Humbert places some emphasis on the idea that he is gradually losing his mind. In addition, this process coincides with his growing paranoia about the presence of Quilty. Believing that Lolita has betrayed him during his solo excursion into Kasbeam, he attacks her, then says that "the scent" he was searching for was "practically undistinguishable from a madman's fancy" (215). After having a flat tire in the mountains, and "rolling down an almost imperceptible grade," Humbert believes he sees his shadow stop fifty yards behind them, gets out to confront this would-be Quilty, when his own car begins to roll away. Lolita insists the car was moving by itself; Humbert is certain she was saving Quilty's identity, and the reader most often sides with Humbert. Nonetheless, Humbert concludes this passage by stating: "Perhaps, I was losing my mind" (229). Humbert himself seems to be rolling down an imperceptible grade, gradually losing his hold on reality.

Toker also argues that Humbert creates these final scenes at the time of writing them. However, she writes, "He is completely unaware of having crossed the line between 'reality' and illusion" (*Nabokov* 211). This is an important difference between her argument and mine. I believe that Humbert is fully aware, on one level, of his approaching madness and that he prepares for writing his text in a way that is analogous to the way he prepares his pistol. At one point, he suggests that he might eventually lose his mind and, if that happens, he might murder "someone": "In fact — said high-and-dry Humbert to floundering Humbert — it might be quite clever to prepare things." He then decides to move the gun into his pocket, so that he will be prepared for that "spell of insanity" (229). High-and-dry Humbert is the narrator of this text; floundering Humbert is its subject, the Humbert of the narrator's memory. This is similar to the formula in that one sentence of Sebastian ("he was already on the other side, if he could see the beach receding") and in the literary structure of *The Eye*: in the process of creativity, which constitutes something of a death to this world, the narrator may watch himself moving away from his own physical being. As Khodasevich wrote, imagination for Nabokov is akin to death, whereby one loses one's hold on this side. One may watch one's self remain

14. Not Quilty: The Problem of Persecution Mania

behind as one drifts toward the imaginative realm. Thus, I half agree with Toker: one Humbert is losing his hold on reality, while the other is drifting to the other side. Humbert believes he can control Lolita's soul, but the truth is that he hasn't even solipsized himself. Nabokov uses the same formula to describe Humbert's state of mind when his first wife left him: "Humbert the Terrible deliberated with Humbert the Small whether Humbert Humbert should kill her or her lover, or both" (29). For Nabokov, one might say, the artistic consciousness creates an exponential self: on one sane level one can be entirely aware of one's own madness. The imaginative mind is its own witness.

As Humbert perceives Quilty coming closer, the bars on his cage become less penetrable. He is well aware that all of these clues may be figments of his own mind: "it was becoming gradually clear that all those identical detectives in prismatically changing cars were figments of my persecution mania" (238). This persecution mania reaches its peak, of course, as Humbert peruses the registers of hotels along the path they had traveled before losing Lolita. I will not go into the details of the various references included in these registers, as scholars have already covered much of this topic. The chapter seems designed to provide a banquet for an annotator, but the bait has lured many readers in the direction of such one-dimensionally deluded critics as Kinbote. As in *Sebastian Knight*, Nabokov is at this point playing on a reader's expectations in regard to a detective novel: the identity must be discovered (V., too, checked the hotel register). We have no choice but to follow Humbert as he looks for clues. We do have a choice, however, as to whether or not we believe his fanatic search for Quilty is a quixotic quest. One register entry reads "Donald Quix, Sierra, Nev."

Stanley Fish has argued that one's expectations formed prior to reading a particular work will predetermine how one will interpret that work. Fish told his students they were reading a poem and "it was the act of recognition which came first — they knew in advance that they were dealing with a poem — and the distinguishing features then followed. In other words, acts of recognition, rather than being triggered by formal characteristics, are their source" (326). The exact same process occurs as Humbert proceeds on his quest for clues to Quilty: every register he reads provides a reference to Quilty, or to himself, or to some literary topic which they presumably have in common. Every entry provides a potential clue — be it due to an idiosyncratic signature, a peculiar license plate number, or even just an odd sounding name — because Humbert has predetermined that they will read in this way. He has decided he will find Quilty, therefore he does.

Were any of these register entries actually Quilty? One would think that "Harold Haze, Tombstone, Arizona" could not be a coincidence. And what about "the anagramtailed entry … Ted Hunter, Cane, NH"? This one too seems almost certainly to be a sign from Quilty, who might have predicted that Humbert would retrace his own steps, searching for clues to who had taken away Lolita. But to follow along this path is to make that imperceptible slide into Humbert's mind. One must decide where to stop the slide, or one will finish by completely coinciding with Humbert. Fish: "To put the matter in either way is to see how unhelpful the terms 'subjective' and 'objective' finally are. Rather than facilitating inquiry, they close it down, by deciding in advance what shape inquiry can possibly take place" (336). We have exactly as many clues that Quilty was following Humbert as we have evidence of Humbert's paranoia.

Immediately after he tells of all the registered names he came across in his quest for Quilty, Humbert describes his return to Beardsley College. In this short scene there is one sentence which indirectly reflects on the absurdity of Humbert's too-literal interpretation of the registered names; for a brief moment of rest and semi-clear thought, he sits on a bench "donated by Cecilia Dalrymple Ramble" (252–253). Had he seen this name in the previous scene, he certainly would have attributed something sinister to its odd sound. Nonetheless, I have yet to find anyone who argues that this marble bench was secretly and pseudonymously donated by Quilty. The oddness of this name helps to convey the distorted state of mind of Humbert Humbert at that point of the novel. Nabokov describes Gogol's use of odd-sounding names: "a singular name to say the least but necessary here to underline utter remoteness from life and the consequent remoteness from life and the consequent irreality of that person, a dream in a dream, so to speak" (83). For Gogol, such names convey a state of "irreality," as well as "a sense of remoteness and optical distortion due to the haze" (85). For Humbert, such names are cause, instead, by the absence

14. Not Quilty: The Problem of Persecution Mania

of Haze, the cause of Humbert's mental imbalance. On the other hand, one should not doubt that there might somewhere exist a Cecilia Dalrymple Ramble who likes to donate marble benches to colleges.

Structurally, this problem can be phrased by asking how close we believe Humbert is to the author, Nabokov. If Humbert's perception is correct, then he stands very close to the creative source, discovering and interpreting objective evidence within Nabokov's created world. If he is wrong, then the manipulative hand of Nabokov must be toying with Humbert, enhancing his delusions with false clues. Many have believed Humbert, at least to the point of believing that Quilty really is somewhere on that path. In fact, some so thoroughly believe Humbert's claim that he has been pursued by Quilty that they seem at times to be sharing his persecution mania.

Appel, for example, sees Quilty in the sound of a flushing toilet. After Humbert and Lolita spend their first night at the Enchanted Hunters hotel, someone in the next room flushes the toilet, creating "a veritable Niagara" (130). Appel connects this to Quilty's flushing of the toilet in the murder scene (a connection which Humbert does not make), and provides a list of all the references to Quilty that he sees in his reading of the novel. He then nudges the reader into Humbert's cage by saying, "A reader armed only with this telescopic list should be able to identify Quilty whenever he appears or is evoked on a page" (*Annotated* 349). Fish might reply by adding that any reader who wishes to identify Quilty whenever "he appears or is evoked on a page" will surely find him on *every* page. Not every toilet flush is a clue to Quilty.[1]

A number of scholars have also seen Quilty in the porch scene at the Enchanted Hunters, but it is the scholars themselves who are enchanted by the hunt for Quilty. In the darkness Humbert describes "somebody" next to him on the porch. In the darkness, he then has a brief comic dialogue with this "somebody" who seems to be asking suggestive questions about Lolita ("'Where the devil did you get her?' 'I beg your pardon?' 'I said: the weather is getting better,'" and so on). Quilty-hunters are certain to make him out in the darkness, though Humbert is unable to distinguish a face until the end of the dialogue. At this point he states: "He struck a light, but because he was drunk, or because the wind was, the flame illumined not him but another person, a very old man, one of those permanent guests of old hotels" (126–127). This scene plays on the reader's expectation of seeing a significant face in that darkness. The structure of the scene seduces one into seeing Quilty: there is no satisfactory discovery if one does *not* see him here. Instead, however, the scene provides a zig-zag away from definite identity. Anticipating this expectation, Nabokov has Humbert tell us that this is "not him." Nabokov gets the last laugh as he leads some readers further into Humbert's persecution mania than even Humbert goes.

The revelation of a definite identity is a plot cliché that Nabokov enjoys manipulating. He appreciates the appearance of peripheral characters, as he expresses in his analysis of Gogol: "Another special touch is exemplified by the chance passer-by — that young man portrayed with a sudden and wholly irrelevant wealth of detail: he comes there as if he was going to stay in the book (as so many of Gogol's homunculi seem intent to do — and do not)" (*Gogol* 76–77). Vivid though peripheral characters, Nabokov explains, tempt one to assign them a greater significance to the events of the book, while they really have none. There are many such characters who arrive with vivid details which have no practical purpose except aesthetic pleasure — like the "plump, glossy little Eskimo girls with their fish smell, hideous raven hair and guinea pig faces" in Humbert's one polar chapter, Lolita's seemingly complicitous nurse Mary Lore in the Elphinstone hospital with her "fundament jigging" and "reeking of urine and garlic," and the amnesiac soldier with the "Brooklynese" accent who wakes up in Humbert and Rita's room and insists that they have "purloined his (worthless) identity," and, indeed, Rita herself (33, 242–243, 260). This "irrelevant wealth" is what Nabokov most enjoys in literature. Only a misguided reader would try to solve all of these presences. Structurally, I have argued that such "subliminal" points are the imaginative details of the top level, far beyond any relevance to the story. An appreciation for Nabokov's sense of literary structure provides a guide to how he believes we should read. Pouncing on every potential clue to the presence of Quilty will only cause one to stumble all over Nabokov's magic carpet: the plot clichés of the pseudo-detective quest do not function as typically expected. This same idea is at work in regard to V. and *Sebastian Knight*. In *Lolita*, Nabokov takes this play on plot clichés a step further by including many phantom clues which lead the reader to share Humbert's paranoia.

14. Not Quilty: The Problem of Persecution Mania

Appel, of course, states without hesitation that this "somebody" on the porch is "Quilty" (*Annotated* 381).[2] Appel's rush to judgment creates a reductive reading by not allowing for the subtle subjectivity of Humbert's mind. A more apt observation about this novel is that Humbert *never* directly encounters Quilty. This is one of the ideas I am relying on to argue that the murder scene is imagined: Humbert never encounters Quilty on any level that can unequivocally be called "real." Even Appel reports,

> Nabokov removed from the final version of *Lolita* three scenes in which Quilty figured conspicuously: a talk before Charlotte Haze's club ...; a meeting with Lolita's friend Mona; and an appearance at a rehearsal of his own play, featuring Lolita. All three scenes were omitted because such foreground appearances interrupted the structure and rhythm of Quilty's pursuit [*Annotated* 349–350].

Elsewhere Nabokov tells us — through Sebastian Knight — that only the final version of an author's work should be relevant to the reader, that drafts should be destroyed (*RLSK* 34). The final version of *Lolita* intentionally eliminates any overt appearance of Quilty.[3] Appel tells us that those scenes disrupted the structure "of Quilty's pursuit." My reading of Nabokovian structure shows that the real question is whether there is any pursuit at all. Nabokov eliminated Quilty's "foreground appearances" because they would have provided objective evidence of Quilty's existence. This is the texture of the novel, not the idea that we see Quilty on the porch, in the registers, and even overhear him flushing the toilet: Quilty never comes into the foreground of the narrative, not once. As I showed regarding his sense of Lolita, this novel is about Humbert's mind, and Humbert's mind often projects the presence of Quilty onto an otherwise innocent world.[4]

Humbert is consumed by "persecution mania," as he states; he therefore casts the shadow of this persecuting presence throughout his text, causing some readers to expect to see the personification of this shadow. Even when Humbert states that he didn't see Quilty, he seems to be thinking that he should have. Once again, these thoughts are the bars of his cage.

I have used Appel's reading as my primary example here because he is often considered to be the official annotator, as his thoughts are attached to one published version of *Lolita*. It seems to me, however, that he guides his interpretation toward a specific reading, rather than annotates. This is another attempt to slam the text shut, rather than accepting the irresolvable

Nabokov's Permanent Mystery

questions of perception inherent in Nabokov's sense of the "real." There are certainly others, in addition to Appel, who have read Quilty into the text in ways that surpass even Humbert's subjectivity.

Carl Proffer is another scholar who says that we must see Quilty on the porch; he writes, "It is important that we do deduce this; otherwise the conversation between Humbert and Quilty would seem purposely mysterious" (64). However, permanent mystery, as well as purposeful mystery, is essential to Nabokov. Many characters, like the old man on the porch, mean little or nothing to the lowest structural level. Those who see multiple Quiltys in the novel often do so because they do not have a complete sense of the inconclusive quality of Vladimir Nabokov's literary structures. Fredson Bowers appropriately puts the following quotation at the front of Nabokov's published lecture notes: "My course, among other things, is a kind of detective investigation of the mystery of literary structures." Thus, Nabokov does see the reader as being in the role of the detective, but a detective who is investigating the mystery, not solving it. Mystery is not a quality which a reader should hope to resolve away. This quotation comes from his lecture on Dickens, and the next sentence of the lecture reads, "But remember that what I can manage to discuss is by no means exhaustive" (*LL* 89). An appreciation of mystery means that one is always ever approaching the text. The right reading of a worthwhile structure is never exhaustive.

I mentioned Foster's explanation of Nabokov's "asymptotic approach"; one can come constantly closer to a complete sense of "real life," though never totally attain it. Applied science, Nabokov writes, creates the illusion of having solved the most profound questions of the universe, but in fact "the greater one's science, the deeper the sense of mystery" (*SO* 44–45). That is, the discoveries of science actually enhance the greatest mysteries. Nabokov's novels should be read the same way, not with the pseudo-science of perfect resolution. Readers are mistaken when they unequivocally solve the essential mystery of *Lolita* by detecting Quilty everywhere.

There is further evidence that the murder of Quilty is a scene which derives solely from Humbert's imagination. When Lolita provides the mythical name of their pursuer, whispering it to Humbert without letting the reader in on the secret, Nabokov uses the same formula of verbal framing which I discussed in the revelation of the dog's name "Floss" in *Speak,*

14. Not Quilty: The Problem of Persecution Mania

Memory and, with more metaphysical resonance, in the idea of revealing "the absolute solution" in *Sebastian Knight*. This same process is repeated early in *Lolita*, long before Humbert uses the device to lead us into believing in Quilty. Describing the time when his wife Valeria left him, Humbert at first says of the taxi-driving other man, "I do not remember his ridiculous name," thus leaving the reader wondering. As the scene nears its conclusion, however, he writes, "Maximovich! his name suddenly taxies back to me" (28, 30). As I argued earlier, this device works by creating an unfilled verbal frame in the reader's mind, a distinct gap where a name should fit, then creating a perfectly satisfactory answer by filling the frame with a name. "Floss!," "Maximovich!": the frame is flawlessly filled, causing the reader to share the narrator's sense of satisfaction.

This process takes on a larger structural dimension when the created frame does nothing less than solve the book itself. In *Sebastian Knight*, that unfilled frame is the place of the celestial essence, the meaning of life and death. The final word is never provided, but the existence of the verbal frame suggests the presence of an unnamable essence. In *Lolita* the entire text builds up an elaborate verbal frame which must be filled in the final chapters. The porch scene is paradigmatic of the entire structure: there is a face in the dark and the reader is led to expect a definite identification of that face. Here is the overly determined way in which Humbert admits to having set up the revelation of this identity: "Quietly the fusion took place, and everything fell into order, into the pattern of branches that I have woven throughout this memoir with the express purpose of having the ripe fruit fall at the right moment..." (272). That is only the beginning of the sentence; it goes on to describe the "monstrous peace" that his literary strategy — his "express and perverse purpose" — should provide now that he is about to provide the absolute solution to his text. (One might wonder if this is a parody of Nabokov's perfect verbal frame strategy or a manipulative use of it in order to "frame" the narrator's guilt elsewhere — or both.) He ends the sentence by insisting that even a resistant reader should, of course, give in to his wonderful literary skill and states that this pure sense of "logical recognition" is what his "most inimical reader should experience now" (272).

"Quietly," he says at the start of the sentence, almost letting the name slip. The presence of Quilty is the pattern which cannot be unseen once it is seen; in fact, it is the pattern which, once seen, is so overt as to pervade the text. Nonetheless, the naming of this all-solving presence is Humbert's imagined resolution of his own irresolvable problems. Humbert's "perverse purpose" is to deceive the reader into sharing his imagined sense of "monstrous peace." He even withholds the name at this point, so that each reader will have to make the "logical recognition" on his or her own. The technique of verbal framing takes over the novel's structure, leading the reader to expect a "real" solution to the plot, a "real" name to fill that frame. The only possible name is, of course, "Quilty." Nabokov, however, once again, is playing with the clichés of discovering a definite identity. For Nabokov conclusions are never as simple as a single word. "Quilty" does not solve the text.

Nonetheless, between Humbert's manipulation and the cooperation of some scholars, many readers have been pulled straight into Humbert's cage. This technique of the verbal frame is one of the ways in which we find ourselves seated right next to the ape. I suggest that one should be an even more inimical reader than Humbert expects, resisting his insistence and recognizing that the fulfillment of this verbal frame is based on Humbert's persecution mania. Humbert has fashioned an artificial frame so that only one illusory identity can make a satisfactory fit. Though not arguing that Quilty is a product of Humbert's mind, Boyd also recognizes that within this text Humbert asserts control over Quilty's presence. In fact, Boyd states that this is one of Humbert's primary purposes for writing the text: "he turns his rival into a puppet who now dances to *his* control of time as he pointedly shapes the pattern of Quilty's appearance and disappearance within the past" (*American Years* 249). It is only a small step from Boyd's argument to the idea that Quilty is Humbert's fabrication. At least within his own text, Quilty is completely controlled by Humbert's pen, regardless of how conscious that control is. Humbert has accurately conveyed his sense of persecution, then imaginatively resolved that sense in his concluding pages.

All of the conclusion is a product of his imagination. In this reading, the structure of the novel, just as that of *Sebastian Knight*, emphasizes mystery and imagination, rather than a resolution of the plot. His text is his dream-catharsis, an extravagant verbal frame which he has fashioned from

14. Not Quilty: The Problem of Persecution Mania

madness and imagination, perfectly and logically filled by that same mysterious mix of madness and imagination. Quilty is the baroque pattern inscribed on the bars of Humbert's cage.

In addition, the scene in which Humbert kills Quilty provides enough evidence on its own that the murder is not "real." There are a number of references to B-movie clichés, highlighting the fictionality of events. These have been noted by readers and scholars. Nabokov's use of clichés in this scene is consistent with his ethical sense of the cliché. The ethical use of clichés, according to Nabokov, involves either breathing new life into dead terms or poking those dead terms with live prose, in an effort to demonstrate their lifelessness. In this scene, as Quilty and Humbert battle each other, Humbert interrupts the battle to prompt the reader's thoughts toward the clichéd conclusion of a Hollywood Western, only to state that this clichéd fight scene is not the kind of fight that he and Quilty carried out, not the kind of fight with "ox-stunning fisticuffs, the flying furniture." Instead of that clichéd cowboy climax the reader of this scene will find a "silent, soft, formless tussle on the part of two literati ... both of us were panting as the cowman and the sheepman never do" (299). This description highlights the pasted-together quality of Humbert's climactic chapter. The soft tussle of two stuffed dummies: at its essence this fight is artificial. Humbert points the reader's attention toward the clichéd battles of Westerns, only to state that *this* battle was nothing of the sort. Once again, a stereotypic structure is evoked for the sole purpose of frustrating the stereotype itself. The "tussle" between Humbert and Quilty is "formless" because the standard fictional form is not functioning at this point. Even at the level of single words Humbert here breaks the standard form: "cowman" is of course a play on the word "cowboy," but what exactly is a "sheepman"?

In addition to the breaking of clichés, Humbert's final scene with Quilty is a concluding dream sequence, much like the final dream-train ride of *Sebastian Knight*. When entering Quilty's house Humbert pushed the front door and "it swung open as in a medieval fairy tale" (294). Nabokov explains, in regard to a moment in *Eugene Onegin*, but as if in explication of this moment in *Lolita*, "There is a dreamlike atmosphere about all this. As in a fairy tale, silent doors open before him. He penetrates into the enchanted castle" (*EO*, vol. 3, 234). In this analysis Nabokov directly connects the idea of a fairy tale to the feeling of dream-logic. The "atmosphere" of this scene provides a complete contrast to the realistic details which come earlier in the novel. Now we are thoroughly inside Humbert's head, his cage, no longer able to catch even a glimpse of the "real" world between the bars.

One more example should suffice to highlight the unreal atmosphere of the murder scene. In addition to the imagery of dreams and nightmares, this sentence demonstrates Humbert's imaginative detachment from himself: "I see myself following him through the hall, with a kind of double, triple, kangaroo jump ... bouncing between him and the front door in a ballet-like stiff bounce" (303). That's a lot of bouncing. A realistic reading of this sentence is not possible; no Hemingway character ever bounced — with a "double, triple" jump — like a balletic kangaroo. Similar to Cincinnatus, Humbert learns that one can escape from one's personal cage through the self-detaching mechanism of imagination. Earlier Humbert states, "I felt curiously aloof from my own self" (33). For some, salvation lies in rendering the "real" world unreal, in perceiving that the bars of the cage are self-projections. In this sense, imagination *is* salvation: one can transcend oneself by expanding one's limited perspective. Elsewhere Nabokov writes, "I've read in myself how the self to transcend" ("Fame," *Poems and Problems* 111). In the above quotation, Humbert is watching himself performing in his own dream ("I see myself..."), which is consistent with Nabokov's structural technique of having the creative author become distanced from his imagined self. We saw Sebastian Knight using the same technique specifically regarding the question of death. Humbert the author is envisioning the Humbert of his dreams carrying out a dream-conclusion.

Here one should also recall the door-imagery in the final pages of *Sebastian Knight*. The half-closed door of the last scene in that novel represents the inconclusive quality of the novel's overall structure. In *Lolita*, as in *Sebastian Knight*, the unclosed dream-door has structural and metaphysical implications. Throughout this scene Humbert keeps attempting to get doors closed, "turning whatever keys in whatever locks there were" (294). Humbert's metaphoric door is not "properly" closed until he creates this final scene. The conclusion, therefore, is only "real" for Humbert. Through this imagined scene he finds some sense of closure.

14. Not Quilty: The Problem of Persecution Mania

Nabokov would never justify a real murder, even a "real" murder within an imagined world. He does, however, let us know that there is "a green lane in Paradise where Humbert is permitted to wander at dusk once a year" (*Despair* xiii). Humbert is killing that quality in himself which he shares with Quilty. Quilty, rather than being "real," represents Humbert's "old nightmare." (This is Humbert's Quilty, regardless of the information we learn from other characters about the actual Quilty. There is, of course, an objectively existing "real" Quilty within the world of this novel — the dentist's nephew, the playwright, etc.) It is less important to state exactly what Quilty might symbolize than to note that Humbert has externalized this aspect of himself, externalized it in order to execute it. In *Despair* Hermann's great crime (in the Nabokovian realm of ethics) is that he believes that he has truly found his double, an identical replication of himself, and that he can therefore get away with the perfect murder. Humbert, in contrast, creates a fictional Quilty who represents that part of himself which he wishes to eradicate, though it is not clear how conscious this process is for him. This imagined murder scene represents something like a personal purification through fiction. Hermann, Nabokov lets us know, earns no otherworldly "parole" (xiii).

In his afterword to *Lolita*, Nabokov states that in writing a book he "has no other purpose than to get rid of that book" (311). I have already argued that he has many more important purposes than simply getting rid of his books. For Humbert, however, getting rid of the Quilty-side of himself may be his primary motive for writing *Lolita*. After Humbert Humbert is rid of one-half of his mirror-self, when Humbert the artist has purged himself of Humbert the monster, he ceases to exist, dying the day he finishes his text. It is not possible to ascertain what amount of Humbert's text is the work of imagination and what amount is prompted by his madness. The two are not easily distinguishable. Alexandrov writes, "Nabokov transvalued earthly madness into otherworldly sense" (*Otherworld* 82). Through madness and imagination Humbert Humbert has detached himself from himself. He has moved beyond this material world, beyond his book, to the other side.

Chapter 15

Ascending Structures

Nabokov often uses the image of an ascending structure, in addition to building a sense of ascension into his overall literary structures. Ascension in his images often represents a potentially unlimited lift, a movement beyond plain material truth. Nabokovian transcendence is connected to such structures or images of ascension.

We can see a failed possibility of ascension in *Lolita*. The problem is that Humbert comes extraordinarily close to Nabokov's sense of the celestial essence in some of his descriptions of Lolita, but then inevitably falls short, as in this description of Lolita on a ski lift: "I would see her floating away from me, celestial and solitary, in an ethereal chairlift, up and up, to a glittering summit...." Here, as in many of Nabokov's images of ascension, Lolita seems to be depicted as an independent being, her image untainted by the control of Humbert's filtering mind. Humbert seems to be on the verge of respecting her "solitary" self, even using the word "celestial" to describe this solitary state. But the sentence ends: "...where laughing athletes stripped to the waist were waiting for her, for her" (160). Humbert's apparent respect for Lolita's solitary, celestial self, reverts, within this one short sentence, to a jealous expression of his own obsession. Thus, this ascension, which seems to have metaphysical potential, becomes in Humbert's mind only a means of landing Lolita in the hands of "laughing athletes." Humbert's double lament — "for her, for her" — stresses the idea that this image of a celestial Lolita has been overcome by Humbert's obsessive mind. Certainly those shirtless "athletes" laughing on top of the ski slope are purely a product of Humbert's paranoia as well as his jealous need to keep Lolita contained. Nympholepsy creates the illusion of transcendence, while ultimately preventing any real transcendence whatsoever.

In the autobiography, Nabokov finishes his discussion of the grammar book by stating that "a real, sensible story unfolded its adult sentences"

15. Ascending Structures

(80). While one might expect, from Nabokov, this to be a lepidopterological reference, the image might refer to birds, rather than butterflies. (Orioles are mentioned in the paragraph just previous to the passage.) Nabokov also relates birds to words in *Sebastian Knight*. With images of birds representing words Nabokov combines three ideas: structures which ascend toward something beyond the book, the materiality of language, and the teleological potential of words.

The first image comes when V. recalls a moment of departure from his half-brother; V. says that "for no earthly reason" he felt a sudden need "to say something real, something with wings and a heart"; however, these hoped-for "birds" only arrive when Knight has left and the words no longer have a purpose (30). As often, V. is more precise with his language than even he realizes: the "real" motivation for sincere words comes for no "earthly" reason. Knight's use of meaningless phrases of farewell has prompted V.'s desire for "real" words. Wood writes, "It is quietly surprising, and entirely in keeping with Nabokov's thought and style, that the birds do land, even if too late and beyond language" (30). The wish for the perfect words is a wish "beyond language." The bird's eventual landing is "in keeping with Nabokov's thought"; equally in keeping with Nabokov's thought is the fact that V. does not present those words for us on the page.

Elsewhere V. quotes a (fictional) critic as comparing one of Sebastian Knight's novels to an "angel mimicking a tumbler pigeon" (89). This is the opposite of the ascending structure of the English grammar book, and yet this reverse image presents essentially the same idea. The angel, a sure sign of the celestial, comes toward earth in the guise of a bird. This pigeon represents the words of the novel. Just as the gem which is plucked from the water turns into a pebble, the angel brought to earth turns into a pigeon. This is the inevitable result of translating the celestial into words. Even the most successful words are celestial tumbler pigeons, though one knows they are actually angels.

Pigeons are again part of an ascending structure in this description of the Arc de Triomphe, where V. describes a moment when he was with his half-brother: a collection of overfed pigeons are walking around their feet, when a passing truck sends them into flight; some of them land on the Arc, and the color of the pigeons lets them blend in with the monument, until some of them fly off again, and it seems as though the Arc itself has come to life. V. tells us that Knight places this image into one of his books, this "stone melting into wing" (72). Here an actual structure ascends into life, and, as they ascend, these pigeons become much more than fat, strutting birds. One might imagine that the "stone melting into wing" ascends further beyond human view and somewhere these pigeons turn back into angels. This is a live, flying structure, the material level "melting" into a higher life. Perhaps one can also toss that pebble back into the water to recreate the gem. There is an interaction between the celestial and the earthly, and words are one means of attempting to convey this interaction. Nabokov believes that words can express a celestial sense, that one can strive to write celestial sentences.

Perhaps this one image of the Arc de Triomphe fluttering into feathered life should be further supported by a few of Nabokov's other ascending structures, to show that this image of ascension is a significant motif in Nabokov's art. As Sebastian Knight looks at a pink house in a green garden, where he believes his mother died, he imagines her moving slowly up some steps that seem to "dissolve into water"; then an orange falls out of a bag on his lap, with a "terrific thump," forcing him to "regain consciousness" (17–18). The material dissolves as it ascends, and one can only imagine what exists past the ascending steps. Once again, water represents a possible means for transcendent communication. Through the mist Knight envisions his mother ascending to some higher realm. But the thumping orange brings Knight back to "consciousness," as the process of transcendence always comes back to the earth. In addition, with a twist that clearly echoes the conclusion of the novel, Knight later learns that he was looking at the wrong house.

There is a related set of ascending steps, in *Speak, Memory*, where Nabokov describes the childhood ritual of ascending the steps with his eyes closed, a ritual which he went through with his mother in preparing for bed. She would say the word "step" as he reached each step, and when she said the word "step" at the very top, his foot "would sink into the phantasm of a step, padded ... with the infinitely elastic stuff of its own nonexistence" (83–84). The "stuff" of "nonexistence" comes after the top step. There are no more actual steps, but one can imagine the infinite possibility of further

15. Ascending Structures

ascension. One senses a "phantasm" step beyond the actual material steps. Nabokov comments, "[T]he whole going-up-the-stairs business now reveals certain transcendental values. Actually, however, I was merely playing for time by extending every second to its utmost." As usual, he does not elaborate on what "transcendental values" are revealed by this process. (Ralph Waldo Emerson might explain by saying that "extending every second to its utmost" is in itself a "transcendental" value.) One could compare this image of ascension to the structure of the grammar book and even to the structure of *Speak, Memory* itself: there is a transcendent potential in words, a celestial essence which transcends the materiality of the words themselves — a structure which suggests an extension beyond itself into some mysterious and transcendent distance.

There is another significant staircase in *Speak, Memory*, an iron staircase in his mother's grandfather's house; after the house burns to the ground, all that remains is those iron steps "still leading up" (100). Again the ascending structure, leading up toward the shining sky, turns out to be the essence of the house. Like Cincinnatus divested of his material body, an essential core remains. Even a house burnt to the ground is not necessarily a desolate sight for Nabokov. Like those steps, the ascending essence of the structure may remain beyond all apparent reason. This is a symbol of optimism, of certain faith. After revolution and fire, the steps still lead toward something, just as his mother's grandfather had intended. Now the steps seem to lead — "up" — toward something beyond themselves.

True, these staircases are regularly patterned structures, and it does not require a great imaginative effort for one to think of the manner in which they might continue beyond themselves. Yet these are elemental examples of the way in which patterns *can* extend beyond themselves. Every close reader of Nabokov quickly becomes aware of various patterns, of course, and I do not wish to elaborate on the patterns themselves, only on the way in which these patterns relate to the structural metaphysics of his works. In some way, the more complicated patterns of his novels can be imagined as extending beyond the book, beyond the perceived "real."

The highest level of Nabokov's literary structures — that implied level which is only approachable — is often represented by the unwritten word. By incorporating the concept of an abstract metaphysical knowledge into his novels, Nabokov attempts to bring his hierarchical structures as close as possible to the celestial essence, to that unwritten word. One can attempt to point toward this unwriteable essence through a written medium. As Wood writes: "Words are among our best routes to what is beyond words" (111). The structures of *Sebastian Knight*, *Pale Fire*, *Lolita*, and other works convey levels which lead beyond the words of the book, like the extended steps of a staircase, leading upward. The novel is not the essence itself, of course, but the means by which Nabokov attempts to illustrate the direction toward something definite.

Thus, the entire complex structure of *Sebastian Knight* tapers toward a final, unspoken word. Or perhaps one could say that the novel broadens into an infinite, all-encompassing final word, best exemplified by the entirety of the structure itself. The entire structure of *The Real Life of Sebastian Knight* embodies this metaphysical idea of the unspoken final word, that word which could encapsulate a "real life." There is no concluding word, but there *is* the idea of a concluding word. (This revelation of an all-encompassing, all-meaningful final word is also the method of the conclusion of Sebastian Knight's final book, *The Doubtful Asphodel* (176–178). There, too, the word is suggested yet never revealed.) This is the greatest verbal frame, extending Nabokov's structural device — concealing then revealing the words "Floss," "Maximovich" and "St. Damier" — to a level where it has metaphysical resonance. Any attempt to fill that frame will by definition be inadequate. "God" is not enough; *potustoronnost'* is only a word. The structure — ranging from the level of unsuccessful clichés to the highest realm, which stands beyond the reach of real words — is similar to a grammar book leading to the unspoken possibilities of the beyond, or pigeons soaring off to a place where they might change into angels. All of these metaphors are apt. Each conveys the idea of a hierarchy pointing toward an unwriteable ideal. Each conveys the idea that mortal structures might lead to further mysteries.

The Permanent Mystery of Pale Fire

This same sense of mystery is essential to that novel which has led so many scholars to search for solutions, *Pale Fire*. In fact, this novel is a

15. Ascending Structures

mockery of explication, a mockery of any arrogant commentator who believes he is capable of offering a solution to another's work of art, a mockery of "answers" offered to solve the puzzle of art. That mockery — that outrageously flawed commentary — only adds to the overall mystery.

The topic on which most scholars have focused concerning this novel is the possible connection between Shade and Kinbote. I want to show that this relationship is not essentially a problem of the plot, but of the literary structure. That is, readers should not concentrate on gathering clues to make an argument about where Shade and Kinbote stand in regard to each other, but recognize that the question itself (rather than any one answer) is essential to the structure.

Many have commented on the textual problem concerning the source of the title "Pale Fire." Here too Kinbote comments, actually comments quite often, on the appropriate source, Shakespeare's *Timon of Athens*, even retranslating the relevant passage from Zemblan back into English, yet seems not to be aware that this is the play in which Shade found the title. It doesn't seem sufficient to say that Kinbote has an acute sense of intuition up to a point — sensing the relevant works — yet absolutely falters when attempting to explain their significance to the poem. It seems more likely that there is another mind at work, a mind which prompts Kinbote up toward the source, then diverts him in the wrong, often comic direction.

The primary structural question, as most readers have seen it, is whether or not this mind can be considered that of Shade. That is, does the text suggest that Shade is the creator of both the poem and the commentary? Other possibilities have been suggested. Stegner thinks that only Kinbote's expansive imagination could have come up with the novel as a whole: "If he [Kinbote] is able to dream up an Arabian Nights tale of his royal life in Onhava and populate that capital city with several dozen fantastic, though imaginary personalities, he is certainly able to dream up John and Sybil Shade and their daughter Hazel" (128). However, this seems like arguing that because Lewis Carroll is capable of creating Wonderland he could certainly, if he chose, write like Robert Frost. Just because Kinbote is capable of elaborately articulating his hallucinations does not mean he is emotionally capable of controlling them.

Even those who do not feel that the question of where Shade stands in regard to Kinbote (and Gradus) is the most relevant issue of the novel feel the need to comment on exactly that topic. D. Barton Johnson, for example, argues that there is no interrelation between the characters, that each is autonomous:

> The Index which resolves a considerable number of problems ... contains nothing to support the assumption that Shade, Kinbote, and Gradus are less than separate identities. In spite of the widespread view that only one of the three protagonists is "real," there is no solid evidence to support this idea [68].

Alexandrov agrees:

> Some readers have attempted to unite the two by championing either Shade or Kinbote (or even an inferred third character) as the wily, and concealed author of the whole thing. But these arguments oversimplify the actual situation in *Pale Fire* because it is inevitably possible to find passages counterbalancing the textual details that are invoked in support of any unitary author [*Otherworld* 188].

Alexandrov is correct to say that any unitary solution to the novel will oversimplify the structure and significance. However, his dismissal of the question is itself an oversimplification. That is, Nabokov very clearly intended for just these questions to be raised in every reader's mind. To dismiss the issue of authorial responsibility by arguing that each character is autonomous is also to oversimplify the structure at exactly the point where Nabokov made it complicated.

Johnson says there is no evidence in the index, but the index begins with a note which explains that the capital letters in the index "stand for the three main characters" (303). Would Kinbote, who supposedly wrote the index, call himself a character? This one word clearly draws our attention to the question of authorial control. From what level of the fiction can the three protagonists be called characters? The questions concerning Shade and Kinbote are raised to draw our attention to the questions themselves, rather than leading us to solve or dismiss them. As with the question of Humbert's perception of Quilty or V.'s hunt for Knight, the problem is raised to evoke the idea of permanent mystery. The argument that Shade and Kinbote are in no way connected seems to be more of a reaction to previous criticism than to the actual novel. However, while a definitive solution cannot be found, the novel does suggest an essential hierarchy.

Though Shade's poem would be capable of standing on its own terms, Kinbote's notes are obviously parasitic. The argument that they are separable

15. Ascending Structures

and autonomous characters overlooks this point. Without the host poem, Kinbote's parasitic commentary — and, thus, Kinbote himself— would not survive. There is at least one hint, however, that Shade's mind may have spawned this extension, that the poem inspires its apparent parasite.

At sixteen years old Shade's daughter Hazel suffered from a unique form of insanity. After their Aunt Maude's death the Shade household was the site of a number of inexplicable occurrences (165). The explanation appears to be that Hazel's insanity was somehow responsible for these actions. Kinbote tells us, "[Shade] and Sybil never doubted that ... [Hazel] was the agent of the disturbance which they saw as representing (I now quote Jane P.) 'an outward extension or expulsion of insanity.'" The implication is that a seemingly autonomous individual — in this case, Hazel — may be responsible for an outward expression of insanity which apparently has no rational connection to her. Of course, one should always question the narrative reliability in this novel: here we have Kinbote telling us what the Shades thought and their secretary said about Aunt Maude's ghost's influence on Hazel's sanity. Whether we believe Kinbote or not, ultimately the idea is placed here by Nabokov for the reader to consider.

Boyd also makes an argument about Hazel's influence on the text: "The evidence Nabokov conceals within *Pale Fire* suggests that Hazel's spirit somehow inspires Kinbote with the idea of Zembla..." (*Nabokov's Pale Fire* 173). This is not another attempt at solving the novel; Boyd is correct to use the verb "suggests." Nabokov's art provides a lesson in reading: one must not be too enticed by one's own ideas. One must be careful not to impose one's own views on the text, thereby oversimplifying the mystery.

Kinbote calls the phenomenon of Hazel's ability to displace her insanity onto surrounding objects "the Hercules springing forth from a neurotic child's weak frame" (167). The key word is "frame": for Nabokov, no frame is capable of containing those irrational and undefinable forces which are a constant quality of real life. I showed that in *Speak, Memory* the word "frame" is also used to refer to one's physical self. Just as an unknown force may spring forth from Hazel's "frame," the frame of Shade's poem may prompt its own mad commentary. It is as though the speaker of Frost's poem had inspired a voice to respond from the other side of those "lovely, dark, and deep" woods, simply by stopping there, a voice which would annotate "Stopping by Woods on a Snowy Evening" into a monstrous novel. *Pale Fire* ventures into those woods with a poem, and comes back with the colorful Kinbote.

Johnson is correct: "there is no solid evidence to support this idea." But I have been trying to show that "solid evidence" is not Nabokov's criteria for explaining otherworldly influences. Irrationality lies at the heart of Nabokov's metaphysics and structures. Logic does not always provide the best evidence. Kinbote coincides with Nabokov when he states that science and the supernatural "are *both* inexplicable" (167). Shade offers this term to describe his own sense of poetic inspiration: "the mystery inborn" (l.865). The point is not that Shade's poem did inspire its own parasite, or that Hazel did create those inexplicable disturbances, but that the possibility is raised. The question of Shade's possible connection to Kinbote is raised to be considered, not logically solved or simply dismissed.

Julia Bader, arguing from the other side of Stegner, says that Shade has written all of *Pale Fire*. She believes that Shade's creation of Kinbote is an extension of his exploration of death. His childhood experience of being "distributed through space and time" is, she says, "the equivalent of authorial omniscience, and foreshadows Shade's ability to transform and nearly obliterate his ordinary surroundings — an ability manifested in the commentary" (46). This would place Shade's "space and time" experience closer to Whitman's experience of "Space and Time!": Shade is also using his semi-transcendent experience to explore another mind. He is afoot with his vision no less than Whitman. Bader connects Shade's creation of Kinbote to an exploration of death, calling his movement into Kinbote's mind a "self-willed creative annihilation" (31). Knight also saw literary creativity as a dying to this world. Khodasevich wrote that this was Nabokov's process of creativity: "the passage from one world into the other, in whichever direction it is accomplished, is akin to death."[1] The shadow of the slain waxwing might fly back through that windowpane to rematerialize — recrystallize — into the body of a bird. The looking glass works both ways. (Might this explain why in the index under the entry for John Shade we find the seemingly misplaced topic "K's views on suicide"?) Similarly, when the commentary is concluded Kinbote is, at least figuratively,

15. Ascending Structures

dead. As he writes toward the end, "My notes and self are petering out" (300). Bader's argument seems consistent with these ideas: Shade is enacting the Nabokovian process of artistic creativity by entering the mind of Kinbote, by traveling away from the material reality of himself. One can also find structural evidence to support this theory.

There is a structural gap between the plot of Shade's poem and the plot conveyed by Kinbote in the commentary. I am not speaking of Kinbote's mental excursions into Zembla, but of a structural overlap between the poem and Kinbote's notes. This gap can help support Bader's claim that Shade created the entire book because it comes precisely at the moment of Shade's apparent death. Shade's death takes place at the time of line 1000. That is when the gardener trundles the emblematic wheelbarrow and a butterfly flies by (l.993–994). However, Kinbote describes the same scene as taking place *after* the poem has been completed. He describes this moment as he carries the completed poem in a large envelope "one minute before [Shade's] death" (290). Kinbote then describes the gardener approaching down the lane and Gradus simultaneously arriving. Thus the commentary claims that the events just moments before Shade's death, as described in his poem, actually take place after the poem had been written. This is quite a gap in the structure.

One might attempt to explain this gap in a number of ways. The simplest, perhaps, is that Kinbote had stolen the poem after Shade's death, and invented his final moments from the final moments of the poem. This would assume that Shade actually did die, but in some manner not presented in the text. Thus we would have no way of ascertaining the means of his "real" death, only of Shade's fabrication and Kinbote's copy. Another possibility is that Shade had a premonition of his own final moments and managed to describe that scene before it took place. This possibility seems even less likely because Kinbote doesn't notice the odd congruity between the poem's final lines and the events of his commentary. Surely he would have read the poem and been struck by Shade's perspicacity. Neither of these explanations is artistically satisfying, yet these are the only two possibilities if Kinbote and Shade are to be considered entirely autonomous figures. Therefore, any argument that the two characters are autonomous must overlook this significant overlap at the moment of Shade's apparent death.

Nabokov's Permanent Mystery

The only possibility which seems in keeping with the themes of *Pale Fire* is that Shade has staged his own death. This is the only way in which the flawed structure of the poem and commentary can coincide with the content. Shade has written the poem and the commentary and has staged his own death in both. Why else would he have chosen the title "Pale Fire" with its theme of theft unless he was also writing of the fictional theft of his poem? There is no theme of theft in the poem. Shade represents the higher consciousness capable of creating both parts of the novel precisely because he is capable of overcoming death with his imagination. "*Other men die; but I/ Am not another; therefore I'll not die*," he writes in italics (l.213–214). When he decides to become "another," this quote suggests, he decides to "die." ("I once read a French detective tale where the clues were actually in italics," writes Humbert [211].) Nabokov has created Shade to explore the interaction between the "real" (poem) and the imaginary (commentary). When taken together, we learn that Gradus exists only in the poet's thoughts; Kinbote directly tells us that we will follow Gradus through the poem (78). The poet controls the presence of death in his imagined world. Or as Nabokov wrote in *Bend Sinister*: "death was but a question of style" (202). Death and style are intimately linked in Nabokov's worlds, yet death is still a "question." Shade has set up his own death as the irresolvable riddle of *Pale Fire*. This is not a solution to that riddle, but perhaps Shade should be granted a higher level of artistic control than Kinbote: the game of worlds is a game of words, and the poet Shade controls the language.

However, this too might oversimplify the text. The structure of *Pale Fire*, just as I argued for the structure of *Sebastian Knight* and of *Lolita*, is not a puzzle which should be resolved away with any one solution. Kinbote's commentary, after all, is not quite a "self-willed creative annihilation" of Shade, as Bader states (31). Shade is not really annihilated by the presence of Kinbote. In fact, we learn more about him and his family from the commentary, often unbeknownst to Kinbote. Kinbote's obtrusive spying does provide some details which Shade would probably not offer on his own. As I showed with the reference to Robert Frost, Kinbote also has some useful ideas about Shade's poem. The seeming parasite at times provides an insightful angle. Rather than an annihilation, Kinbote's world is

15. Ascending Structures

more of a mad extrapolation of the "real," much like Carroll's Wonderland. This overlap at the time of death demonstrates a definite interdependence between poem and commentary, as does much other evidence, but even the strongest argument — that Shade wrote everything — does not provide a perfect solution to all the intricacies of the novel. Kinbote's existence cannot be explained by any rational argument.

Nonetheless, there does exist a hierarchy of creative control in the text. Through Kinbote's commentary we catch glimpses of Shade; through Shade's poem we can see nothing of Kinbote. The parasite stands below the host in the artistic hierarchy. Shade rises above Kinbote, into a solitary atmosphere, like Lolita on her ski lift. Marilyn Edelstein agrees: "John Shade is the only character in *Pale Fire* conscious of the Nabokovian tenet that we each devise our own reality; thus, he is the most conscious character.... But Shade, in spite of all his attempts at creation of a perceptible pattern, is still at the mercy of his aesthetic captor/creator, Nabokov" (221). Such arguments may seem circular: one must be aware of the "Nabokovian tenet" in order to make sense of the Nabokovian novel. But the main point of my argument is that the "tenet" is inherent in the structure. The structure of the novel is also what the novel is about: the structure embodies the metaphysics. In *Pale Fire* there is a hierarchy of consciousness — and of aesthetic appreciation[2] — which leads to Nabokov who, of course, composes the overall structure. That hierarchy then suggests an even higher, less easily labeled level above the real author.

The hierarchy of consciousness needs to be recognized in order to see the value structure of the novel. Boyd explains this upper level of the structure:

> The more we accept Shade as the author of both poem and commentary, the less we can be sure that someone who has invented Zembla and his own murder has not already transformed the life he presents in the poem in order to make poem and commentary fit. The more autonomy we see in Shade the artist, the less distinct become the outlines of Shade the man. He begins, in other words, to grade into Nabokov [*American Years* 455].

The more creative control we attribute to Shade, the closer he comes on the structural hierarchy to Nabokov. Nabokov, who stands higher on the structure than either Shade or Kinbote, has made certain that no facile solution is completely supportable.

Nabokov's Permanent Mystery

Those who place too much emphasis on resolving these questions of Kinbote and Shade, on turning *Pale Fire* into an easily manageable straight line, rather than the mad zig-zag that it is, are wrongly placing the emphasis on plot. Nabokov has created a literary work which raises irresolvable plot problems in order to transcend plot. One might quote Alexander Pope, the subject of one of Shade's books: "A mighty maze! but not without a plan" (129).[3] The plan, however, precludes any definitive solution at this level of the structure. One cannot settle *Pale Fire* onto a "real" level when looking at the interaction of Kinbote and Shade. Nabokov has a knack for drawing critics into his Wonderlands, but at some point one must step above the constant questions about Kinbote's character and Shade's responsibility. The questions are the point; mystery is the theme. The questions concerning Shade and Kinbote draw the "reality" of the novel into doubt, stretching our suspension of disbelief to the point where we must necessarily recognize a higher creative source, a mind that has created this mystery.

Chapter 16

The Conjurer's Rented Rabbit

Lewis Carroll often shows up as a representative of the world of imagination in Nabokov's work. This may be why — in *Sebastian Knight*— that cat with blue eyes appears "from nowhere" in response to *The Laws of Literary Imagination*: a cat from nowhere is quite Carrollian (45). There are, the cat would seem to suggest, no such laws. Cats can be blue and can appear from nowhere, especially literary cats. Its presence alone should be commentary enough on the idea of placing restrictive laws on the imagination. When coupled with this cat's suddenly disagreeable demeanor in response to a backhanded compliment about Knight (48), it would seem that the cat could represent the presence of Knight. At the very least, the cat — like Knight — makes a subtle statement in favor of imagination. The presence of Lewis Carroll — or allusions to him — usually suggests the highest level of a Nabovian structure, the level that transcends mere earthly terms.

The images of *Lolita*, however, once again present the failed possibility of Nabokovian transcendence. Here Humbert describes Lolita's possessions: "Lo's little belongings that had wandered to various parts of the house to freeze there like so many hypnotized bunnies" (81). What could be a better image for this reverse wonderland? The rabbit leads Alice down the hole is, in this novel, frozen in the narrator's gaze, rendered almost lifeless in Humbert's presence. Little Lo's childhood is a failed Carrollian possibility.

The idea that Nabokov uses the rabbit as a sign of the celestial potential — of Carroll-like imagination — also makes one scene of the *Lolita* screenplay more significant. As Humbert discusses his favorite poem with Lolita, the stage directions state, "A more or less tame rabbit stops, nibbles, lopes on." As Humbert continues the discussion, Lolita disappears: "He looks for her among the trees and shrubs. He is in a state of distress and distraction.... She has wandered away in dim-smiling, stooping pursuit of the soft elusive rabbit" (121–122). Carroll's story begins with Alice following a rabbit down a hole under a hedge. She, of course, has no Humbert to prevent her from exploring that imaginative other world. Lolita, however, can only be tantalized by her brief pursuit of this rabbit from Wonderland. The path toward the celestial side of the imagination seems, for Lolita, to be cut short. The rabbit of the imagination is always an "elusive" presence, but a child with Humbert as guardian has almost no hope of exploring that imaginative side.

As Lolita does assert her independence, however, by skipping a piano lesson, Humbert reports that she has something which is "locally known as a 'rabbit cold'" (204). Even more locally, within Nabokov's lexicon, such a cold would suggest that she has, if only temporarily, freed herself from Humbert's paralyzing perspective. In case we miss the subliminal bunnies of *Lolita*, Nabokov provides another clue in *Strong Opinions*: "Dolly ... went nicely with the surname 'Haze,' where Irish mists blend with a German bunny—I mean, a small German hare" (25). (Victor Fet points out the Ada and Lucette have a teacher whose name—Krolik—is "Russian for Rabbit" [61].) Nabokov often portrays the other side as something seen through a mist. Here, through the mist, Dolores Haze herself takes on the symbolic role of a rabbit. Despite Humbert's hypnotizing perspective, celestial potential is an internal quality of every life. In this novel, though, it is only through the looking glass that we can see this Dolores has an original life of her own.

Quite a few references to Lewis Carroll also pop up in *Sebastian Knight*, both directly and indirectly. Susan Fromberg has pointed out that the final paragraph "is a deliberate and conscious echo of the final speech of *Alice in Wonderland*" (439). A hotel manager is said to speak in a similar manner to the caterpillar created by Lewis Carroll (121). Within his final dream sequence, V. writes, "for some reason unknown, I went to the bathroom and stood there for a moment in front of the looking-glass" (189). On the final train ride, V. repeats, "I must, I must get there in time," perhaps recalling Carroll's Mad Hatter (191). Madame Lecerf says to V., "The

16. The Conjurer's Rented Rabbit

past makes noble fuel. Would you like a cup of tea?" (146). This might seem an obvious reference to Proust, but perhaps this tea is a less obvious reference to *Alice*, where, during the Mad Tea Party, Alice says, "I think you might do something better with the time ... than waste it asking riddles with no answers" (59). The logic of this novel is closer to that of Lewis Carroll than Marcel Proust, though both are on Knight's shelf.

Foster, in his study of Nabokov's changing "art of memory," has argued that Nabokov developed "toward Proust" in his earliest novels, and he also sees some "fleeting analogies with Proust" in Knight's writing (54).[1] Nabokov's interest in Lewis Carroll, on the other hand, is one which did not alter over the course of his career. He makes reference to Carroll (and Charles Dodgson) in his later novels, *Ada* (1969) and *Look at the Harlequins!* (1974). He translated and published a Russian version of *Alice in Wonderland* in 1923. Beverly Lyon Clark has argued that in this translation Nabokov places a greater emphasis on the fantastic quality of "reality" than does Carroll's original. Carroll's story shows a clear demarcation between Wonderland and Alice's reality. Alice's sister senses that without the imagination of Wonderland "all would change to dull reality" (103). "In Nabokov's Wonderland," Clark writes, "fantasy is kept less firmly in its place as something to be carefully differentiated from and excluded from 'reality'" (72).[2] Nabokov is more interested in infusing the fantastic into the "real," rather than contrasting "dull reality" to a Wonderland or another world.[3]

Nabokov could have been speaking about the title of this novel — *The Real Life of Sebastian Knight*—when he made the following statement about "dull reality":

> The notion of "real life" ... is based on a system of generalities, and it is only as generalities that the so-called "facts" of so-called "real life" are in contact with a work of fiction. The less general a work of fiction is, then, the less recognizable it is in terms of "real life." Or to put it the other way around, the more vivid and new details in a work of fiction, then the more it departs from so-called "real life," since "real life" is the generalized epithet, the average emotion, the advertised multitude, the commonsensical world [*LDQ* 1].

This may be the final irony of the title of *The Real Life of Sebastian Knight*: Nabokov is intentionally setting up some "generalized" expectations with the title. He knows that in claiming to tell the story of someone's "real life," he is not at all advertising what the reader will find in this novel. Thus, the title itself is the greatest frustrated cliché. Anyone who expects to find the entirety of another person's "real life" between the pages of a book will probably be satisfied with an average portrayal of reality, a collection of clichés. Instead, one finds in Nabokov's novel a twisted, meandering, pseudo-scientific quest that leaves one with a number of unanswered questions and perhaps only a glimpse of the original Knight. Real "real life," Nabokov suggests, contains an essential mystery that raises it above common perception.

Great literature, according to Nabokov, is always more than merely "real." It is not so much that Nabokov is opposed to "realism," but that in his mind there is no such thing as "realism": "Average reality begins to rot and stink as soon as the act of individual creation ceases to animate a subjectively perceived texture" (*SO* 118). Imagination is the necessary ingredient for reinvigorating accurate — as opposed to accepted — perception. Some readers have been befuddled as to how, in discussing the work of Jane Austen, Charles Dickens and Gustave Flaubert, Nabokov could say, "The truth is that great novels are great fairy tales — and the novels in this series are supreme fairy tales" (*LL* 2). However, by "fairy tales" Nabokov means creations of the imagination which are sustainable only on their own terms. If those terms happen to correspond to those of the "real" world as perceived by the reader, the works are nonetheless self-enclosed fairy tales, products of a convincing conjurer. "Realism" is only one type of illusion. Verisimilitude is deception. What might seem to be the most realistic recreation of a world is still a fantasy world, an act of a single creative mind. With this view, *Alice in Wonderland* is no more or less realistic than *Madame Bovary*, Lewis Carroll's fantasies no more or less fantastic than those of Flaubert.

For Nabokov, the "real" should never be confused with inspired art. The two should be considered separate entities. Charles Kinbote mentions the artist "Eystein" who was a "master of the trompe l'oeil." Eystein would sometimes put a real object into his paintings, a piece of "wood or wool, gold or velvet." He describes the effect, and concludes that this method helps to illustrate "the basic fact that 'reality' is neither the subject nor the object of true art which creates its own special reality having nothing to

16. The Conjurer's Rented Rabbit

do with the average 'reality' perceived by the communal eye" (*PF* 130). Eystein was not attempting to create a ready-made work of art, drawing the viewer's definition of "art" into question. Rather, he was attempting to enhance his paintings by simply inserting a "real" object alongside the painted one. This, Kinbote and Nabokov both tell us, represents a fundamental misunderstanding of art. Eystein seems only to be hoping that his painting can accurately mimic that which everyone is able to perceive. All art, in fact, is a trick to the eye which makes an invented world come to life, but the best worlds infuse a degree of imagination to raise them above what is typically considered "real."

V. reports that one writer criticized Knight's work for being overly "Conradish" and gives the advice that Knight should get rid of the "con" and pay more attention to the "radish" (40). Earlier in the same chapter, V. states that "food" is our primary connection to "the common chaos of matter rolling about us" (35). Thus, this "radish" which the critic wishes Knight would cultivate represents realism. The critic wishes that Knight would further engage the real world "rolling about us," rather than continuing to "con" the reader.

The "con," on the other hand, is represented by the "conjuror,"[4] an important presence in a number of Nabokov's novels and one who comes to the foreground three times in *Sebastian Knight*. Walter Evans has explained the distinction implicit in Nabokov's choice of the word "conjuror" rather than "magician": "Nabokov deliberately emphasize ... [the] creative power to 'conjure up' rather than merely manipulate" (76). The conjuror represents the creative spirit, which for Nabokov is also interlinked with the spirit of deception (hence "con"). Knight is more apt to abandon the radish and cultivate the con.

A "conjuror" is mentioned at the end of the first and the last chapters: the first as a character in a comic book that Knight describes himself reading as a young boy, the last as an off-stage presence who is waiting with his "hidden rabbit." These two brief though strategic appearances create the impression that this "conjuror" may have a greater significance to the novel (and its structure) than is initially apparent. In one of Knight's novels a character named William offers to buy his neighbor the conjuror a rabbit. It is an odd moment, with William insulting the conjuror, and the conjuror in reply turning out the lights. The scene ends with the conjuror snoring (98). The details of this odd passage are less significant to my argument than the placement of the conjuror in this place of the overall structure. This appearance of the conjuror occurs at the end of the tenth chapter (of twenty). Thus, the conjuror's three appearances become a semi-secret aspect of the novel's frame (first, last and center), a part of the structure which at first glance may seem to have little significance.[5] In other Nabokov novels the conjuror's presence is more overt and more clearly connected to the role of the "real" Nabokov. As Dabney Stuart writes of the conjuror in *Sebastian Knight*, "[H]e isn't even annagramatical" (36). Nonetheless, the conjuror provides an almost-hidden symmetry to this structure.

The conjuror's rented rabbit also makes some subtle appearances in *Sebastian Knight*. At one point Knight is described as having a "finely-shaped white face" and "large slightly pointed ears" (70). The conjuror Nabokov can make his rabbit Sebastian appear at will. The conjuror is a stand-in for the real author; both roles are representative of Nabokov's structural status as creator of the text. The conjuror is not an apt image for any author, only for the author who comprehends the magic aspect of the literary endeavor, the type of author who can subtly transform a character into a rabbit or bring in a blue cat from nowhere. This, too, is Lewis Carroll's type of world. At lunch, the secretive Madame Lecerf, while stalling to inform V. that she is the woman he is looking for, explains that she has a "special way of preparing rabbit" (165). Lecerf's manipulation of the narrator is thereby connected with Nabokov's manipulative control. He is preparing to pull the special rabbit from his authorial top hat just as Madame Lecerf is planning her surprise.

The conjuror's rented rabbit may be another means of commenting on a reader's need for a "solution." The conjuror creates many illusive solutions, to which some have clung, but they are all rented rabbits, final ideas pulled from a hat. Nabokov seems to be suggesting that people need solutions to novels as much as they need metaphysical "solutions" to real life. The average mind does not like unsolved mysteries. Therefore the hidden rabbit can be read as a metaphor for real "real life," that magic last word which one can never hear spoken on this side. In *Sebastian Knight* subliminal bunnies, Nabokovian delegates of the Carrollian other side, stand-

16. The Conjurer's Rented Rabbit

ins for the imagination, are scattered throughout the text, sometimes hidden, and represent the top level of the structure.

A systematic guidebook to what the imagination can and cannot do is as antithetical to Nabokov's thought as would be a systematic religion with which one is supposed to capture that original essence, that chill along the spine. Imagination is the ability to perceive the fantastic in the everyday. Imagination, therefore, is a metaphysical tool. "I cannot imagine (and that is saying a good deal) such circumstances as might impinge on the lovely and lovable world," says Nabokov (*LL* 373). "I can imagine anything," says *Ada*'s Van Veen (478). Imagination is the direct connection between the authorial level of the literary structure and the highest level: "imagination — the muscle of the soul" (*RLSK* 81). An imaginative attempt to find a new approach to "real life" is, within Nabokov's metaphysics, the greatest tribute one can offer to real life.

Chapter 17

The Metaphysics of Imagination

See under Real is one of the fictional novels written by Vadim Vadimovich, the narrator of Nabokov's *Look at the Harlequins!*, a novel which presents the story of an author whose life is semi-parallel to Nabokov's life. Perhaps the closest parallel between Vadimovich and Nabokov's lives is in the list of the author's books, which makes some fairly obvious references to Nabokov's books. *See under Real* is said to have been published in 1939, and Vadim calls it "my first novel in English"; *Sebastian Knight* was published in 1941, though Nabokov attempted to have it published earlier, and it was of course his first novel in English (226). The instruction to "see under real" seems like a footnote in some metaphysical encyclopedia for someone who had looked up the word "life" or "God." This title also suggests that the meaning of the book must be searched for somewhere underneath that which might at first appear to be the "real" significance. Laurie Clancy writes of *See under Real*,

> It is perhaps the wittiest of Nabokov's unwritten books, the purpose of the method being to satirise that kind of biography in which every detail of the great man's life, from his bus tickets to his bowel movements, is meticulously documented, the kind of biography represented, for instance, by Joseph L. Blotner's massive tome on William Faulkner [161].

One must "see under" the accumulation of mundane details in order to approach a more valid sense of "real life." One must at least attempt to glimpse "the lining of life," as Cincinnatus is able to do, if only for a moment.

Another method Nabokov uses to lead one to "see under real" is to make the material of "reality" seem less real. In many novels he does this by associating the image of a top hat with death. The euphemism for execution

17. The Metaphysics of Imagination

in *Invitation to a Beheading* is "to don the red tophat" (21); in *King, Queen, Knave* we see "pale, top-hatted city fathers driving to the execution" (207); *Despair* describes "the burly executioner in his top hat" (103). When V. accidentally intrudes on the aftermath of a funeral he notices "two solemn top hats" (132). One would ask, of course, what Nabokov's purpose is for so often juxtaposing top hats and death. In some of the above images it is clear in context that he is combining images of execution by guillotine with the idea of heads as easily removable as hats. Nabokov's book on Nikolai Gogol suggests that he may have borrowed this idea, as he mentions Gogol's creation of a "sham world where hats are heads" (53). Nabokov's juxtaposition of top hats and death creates a sense of the unreality of the head itself, thus the unreality of death. Material is less real than one might assume, even the material of one's own head.

In *Bend Sinister*, Krug notices this object: "Cute little model of guillotine (with stiff top-hatted doll in attendance)" (192). That a guillotine could be considered "cute" is a comment on the world of that novel, where death is the plaything of tyrants. At the same time, however, the image suggests that death is not as all powerful as it may initially seem. Terror is less effective to those who consider death unreal. Here we might recall V.'s inability to understand the reaction of Sebastian Knight's last love to Knight's death, that she had "special views about death" which do not include the standard emotional response (154). Those who are firm believers in the material world may not understand the reactions to death of those who are not.

Nabokov also disrupts any common view of what is "real" with the image of toys, such as the above guillotine. John Shade's early experience of death is somehow associated with — or prompted by — a toy wheelbarrow. The final written line of his poem, moments before his more "real" death at the hands of Gradus, tells of a gardener "trundling an empty barrow up the lane."[1] There is a structural movement from a "toy" object to a "real" one. A similar technique is used in *Bend Sinister*: "What looked like a fluffy piebald toy dog was prettily placed at the foot of the bed. Before rushing out of the ward, Krug knocked this thing off the blanket, whereupon the creature, coming to life, gave a snarl of pain and its jaws snapped, narrowly missing his hand" (201). The pretty toy dog turns into a snapping animal: levels of reality are brusquely juxtaposed. In Cincinnatus' cell, which he shares with a spider, the process is reversed: "he pulled down the thick gray cobweb and with it the spider, which he had once nursed with such care ... it consisted of a round plush body with twitching legs made of springs, and, there was, attached to the middle of its back, a long elastic" (210). This moment is a paradigm for the structure of *Invitation to a Beheading*: what had seemed to be most "real," most worthy of one's personal care and attention, turns out to be a toy, a sham world where reality is "crudely but cleverly made." The conclusion of that novel, of course, shows Cincinnatus' entire world revealing itself to be a sham construction: "[trees] barely held on with their branches to the ripping mesh of the sky" (223). There is a similar hint of the world revealing itself to be a false construct in John Shade's second described death experience: "A sun of rubber was convulsed and set" (l.702). Whatever essential quality had made an object seem most real in life is drained away in the experience of death. One would think that a rubber sun couldn't reflect even the palest of fires.

Perhaps the purpose of all this is to convey the sense that one's inner world may be more real than the world of outside objects. Victor Shklovsky, the Russian Formalist critic, famously states: "art exists that one may recover the sensation of life; it exists to make one feel things, to make the stone *stony*" (12). Nabokov, however, makes the stone stony, then makes it evaporate, perhaps, or has it sprout feathers and fly off in a new form, like the "stone melting into wing" in *Sebastian Knight*. The Nabokovian stone is *more* than stony. Irrational imagination is a force capable of transforming the rational world.

The final metaphysical point which a structural study of Nabokov's narratives leads to, then, is an optimism based on an imaginative perception of real life. Those who most appreciate "real life" will also have the most certainty of a beyond; those who perceive the presence of the celestial essence on this side will be assured of the existence of an ultimate creative source. Barabtarlo writes, "Nabokov ... does not know or view the world as ... existence without essence" (*Aerial* 236). The details of this world are capable of conveying that otherworldly essence. As Nabokov writes in one story, "Actually he was a pessimist and, like all pessimists, a ridiculously

17. The Metaphysics of Imagination

unobservant man" ("An Affair of Honor," *Stories* 218). The pessimist has a ridiculous inability to see his or her surroundings. The following paragraph from *Laughter in the Dark* assures us, once we see Nabokov's sense of the importance of perception, that Margot is another unobservant pessimist: "She walked to the window while the baggage was being brought in. There was a big star in the plum-colored sky, the black tree-tops were perfectly still, crickets chirped ... but she saw and heard nothing" (204, ellipsis in the original, forming a blank transition between the vibrant natural world and her empty perception). Here one might recall the hiker carrying Camus who failed to see the butterflies swarming on the mountainside; one might note that Gradus, the embodiment of death, is also "exceptionally unobservant" (*PF* 251). A pessimist is a person who is persistently blind to the creative details of real life. A nihilist is a person who sees nothing, even when a "big star" and a "plum-colored sky" are right overhead.

Optimism is a view of the world which asserts the persistence of the imagination in the presence of the greatest conceivable disasters: "I can very well imagine that my fellow dreamers, thousands of whom roam the earth, keep to these same irrational and divine standards during the darkest and most dazzling hours of physical danger, pain, dust, death" (*LL* 373). The imagination must be a force which is more than rational; only then can one be capable of seeing under the "real" and perhaps achieving "the happy impression of enchanting irrationality" (*Butterflies* 223).

He further explains the ideal of irrational perception by again bringing up Lewis Carroll's character:

> We all are crashing to our death from the top story of our birth to the flat stones of the churchyard and wondering with an immortal Alice in Wonderland at the patterns of the passing wall. This capacity to wonder at trifles — no matter the imminent peril — these asides of the spirit, these footnotes ... are the highest form of consciousness [*LL* 373–374].

The "imminent peril" is pretty compelling, and one must have a lack of logic to appreciate the ever-peripheral presence of the celestial essence. This, once again, is a metaphysical statement: the imaginative mind is assured that real life is everywhere infused with the fantastic.

John Shade also discusses what one might do when faced with imme-

Nabokov's Permanent Mystery

diate mortality, what the heroic mental response would be when one is marched up to the wall for execution by some political thug: "We'll think of matters only known to us —" (l.601). Rather than lament the situation, in those final moments, one might "discern/ Upon the rough gray wall a rare wall fern" (l.604). Nabokov often returns to this image of one facing a wall, facing execution, while appreciating the details of real life. Fyodor of *The Gift* imagines his father facing execution and is certain that he would appreciate a passing moth at that moment: "if a whitish moth had hovered among the shadowy burdocks he would, even at the moment, I *know*, have followed it with [a] glance of encouragement..." (137, emphasis in original). While making that fall with Alice, one might perceive a "rare wall fern" or "a whitish moth." The appreciation of details is one means for achieving a sense that is greater than the typically "real": one has no idea what one might discover while falling alongside that Wonderland wall.

Recognizing a rare fern, contemplating a moth, these images show that precision and understanding are good ways of approaching "real life," of understanding the presence of the otherworld in this world. These are two ways, then, by which Nabokov believes one can transcend the everyday material world: one, by the precise perception of seemingly trivial details and, two, by revealing the material world to be of less importance than the world of imagination. These might seem contradictory, but the aim of each is to move beyond the usual view of objective reality. It may even be true that the "flat stones" at the bottom are not the conclusion.

Nabokov's best literary structures are fused together by intuition and imagination, and they use a number of devices to lead to a sense of an unreachable beyond. These structures suggest the presence of a poetic mystery, a mystery which Nabokov sees as the essence of the beyond and of "real life." Elsewhere he writes of the "faint something that reaches the ears of good poets, penetrating our being with the beyond's fresh breath and conferring upon art that mystery which more than anything characterizes its essence" (*SO* 227). Nabokov's structures attempt to convey the intuitive sense of that fresh breath, that faint something, that mysterious essence.

Chapter Notes

Introduction

1. Nabokov stresses the significance of "structure" in nearly all of his lectures. Dostoevski's fiction "has no structural power"; Gorki's stories are weighed down by a "mechanical structure" (*LRL* 116, 305). On James Joyce's novel: "*Ulysses* is a splendid and permanent structure" (*LL* 287). Nabokov tries to state succinctly what he means by "structure" in his lecture on Dickens' *Bleak House*: "In a word, we mean the planned pattern of a work of art. This is structure" (*LL* 113). In regard to "the enchantment" of Stevenson's "Dr. Jekyll and Mr. Hyde," Nabokov writes that "the structure" of that work contains that same quality (*LL* 252). There are plenty of more examples.

2. Nabokov uses the same term in reference to Cervantes and the writing of *Don Quixote*. He says Cervantes "had alternate phases of lucidity and vagueness, deliberate planning and sloppy vagueness" and "the intuition of genius saved him." This statement is also in a section entitled "Structural Matters" (*LDQ* 28–29).

3. The term "imagination" here includes and moves beyond mere rational thought: the "more than rational ... energy of the imagination" (Hartman 319). This—"more than rational"—corresponds to Nabokov's sense of imagination, a force that is greater than that which is commonly perceived to be "real."

4. In the afterword to *Lolita*, Nabokov states that "reality" is "one of the few words which mean nothing without quotes" (312).

5. Stephen Greenblatt discusses this quality of mystery in *Hamlet* in terms that could be applied to novels such as *Sebastian Knight* or *Pale Fire*. He writes of the "intricate arguments ... that ... are almost certainly doomed to inconclusiveness" (239). While acknowledging that the many inconclusive arguments can shed various angles of light on the play, he argues that there is a planned pattern of mystery built into the art: "There is ... a pervasive pattern, a deliberate forcing together of radically incompatible accounts of almost everything that matters in *Hamlet*" (240).

6. My translation. The original reads:

Mariposa de luz,
la belleza se va cuando yo llego
a su rosa.
Corro, ciego, tras ella...
La medio cojo aquí y allá...
¡Sólo queda en mi mano
la forma de su huída! [Jiménez 109].

7. Here and elsewhere Nabokov makes clear that his ideal translator is male. In a letter concerning the translation of *Invitation to a Beheading* he states that his number one requirement is that the translator be male: "Two things the translator must be: 1) male, 2) American-born or English." He specifically stresses this point: "the translator *must not* be a Russian-born lady" (emphasis in the original). The reasons for Nabokov's sexism seem unclear, especially in light of the many statements he made against various male-translated works (*SL* 258).

Chapter 1

1. Moriarty writes that Barthes' text is an attempt to break down the "glorified agglomeration of stereotypes" accumulated by Balzac.

Chapter Notes

2. Vladimir Nabokov's first novel in English, *The Real Life of Sebastian Knight*, is greatly underrated. Lucy Maddox calls it "a perplexing failure" (47). Stacy Schiff calls it "the greatest English-language novel to have been written on a bidet" (98). Her point with this backhanded complimented is that Nabokov was "nationally fragmented" at the time of writing this novel: composing in English while writing atop "that ultimately European fixture." Neil Cornwell writes of "the still lingering desire for a career move to England" when Nabokov wrote *Sebastian Knight* (157). The novel was written in a period of uncertainty for Nabokov, between his Russian period and his American one. One might consider it his one-novel British period. Gennady Barabtarlo says that it is "the first and weakest of Nabokov's English novels" ("Narrative Stance" 60). Jonathan Sisson overviews a number of the less flattering evaluations of the novel, including one of Nabokov's own, quoting from Andrew Field's *Nabokov: His Life in Art*: "It is perhaps the weakest of Nabokov's longer works written after 1931, and in a foreword to the Russian version on [sic] his memoirs, *Other Shores*, he refers to the 'unbearable imperfections' he now sees in *The Real Life of Sebastian Knight*" ("*Knight*" 634). Brian Boyd, noting the developing complexity of Nabokovian structures, writes that Nabokov had never before "packed such a complex structure into such a small space with such seeming ease" (*Russian Years* 496). Structurally, *The Real Life of Sebastian Knight* is as subtly complicated as any of Nabokov's novels. In fact, the novel is packed (to use Boyd's word) with a great number of devices. I intend to look at many of these devices, with the implied argument being the value of *The Real Life of Sebastian Knight* as a novel and as a place to discover many of Nabokov's metaphysical and structural techniques.

3. In discussing the significance of the detective genre for *Sebastian Knight*, Charles Nicol points out that V.'s odd sense of a murdered body being buried in "just such a garden as this" seems to be a leftover plot point from some typical detective text (Nicol 88; Nabokov, *RLSK* 167).

4. Shlomith Rimmon makes the same point (114). Susan Elizabeth Sweeney also writes about Bohemsky, arguing that her name refers to Arthur Conan Doyle's "A Scandal in Bohemia," a "stolen" version of Poe's "Purloined Letter." Sweeney discusses the significance of the many letters in *Sebastian Knight*, especially those whose contents remain undisclosed even as their form is described, just as the letter in Poe's story (Sweeney, "Purloined" 231).

5. A source for one of these descriptive details, for the young Nabokov, may be Mayne Reid's *The Headless Horseman*. In *Speak, Memory*, Nabokov recounts his sense of one character in that book, Louise Poindexter, with "her twin breasts sinking and swelling in quick, spasmodic breathing, her twin breasts, let me reread..." (202). Here Nabokov displays the adolescent sense of rereading and the poignancy of clichés to a reader of that age. This passage shows the "live source" as seen by a reader not yet old enough to find clichés unconvincing, while the irony in the presentation—"let me reread"—reveals the insight of the older writer looking back at his inexperienced enticements. This quote ends with the three suspension dots in the original, suggesting the possibility of an endless and satisfying repetition for the ten-year-old Nabokov.

6. A number of scholars have discussed the Cinderella theme in *Pnin*, including Charles Nicol in "Pnin's History" and Boyd in *American Years*, page 283.

7. This thirty-second chapter of Part II is full of such manipulated "revelations."

Chapter 2

1. Will Norman has shown that this contrast also exists within Knight alone: "In contrast to Sebastian's history-defying composition and aesthetic, however, there remains the jarring narrative of his awkward existence within a time-bound, historical moment" (68).

2. Jane Grayson offers this "fancy frame" as one of many examples of Nabokov's increasing use of alliteration, especially when translating his own work from Russian to English (*Nabokov Translated* 153). (In an ear-

lier version, this was a "noble frame.") Between *Conclusive Evidence* (1951) and *Speak, Memory: An Autobiography Revisited* (1966) is the Russian *Drugie Berega* (1954).

3. Perhaps V. fears the threat of losing earth-bound measures of time because he fears that such a loss would mean losing his sanity, like Luzhin in *The Defense* who "lingered long in those heavens where earthly lines go out of their mind" (37).

Chapter 3

1. Still, Nabokov found most "creative" attempts at biography to be uninspired: "we get the subject's psychology, the Freudian frolics, the bedaubed descriptions of what the protagonist was thinking at a given moment: a jumble of words akin to the wire holding together a skeleton's poor bones, a literary vacant lot" ("Plausible" 39).

Chapter 4

1. The idea that this is "the time of the culture of narcissism" makes Field sound surprisingly like Mr. Goodman in *Sebastian Knight*, categorizing his topic in terms of his clichéd assessment of the era and its interests.

Chapter 5

1. In this sense *The Real Life of Sebastian Knight* could be seen as a precursor to the "oral biographies" with which George Plimpton has been involved. In his biography of Truman Capote, for example, he collects all the various versions of Capote's life as related by family, friends, acquaintances, and so on. This is virtually the same method V. ends up with, although it was not his goal. Plimpton describes the method: "our reader moves from group to group and listens in on personal reminiscences, opinions, vitriol, and anecdote." He adds, "First-time readers may be put off by the idiosyncrasies of the form—the staccato rhythms of the text, the contradictions in the evidence about a particular episode, and especially the fact that the editors of oral biography do not have the luxury of being guides and interpreter's of the subject's life" (Plimpton ix). These same thoughts could be applied to V.'s accidental biographical method. Stuart discusses the significance of this method and V.'s collection of "angles of perception" (35–53).

2. Nonetheless, Toker is correct that Dolores Haze's choice of names would be "Dolly." There is further evidence of this in the text. Humbert receives a phone call while watching "golden Lolita" play tennis. When he returns, he sees that another person had intruded on the game. As he writes, he looks back on the scene and wonders who that man was; then he ends a sentence and begins the next paragraph with these two words: "Dolly? Dolly." When distanced from his control, "Lolita" turns to "Dolly." His repetition of the name makes that point. After she appeases him, suggesting that they spend the day by the pool, he ends the chapter by re-naming her "Lolita!" (236). Humbert laments that he has "only words to play with," but that is more than Dolly has, and words are no mean toy.

3. Lolita further asserts her authority over names on the next page, telling Humbert, "I loathe your name. It's a clown's name: Humlet Hambert. Omelette Hamburg."

Chapter 6

1. The similarity between Shade's description and that of Whitman is probably intentional. Nabokov calls Shade's *Pale Fire* an "American poem" (*SO* 55). This may even represent Shade's response to Whitman: as a good American poet Shade should be aware of the tradition in which he is working.

2. In V.'s dream about his dead half-brother, Knight also appears to be "ashamed" (186).

Chapter 8

1. Those who have written on this novel seem split, as am I, as to whether he should be called "Sebastian," following V.'s lead, or "Knight." The latter, I believe, should be used when we are stressing our unfamiliarity with Mr. Knight. The use of the first name

could be a sign that one has been duped by V.'s deceptively familiar attitude toward him.

2. There is also a suggestion that this disturbed bulldog might be Knight: Knight's last planned book was a "fictitious biography" for which he had gathered photographs of a "bulldog type of man" (38). Rowe argues that bulldogs — and other dogs — in Nabokov's work are often "agents of fate" (*Patterns* 88). However, Madame Lecerf says that Knight "did not turn into a sentimental pup" (157).

3. Nabokov's translation is, "A thought once uttered is untrue" (Tyutchev 34). Alexandrov also connects this line to Nabokov's metaphysical sense and "the mystical and Romantic notion of the incommunicability of ultimate 'religious' or 'spiritual' experiences" (5).

Chapter 9

1. In different novels the word "zig-zag" is alternately hyphenated or not. I will remain faithful to each text, while using the hyphenated word in my own sentences.

Chapter 11

1. Sisson also compares Nabokov's *Invitation* to the work of Wells: "*Invitation to a Beheading*... is a book-length elaboration of the themes of H. G. Wells's short story 'The Country of the Blind'" ("Cosmic Synchronization and Other Worlds" 140). He develops many other comparisons between these two writers (134–153).

Chapter 12

1. There is a moment in *The Invisible Man* which contains a couple of interesting similarities to this scene. The Invisible Man describes one young man who was searching for him, "His staring eyes and thick-lipped bearded face came a foot from my face. I was half minded to hit his silly countenance, but I arrested my doubled fist" (91). Were we to read the same sentence as written by Nabokov we would certainly see a further significance in the word "doubled." As I ar-gued above, however, the final value of a comparison between these two characters is to show the essential quality of Cincinnatus' ability to transcend — temporarily — materiality, whereas the Invisible Man is hopelessly entrapped in his physical body, regardless of whether or not others can see him.

2. I have been informed that this pun does not exist in the Russian original. That, of course, only demonstrates that Nabokov discovered the pun in English, perhaps while writing *Bend Sinister*, which was published in 1947 (the translation of *Invitation to a Beheading* was published after that work, in 1959). Jane Grayson shows that "Nabokov is a compulsive reviser and when translating his own work he frequently takes the opportunity to incorporate substantial modifications and reworkings" (*Nabokov Translated* 3). She argues, "The creative writer remains active even in the minor reworkings" (131).

3. Humbert describes the same type of conscious-free dream responses in the conclusion of *Lolita*, although his, of course, are more malicious than those of Cincinnatus. For example, speaking to the mother of one of Lolita's acquaintances from Camp Q., he says, "By the way, did she ever tell you how Charlie Holmes debauched there his mother's little charges?" (290). He then responds to the news that Charlie Holmes has "just been killed in Korea" with a comment about French vs. English grammar. The idea that part of the double may be imaginary also has implications for the continued debate over whether or not the murder of Quilty is "real."

4. Elsewhere Toker shows that some Nabokovian protagonists have a real resistance to this carnivalesque mode, this "removal of partitions" between discrete selves. In *Mary*, for example, she convincingly shows that Ganin displays "the need for a balance between sympathy and detachment" and refuses to cross "the threshold beyond which sympathy... threatens to become merger" (46). Toker pursues this topic of the "carnivalesque" in a more recent article where she argues that Nabokov often presents a tension "between the carnivalesque and the anti-carnivalesque narrative modes." In this article she discusses some Nabokovian characters' resistance to crowds and briefly argues against the indi-

viduality of Nabokovian ghosts. She recognizes that many of Nabokov's characters have an inclination toward individuality, but she also sees his metaphysics as one where all individual selves ultimately merge: "studies of the ubiquitousness of ghosts in Nabokov's fiction ... strike me as undue literalizations of the persistence of a character's leitmotifs after the character's death in the fabula" ("'The Dead are Good Mixers': Nabokov's Versions of Individualism" 92, 106–107). In the most recent touch on this topic, Toker discusses Nabokov's desire to escape from "the prison-house of the self" in *Speak, Memory*: "From this prison-house Nabokov had tried to escape by surrendering some of the water-tight discreteness of his ego" ("Nabokov and Bergson on Duration and Reflexivity" 137).

5. However, Sisson also agrees with Toker about the idea of being able to inhabit other people's souls:

> In *The Real Life of Sebastian Knight* Nabokov urges the reader to imagine the soul not as an irreducible element, analogous to a physical object in space, but as a combinational and metamorphic process, a movement in time analogous to music ... thus expanding consciousness and perhaps enabling us ... to inhabit the soul of another ["Knight" 642].

"Perhaps" is the key word. However, Cincinnatus shows that the soul is "analogous to a physical object in space," a pearl. Also, although Nabokov does suggest that the soul is analogous to music — recall that "violin in a void" — I do not see how that supports the argument about being able to inhabit another's soul. In fact, "inhabit" certainly seems to be too strong of a word.

6. See Toker's discussion of this "something" (*Structures* 130–132). Here she notes the inability of language to capture metaphysical "essence" in *Invitation to a Beheading*: "the conventional arbitrariness of the language ... block[s] one's access to the essence that is beyond things and words" (132). Cincinnatus is another character, like Ganin, who she does not argue as being cancelled out.

7. Barabtarlo pursues this line by arguing that Sebastian Knight's name is an anagram for "Knight is absent" (*Aerial* 216). The anagram does not quite work, of course, as there is an A left over from the name Sebastian. (Perhaps this could be considered a slant anagram — to steal a term from Emily Dickinson.) Barabtarlo gives further evidence for this idea in a more recent article, "Narrative Stance in Nabokov's *The Real Life of Sebastian Knight*."

8. An interesting related topic to the difficulty of mingling souls in Nabokov's fiction is Stephen Blackwell's discussion of the "interpenetration of souls" that is the ideal "author-reader interaction," an idea that Blackwell argues is shared by Nabokov and Iulii Aikhenvald (Blackwell 29–36).

9. See Field's *VN: The Life and Art of Vladimir Nabokov* and Oates' "A Personal View of Nabokov," although Oates slightly changes her mind in her "Postscript to a Personal View of Nabokov."

Chapter 13

1. My translation; the original reads: "No sólo costaba comprender que el símbolo genérico perro abarcara tantos individuos dispares de diversos tamaños y diversa forma; le molestaba que el perro de las tres y catorce (visto de perfil) tuviera el mismo nombre que el perro de las tres y cuarto (visto de frente)."

2. Foster places this scene in the context of Bergson's concept of verbal "frames," and compares this recollection of the name "Floss" to a similarly recalled dog's name in Nabokov's story "Reunion."

Chapter 14

1. Appel also misreads the passage where Humbert describes hiring a private detective. Humbert hires an "ex-pugilist" to help with his search only to have him, two years later, discover a match with one of the hotel registries: "an eighty-year-old Indian by the name of Bill Brown" (Nabokov, *Lolita* 253). Appel writes, "Nabokov immediately mocks such doggedly persistent literalism by having H.H. hire Bill Brown" (*Annotated* 429).

Chapter Notes

Nabokov does mock the literalism, but Humbert never hires the old Indian for anything.

2. Even on the level of plain "story" it is a stretch to state that Quilty was trailing Humbert and Lolita only a few days after Charlotte's death. This porch scene comes right at the start of that "fatal summer," not on their second cross-country drive, after Quilty had ostensibly become attracted to Lolita while directing the school's play.

3. Ironically, Kubrick's version takes the exact opposite approach, where Quilty, played by Peter Sellers, appears in a variety of disguises and roles, even playing a Freudian parody of a school principal. In this film version, Quilty is everywhere.

4. The screenplay is a different story: in that work Clare Quilty does appear, at a school dance, for example, where he has a brief conversation with Charlotte: "CHARLOTTE: She's dancing down there. And tomorrow she'll be having a cavity filled by your uncle. QUILTY: I know; he's a wicked old man" (Nabokov, *Screenplay* 57). Later Humbert clearly hears Quilty's voice on the porch, after the bellboy identifies him for Humbert in the lobby beforehand (105–106). The screenplay is much less enigmatic about Quilty's presence and raises fewer doubts about Humbert's sanity. In fact, the problem of persecution mania — so significant to the novel — is barely present in the screenplay at all.

Chapter 15

1. Khodasevich, writing in 1937, predicted this theme of *Pale Fire*: "I think — I am even almost convinced — that Sirin ... will someday give himself rein and favor us with a merciless satiric portrayal of a writer. Such a portrayal would be a natural development in the unfolding of the basic theme with which he is obsessed" (101). This "basic theme" is the interaction of the created and "real" worlds.

2. The difference in aesthetic appreciation between Shade and Kinbote can be shown in their views of race. Kinbote sometimes relies on ideas such as "all Chinese look alike" (265). Shade's is the highest mind of the novel, approaching that of Nabokov. He does not make generalities: "we, whites, are not white at all, we are mauve at birth, then tea-rose, and later all kinds of repulsive colors" (218).

3. This essay contains many lines which might be significant to an interpretation of *Pale Fire*, including a reference to "Zembla." Pope's view of the universe corresponds very closely to Nabokov's sense of fiction: "The great directing Mind of All ordains" (137).

Chapter 16

1. Stuart also discusses the role of Proust in *Sebastian Knight*, arguing that Nabokov — in the biographical method of accumulated reflections — develops Proust's ideas about subjectivity and the self. Will Norman has also shown some ways in which Proust is present in this text, explaining, "The Proustian work that V finds on Sebastian's bookshelf is not simply *A la recherché du temps perdu*, but emphatically the last part of that series, *Le temps retrouvé* (*Time Recovered*), in which the novel's narrator finally realizes that the true mechanism by which time is recovered is through 'involuntary memory,' through accident rather than conscious intention" (74).

2. Her larger argument concerns the gradually increasing chaos in imaginative fiction, from Carroll to Nabokov to Pynchon (Clark, "Abstract").

3. Julian Connolly discusses many interesting details of Nabokov's *Alice* translation in "Ania v strane chudes."

4. Conjurer is spelled with an -er in *Pale Fire*, with an -or in *Sebastian Knight*.

5. Maddox suggests that the silent man who shares the meal — of rabbit — with V. and Madame Lecerf may secretly be the conjuror as well (Maddox 45–46).

Chapter 17

1. A wheelbarrow is also associated with death in *Sebastian Knight* (23). Thus, the wheelbarrow may represent something like the burden of material reality.

Works Cited

Alexandrov, Vladimir. *Nabokov's Otherworld*. Princeton: Princeton University Press, 1991.

———, ed. *The Garland Companion to Vladimir Nabokov*. New York: Garland, 1995.

Appel, Alfred, Jr., ed. *The Annotated* Lolita. New York: Vintage, 1991.

———. "Nabokov: A Portrait." In *Nabokov's Fifth Arc*, edited by Charles Nicol and J. E. Rivers, 3–21. Austin: University of Texas Press, 1982.

Bader, Julia. *Crystal Land: Artifice in Nabokov's English Novels*. Berkeley: University of California Press, 1972.

Barabtarlo, Gennady. *Aerial View: Essays on Nabokov's Art and Metaphysics*. New York: Peter Lang, 1993.

———. "*Taina Naita*. Narrative Stance in Nabokov's *The Real Life of Sebastian Knight*." *Partial Answers: Journal of Literature and the History of Ideas* 6 (Jan. 2008): 57–80.

Barthes, Roland. *S/Z*. New York: Noonday, 1991.

Bethea, David. *Khodasevich*. Princeton: Princeton University Press, 1983.

Blackwell, Stephen. *Zina's Paradox: The Figured Reader in Nabokov's* Gift. New York: Peter Lang, 2000.

Bodenheimer, Rosemarie. *The Real Life of Mary Ann Evans: George Eliot, Her Letters and Fiction*. Ithaca: Cornell University Press, 1994.

Borges, Jorge Luis. "Funes el memorioso." In *Ficciones*, 121–132. Madrid: Emecé, 1956.

Boyd, Brian. "Nabokov as Storyteller." In *The Cambridge Companion to Nabokov*, edited by Julian Connolly, 31–48. Cambridge: Cambridge University Press, 2005.

———. *Nabokov's* Ada: *The Place of Consciousness*. Ann Arbor, MI: Ardis, 1985.

———. *Nabokov's* Pale Fire: *The Magic of Artistic Discovery*. Princeton: Princeton University Press, 1999.

———. *Vladimir Nabokov: The American Years*. Princeton: Princeton University Press, 1991.

———. *Vladimir Nabokov: The Russian Years*. Princeton: Princeton University Press, 1993.

Brenner, Conrad. Introduction. *The Real Life of Sebastian Knight*. Norfolk: New Directions, 1941.

Carroll, Lewis. *Alice in Wonderland*. Rutland: Everyman, 1991.

Carroll, William. "The Cartesian Nightmare of *Despair*." In *Nabokov's Fifth Arc*, edited by Charles Nicol and J. E. Rivers, 82–104. Austin: University of Texas Press, 1982.

Clancy, Laurie. *The Novels of Vladimir Nabokov*. New York: St. Martins, 1984.

Clark, Beverly Lyon. "Abstract." *The Vladimir Nabokov Research Newsletter* (Fall 1979): 24–26.

———. "Nabokov's Assault on Wonderland." In *Nabokov's Fifth Arc*, edited by Charles Nicol and J. E. Rivers, 63–74. Austin: University of Texas Press, 1982.

Connolly, Julian. "Ania v strane chudes." In *The Garland Companion to Vladimir Nabokov*, edited by Vladimir Alexandrov, 18–24. New York: Garland, 1995.

———. "'Nature's Reality' or Humbert's 'Fancy': Scenes of Reunion and Murder in *Lolita*." *Nabokov Studies* 2 (1995): 41–61.

———. "*Pnin*: Recurrence and Transformation." In *Nabokov's Fifth Arc*, edited by Charles Nicol and J. E. Rivers, 195–210. Austin: University of Texas Press, 1982.

Works Cited

———, ed. *The Cambridge Companion to Nabokov*. Cambridge: Cambridge University Press, 2005.

Cornwell, Neil. "From Sirin to Nabokov: The Transition to English." In *The Cambridge Companion to Nabokov*, edited by Julian Connolly, 151–169. Cambridge: Cambridge University Press, 2005.

De la Durantaye, Leland. *Style Is Matter*. Ithaca: Cornell University Press, 2007.

Dickinson, Emily. *Selected Letters*, edited by Thomas Johnson. Cambridge: Harvard University Press, 1958.

Edelstein, Marilyn. "Pale Fire: The Art of Consciousness." In *Nabokov's Fifth Arc*, edited by Charles Nicol and J. E. Rivers, 213–223. Austin: University of Texas Press, 1982.

Evans, Walter. "The Conjuror in 'The Potato Elf.'" In *Nabokov's Fifth Arc*, edited by J. E. Rivers and Charles Nicol, 75–81. Austin: University of Texas Press, 1982.

Fet, Victor. "Beheading First: On Nabokov's Translation of Lewis Carroll." *The Nabokovian* (Fall 2009): 52–63.

Field, Andrew. *VN: The Life and Art of Vladimir Nabokov*. New York: Crown, 1986.

Fish, Stanley. *Is There a Text in this Class?* Cambridge: Harvard University Press, 1980.

Fitzgerald, F. Scott. *The Crack Up*. New York: New Directions, 1956.

Foster, John Burt, Jr. *Nabokov's Art of Memory and European Modernism*. Princeton: Princeton University Press, 1993.

Fromberg, Susan. "The Unwritten Chapters in *The Real Life of Sebastian Knight*." *Modern Fiction Studies* XIII (1967–1968): 427–442.

Frost, Robert. "The Figure a Poem Makes." *The Robert Frost Reader: Poetry and Prose*, 439–442. New York: Holt, 1972.

Grayson, Jane. *Nabokov Translated: A Comparison of Nabokov's Russian and English Prose*. Oxford: Oxford University Press, 1977.

———, Arnold McMillin, and Priscilla Meyer, eds. *Nabokov's World: Volume One: The Shape of Nabokov's World*. New York: Palgrave, 2002.

Greenblatt, Stephen. *Hamlet in Purgatory*. Princeton: Princeton University Press, 2001.

Hartman, Geoffrey. *Beyond Formalism*. New Haven: Yale University Press, 1970.

Hemingway, Ernest. *Death in the Afternoon*. New York: Scribner's, 1932.

Irwin, John. *The Mystery to a Solution*. Baltimore: Johns Hopkins University Press, 1994.

Jiménez, Juan Ramón. *Piedra y Cielo*. Madrid: Imprenta de Fortanet, 1919.

Johnson, D. Barton. *Worlds in Regression: Some Novels of Vladimir Nabokov*. Ann Arbor, MI: Ardis, 1985.

Khodasevich, Vladislav. "On Sirin." In *Nabokov*, edited by Alfred Appel, Jr., and Charles Newman, 96–101. New York: Simon and Schuster, 1970.

Kuzmanovich, Zoran. "'Splendid Insincerity' as 'Utmost Truthfulness': Nabokov and the Claims of the Real." In *Nabokov Translated: A Comparison of Nabokov's Russian and English Prose*, edited by Jane Grayson, 26–46. Oxford: Oxford University Press, 1977.

Maddox, Lucy. *Nabokov's Novels in English*. Athens: University of Georgia Press, 1983.

Meyer, Priscilla. "Black and Violet Words: *Despair* and *The Real Life of Sebastian Knight* as Doubles." *Nabokov Studies* 4 (1997): 37–60.

Moriarty, Michael. *Roland Barthes*. Stanford: Stanford University Press, 1991.

Nabokov, Dmitri. "Translating with Nabokov." *The Achievements of Vladimir Nabokov*, edited by George Gibian and Stephen Jan Parker. Ithaca: Cornell University Press, 1984.

Nabokov, Vladimir. *Ada*. 1969. Reprint, New York: Vintage, 1990.

———. *Bend Sinister*. 1947. Reprint, New York: Vintage, 1990.

———. *Conclusive Evidence*. New York: Harper, 1947.

———. *The Defense*. 1930. Reprint, translated by Michael Scammell and Vladimir Nabokov, 1964. Reprint, New York: Vintage, 1990.

———. *Despair*. 1936. Reprint, translated by Vladimir Nabokov, 1966. Reprint, New York: Vintage, 1989.

———. *The Eye*. 1930. Reprint, translated

Works Cited

by Dmitri Nabokov and Vladimir Nabokov, 1965. Reprint, New York: Vintage, 1990.

———. *The Gift*. 1938. Reprint, translated by Michael Scammell and Vladimir Nabokov, 1963. Reprint, New York: Vintage, 1991.

———. *Glory*. 1932. Reprint, translated by Dmitri Nabokov and Vladimir Nabokov, 1971. Reprint, New York: Vintage, 1991.

———. *Invitation to a Beheading*. 1938. Reprint, translated by Dmitri Nabokov and Vladimir Nabokov, 1959. Reprint, New York: Vintage, 1989.

———. *King, Queen, Knave*. 1928. Reprint, translated by Dmitri Nabokov and Vladimir Nabokov, 1968. Reprint, New York: Vintage, 1989.

———. *Laughter in the Dark*. 1938. Reprint, New York: Vintage, 1989.

———. *Lectures on Don Quixote*, edited by Fredson Bowers. New York: Harcourt, 1983.

———. *Lectures on Literature*, edited by Fredson Bowers. New York: Harcourt, 1980.

———. *Lectures on Russian Literature*, edited by Fredson Bowers. New York: Harcourt, 1981.

———. *Lolita*. 1955. Reprint, New York: Vintage, 1989.

———. *Lolita: A Screenplay*. New York: McGraw-Hill, 1961.

———. *Look at the Harlequins!* 1974. Reprint, New York: Vintage, 1990.

———. *Mary*. 1926. Reprint, New York: Vintage, 1989.

———. "Mr. Williams' Shakespeare." *The New Republic* (19 May 1941): 702.

———. *Nabokov's Butterflies*, edited by Brian Boyd and Robert Pyle. Boston: Beacon, 2000.

———. *Nikolai Gogol*. New York: New Directions, 1944.

———. *The Original of Laura*. New York: Knopf, 2009.

———. *Pale Fire*. 1962. Reprint, New York: Vintage, 1989.

———. *Pnin*. 1957. Reprint, New York: Vintage, 1989.

———. *Poems and Problems*. New York: McGraw-Hill, 1970.

———. "Pushkin, or the Real and the Plausible." *The New York Review of Books* (31 March 1988): 38–42.

———. *The Real Life of Sebastian Knight*. 1941. Reprint, New York: Vintage, 1992.

———. *Selected Letters 1940–1977*. New York: Harcourt, 1989.

———. *Speak, Memory*. 1967. Reprint, New York: Vintage, 1989.

———. *The Stories of Vladimir Nabokov*, edited by Dmitri Nabokov. New York: Knopf, 1995.

———. *Strong Opinions*. 1973. Reprint, New York: Vintage, 1990.

———. *Transparent Things*. 1972. Reprint, New York: Vintage, 1989.

———, trans. *The Song of Igor's Campaign*. New York: Vintage, 1960.

———, and Edmund Wilson. *The Nabokov-Wilson Letters*, edited by Simon Karlinsky. New York: Harper, 1979.

Nicol, Charles. "The Mirrors of Sebastian Knight." *Nabokov: The Man and His Work*, 85–94. Madison: University of Wisconsin Press, 1967.

———. "Pnin's History." In *Critical Essays on Vladimir Nabokov*, edited by Phyllis Roth, 134–156. Boston: GK Hall, 1984.

———, and J. E. Rivers, eds. *Nabokov's Fifth Arc*. Austin: University of Texas Press, 1982.

Norman, Will. "*The Real Life of Sebastian Knight* and the Modernist Impasse." *Nabokov Studies* 10 (2006): 67–97.

Oates, Joyce Carol. "A Personal View of Nabokov." In *Critical Essays on Vladimir Nabokov*, edited by Phyllis Roth, 105–108. Boston: GK Hall, 1984.

Packman, David. *Vladimir Nabokov: The Structure of Literary Desire*. Columbia: University of Missouri Press, 1982.

Pifer, Ellen. *Nabokov and the Novel*. Cambridge: Harvard University Press, 1980.

Plimpton, George. *Truman Capote*. New York: Doubleday, 1997.

Pope, Alexander. "Essay on Man." *Selected Poetry and Prose*, 127–167. New York: Holt, 1951.

Proffer, Carl. *Keys to* Lolita. Bloomington: Indiana University Press, 1968.

Pushkin, Aleksandr. *Eugene Onegin*, vol. 1–4, translated by Vladimir Nabokov. Princeton: Princeton University Press, 1975.

Works Cited

———. "Mozart and Salieri." *Three Russian Poets*, translated by Vladimir Nabokov, 20–29. Norfolk: New Directions, 1944.

Rimmon, Shlomith. "Problems of Voice in Nabokov's *The Real Life of Sebastian Knight*." In *Critical Essays on Vladimir Nabokov*, edited by Phyllis Roth, 109–129. Boston: GK Hall, 1984.

Rivers, J. E., and Charles Nicol, eds. *Nabokov's Fifth Arc*. Austin: University of Texas Press, 1982.

Roth, Phyllis, ed. *Critical Essays on Vladimir Nabokov*. Boston: GK Hall, 1984.

Rowe, W.W. "The Honesty of Nabokovian Deception." *A Book of Things About Vladimir Nabokov*, edited by Carl Proffer, 171–181. Ann Arbor, MI: Ardis, 1974.

———. *Nabokov and Others: Patterns in Russian Literature*. Ann Arbor, MI: Ardis, 1979.

Rydel, Christine. "Semantic Hierarchies of Nabokov's God." MLA Convention. Toronto, 30 Dec 1993.

Salomon, Roger. *Desperate Storytelling*. Athens: University of Georgia Press, 1987.

Schiff, Stacy. *Vera (Mrs. Vladimir Nabokov)*. New York: Random House, 1999.

Shadows and Fog. Directed by Woody Allen. Orion, 1992.

Shklovsky, Victor. "Sterne's *Tristram Shandy*: Stylistic Commentary." In *Russian Formalist Criticism: Four Essays*, edited and translated by Lee Lemon and Marion Reis, 25–57. Lincoln: University of Nebraska Press, 1965.

Sisson, Jonathan. "Cosmic Synchronization and Other Worlds in the Work of Vladimir Nabokov." Diss., University of Minnesota, 1979.

———. "Cosmic Synchronization and 'Something Else.'" *Nabokov Studies* 1 (1994): 155–177.

———. "*The Real Life of Sebastian Knight*." In *The Garland Companion to Vladimir Nabokov*, edited by Vladimir Alexandrov, 633–643. New York: Garland, 1995.

Stegner, Page. *Escape into Aesthetics: The Art of Vladimir Nabokov*. New York: Dial, 1966.

Stevens, Wallace. *The Collected Poems*. New York: Vintage, 1954.

Stuart, Dabney. *Nabokov: The Dimensions of Parody*. Baton Rouge: Louisiana State University Press, 1978.

Tammi, Pekka. *Problems of Nabokov's Poetics*. Helsinki: Suomalaienen Tiedeakatemia, 1985.

Toker, Leona. "'The Dead are Good Mixers': Nabokov's Versions of Individualism." In *Nabokov and His Fiction*, edited by Julian Connolly, 92–108. Cambridge: Cambridge University Press, 1999.

———. "Nabokov and Bergson on Duration and Reflexivity." In *Nabokov Translated: A Comparison of Nabokov's Russian and English Prose*, edited by Jane Grayson, 132–140. Oxford: Oxford University Press, 1977.

———. *Nabokov: The Mystery of Literary Structures*. Ithaca: Cornell University Press, 1989.

Tyutchev, Fedor. "Silentium." In *Three Poets*, translated by Vladimir Nabokov, 33–34. New York: New Directions, 1944.

Wells, H. G. *The Invisible Man*. New York: Bantam, 1970.

Whitman, Walt. *The Complete Poetry and Selected Prose*, edited by James Miller, Jr. Boston: Riverside, 1959.

Wood, Michael. *The Magician's Doubts*. Princeton: Princeton University Press, 1994.

Wyllie, Barbara. *Nabokov at the Movies*. Jefferson, NC: McFarland, 2003.

Yeats, W. B. *The Collected Poems of W. B. Yeats*, edited by Richard J. Finneran. New York: Collier, 1983.

Index

Ada (Nabokov) 8, 36, 53, 91–91, 176, 177, 181
"An Affair of Honor" (Nabokov) 184–185
Aikhenvald, Iulii 191*n*
Alexandrov, Vladimir 7, 46, 47, 51, 54–55, 70–71, 94, 109–110, 143, 144, 161, 168, 190*n*
Alice in Wonderland (Carroll) 20, 175–176, 177, 178, 185–186, 192*n*
Allen, Woody 10
Appel, Alfred 28, 63, 153, 155–156, 191*n*
"The Art of Translation" (Nabokov) 11–14, 55, 84–85, 87, 124, 140

Bader, Julia 170–172
Barabtarlo, Gennady 45, 120–121, 139, 184, 188*n*, 191*n*
Barthes, Roland 15–16, 49–50, 187*n*
Bend Sinister (Nabokov) 79–80, 93, 112–113, 121, 133–134, 136–139, 141, 172, 183–184, 190*n*
Bethea, David 11
Blackwell, Stephen 191*n*
Bleak House (Dickens) 120, 187*n*
Bodenheimer, Rosemarie 115–116, 124
Borges, Jorge Luis 67, 142–143
Boyd, Brian 9, 28, 40, 43, 48–49, 51, 58–59, 60–61, 68, 71, 77, 81, 86, 89, 92, 109, 123, 140, 158, 169, 173, 188*n*
Brenner, Conrad 66–67
"Butterfly of Light" (Jiménez) 10–11, 25, 104, 144, 146, 187*n*

Camus, Albert 103, 185
Carroll, Lewis 96, 167, 173, 175–178, 180, 185, 192*n*
Carroll, William 88–89
Cervantes, Miguel de 3, 14, 18–20, 118, 177, 187*n*
Clancy, Laurie 182

Clark, Beverly Lyon 177, 192*n*
Conclusive Evidence (Nabokov) 34–36, 189*n*
Connolly, Julian 40–41, 112–113, 192*n*
Cornwell, Neil 188*n*

The Defense (Nabokov) 80, 105, 189*n*
de la Durantaye, Leland 63
Despair (Nabokov) 20, 48, 53, 57, 105, 123, 133, 161, 183
Dickens, Charles 14, 156, 178, 187*n*
Dickinson, Emily 11, 191*n*
Don Quixote (Cervantes) 17, 19–20, 118, 187*n*
Dostoevski, Fyodor 187*n*

Edelstein, Marilyn 173
Emerson, Ralph Waldo 165
Eugene Onegin (Pushkin) 2–5, 8, 12, 51, 55, 59, 86, 119–120, 159
Evans, Walter 179
The Eye (Nabokov) 76, 97–98, 106–107, 150

"Fame" (Nabokov) 137, 160
Fet, Victor 176
Field, Andrew 59, 141, 188*n*, 189*n*, 191*n*
"The Figure a Poem Makes" (Frost) 86
Fish, Stanley 17, 151, 153
Fitzgerald, F. Scott 44, 60
Flaubert, Gustave 14, 22, 32, 120, 178
Foster, John Burt, Jr. 20, 110, 116, 142, 156, 177, 191*n*
Fromberg, Susan 77, 101, 128, 176
Frost, Robert 86–87, 167, 169–170, 172
"Funes, el Memorioso" (Borges) 142–143

The Gift (Nabokov) 27, 31, 34, 55, 82–84, 90–91, 126, 135, 146–147, 186, 188

197

Index

Glory (Nabokov) 84, 90–91, 109
Gogol, Nikolai 14, 152, 154, 183
Gorki, Maxim 187*n*
Grayson, Jane 188*n*, 190*n*
Greenblatt, Stephen 187*n*

Hamlet (Shakespeare) 10, 63–64, 187*n*
Hartman, Geoffrey 4, 187*n*
Hemingway, Ernest 80, 85, 160

"The Idea of Order at Key West" (Stevens) 4
"In Memory of L.I. Shigaev" (Nabokov) 111
Invisible Man (Wells) 129–130, 190*n*
Invitation to a Beheading (Nabokov) 27, 54–55, 65, 80, 84, 88, 104, 127–130, 134, 136–137, 141, 160, 165, 182–184, 190*n*, 191*n*
Irwin, John 79, 108

Jiménez, Juan Ramón 10–11, 187*n*
Johnson, D. Barton 7, 168, 170
Joyce, James 15, 18–19, 46, 187*n*

Khodasevich, Vladislav 8, 11, 74, 150, 170, 192*n*
King Lear (Shakespeare) 63–64
King, Queen, Knave (Nabokov) 105–107, 110, 142–143, 183
Kuzmanovich, Zoran 7

Laughter in the Dark (Nabokov) 17, 88–89, 107–108, 185
Lectures on Don Quixote (Nabokov) 3, 18–20, 118, 177, 197*n*
Lectures on Literature (Nabokov) 3, 8, 15, 22, 25, 49–50, 83, 87, 117–118, 156, 178, 181, 185, 187*n*
Lectures on Russian Literature (Nabokov) 9, 11–14, 39, 93, 113, 118–120, 187*n*
Libro de Arena (Borges) 67
Lolita (Nabokov) 1, 3, 16, 22–29, 31–32, 34, 39–42, 47–48, 53, 58, 68–73, 79–80, 82, 84, 94–96, 139–140, 148–162, 166, 172–173, 175–176, 187*n*, 189*n*, 190–192*n*
Lolita: A Screenplay (Nabokov) 70, 95, 175–176, 192*n*
Look at the Harlequins! (Nabokov) 45, 83, 177, 182

Madame Bovary (Flaubert) 22, 178
Maddox, Lucy 144, 188*n*, 192*n*
"Mariposa de Luz" (Jiménez) 10–11, 187*n*
Mary (Nabokov) 42–43, 65, 190*n*
Meyer, Priscilla 138
"Mr. Williams' Shakespeare" (Nabokov) 17
Moriarty, Michael 15–16, 187*n*
"Mozart and Salieri" (Pushkin) 128–129

Nabokov, Dmitri 7
Nabokov, Vladimir: *Ada* 8, 36, 53, 91–91, 176, 177, 181; "An Affair of Honor" 184–185; "The Art of Translation" 11–14, 55, 84–85, 87, 124, 140; *Bend Sinister* 79–80, 93, 112–113, 121, 133–134, 136–139, 141, 172, 183–184, 190*n*; *Conclusive Evidence* 34–36, 189*n*; *The Defense* 80, 105, 189*n*; *Despair* 20, 48, 53, 57, 105, 123, 133, 161, 183; *Eugene Onegin* (translation and commentaries) 2–5, 8, 12, 51, 55, 59, 86, 119–120, 159; *The Eye* 76, 97–98, 106–107, 150; "Fame" 137, 160; *The Gift* 27, 31, 34, 55, 82–84, 90–91, 126, 135, 146–147, 186, 188; *Glory* 84, 90–91, 109; "In Memory of L.I. Shigaev" 111; *Invitation to a Beheading* 27, 54–55, 65, 80, 84, 88, 104, 127–130, 134, 136–137, 141, 160, 165, 182–184, 190*n*, 191*n*; *King, Queen, Knave* 105–107, 110, 142–143, 183; *Laughter in the Dark* 17, 88–89, 107–108, 185; *Lectures on Don Quixote* 3, 18–20, 118, 177, 197*n*; *Lectures on Literature* 3, 8, 15, 22, 25, 49–50, 83, 87, 117–118, 156, 178, 181, 185, 187*n*; *Lectures on Russian Literature* 9, 11–14, 39, 93, 113, 118–120, 187*n*; *Lolita* 1, 3, 16, 22–29, 31–32, 34, 39–42, 47–48, 53, 58, 68–73, 79–80, 82, 84, 94–96, 139–140, 148–162, 166, 172–173, 175–176, 187*n*, 189*n*, 190–192*n*; *Lolita: A Screenplay* 70, 95, 175–176, 192*n*; *Look at the Harlequins!* 45, 83, 177, 182; *Mary* 42–43, 65, 190*n*; "Mr. Williams' Shakespeare" 17; "Mozart and Salieri" (translation) 128–129; *The Nabokov-Wilson Letters* 24, 27, 53–55; *Nikolai Gogol* 18, 26, 63, 99, 152, 154, 183; *The Original of Laura* 97, 141; *Pale Fire* 3, 7, 27, 56–59, 72, 77–89, 93, 105, 113, 125–128, 132, 141, 151, 166–174, 178–

Index

179, 185–186, 189n, 192n; "The Passenger" 108, 112; *Pnin* 26, 45, 53, 84, 93, 112–113, 136–139, 141, 147, 188n; *The Poetry of Prose* 14; "Pushkin, or the Real and the Plausible" 46–47, 189n; *The Real Life of Sebastian Knight* 1, 16–22, 27, 34–35, 37–39, 43–47, 49, 52–55, 60–68, 70–71, 74–80, 86, 88, 92–94, 98–106, 110–111, 113, 115–117, 122–125, 127–128, 130- 140, 142–145, 154, 157–160, 163–164, 166, 168, 172, 175–182, 188–192n; *Selected Letters* 2, 6, 13–14, 97, 187n; *The Song of Igor's Campaign* (translation and commentary) 129; *Speak, Memory* 227, 145–147, 29–31, 34–37, 60–61, 70, 79, 81–82, 84, 103, 109–110, 142, 146–147, 157, 162, 164–166, 169, 188–189n, 191n; "Spring in Fialta" 42; *Strong Opinions* 4, 6, 9–10, 27, 42, 51–52, 55–56, 68, 81, 84, 86, 156, 178, 186, 189n; *Transparent Things* 143, 106; "Tyrants Destroyed" 8; "Ultima Thule" 91; "The Vane Sisters" 59, 93; "Wingstroke" 39
The Nabokov-Wilson Letters 24, 27, 53–54
Nabokov's Butterflies 103, 185Nicol, Charles 21, 61, 101, 188n
Nikolai Gogol (Nabokov) 18, 26, 63, 99, 152, 154, 183
Norman, Will 188n, 192n

Oates, Joyce Carol 59, 141, 191n
The Original of Laura (Nabokov) 97, 141

Packman, David 18
Pale Fire (Nabokov) 3, 7, 27, 56–59, 72, 77–89, 93, 105, 113, 125–128, 132, 141, 151, 166–174, 178–179, 185–186, 189n, 192n
"The Passenger" (Nabokov) 108, 112
Pifer, Ellen 105
Plimpton, George 189n
Pnin (Nabokov) 26, 45, 53, 84, 93, 112–113, 136–139, 141, 147, 188n
The Poetry of Prose (Nabokov) 14
Pope, Alexander 174, 192n
Proffer, Carl 2, 58, 156
Proust, Marcel 14, 117–119, 177, 192n
Pushkin, Alexander 2–3, 5, 13–14, 46–47, 51, 55, 86, 119–120, 128–129

"Pushkin, or the Real and the Plausible" (Nabokov) 46–47, 189n

The Real Life of Sebastian Knight (Nabokov) 1, 16–22, 27, 34–35, 37–39, 43–47, 49, 52–55, 60–68, 70–71, 74–80, 86, 88, 92–94, 98–106, 110–111, 113, 115–117, 122–125, 127–128, 130–140, 142–145, 154, 157–160, 163–164, 166, 168, 172, 175–182, 188–192n
Rimmon, Shlomith 115, 188n
Rowe, W.W. 18, 133, 190n
Rydel, Christine 6

Salomon, Roger 57–58
Schiff, Stacy 188n
Selected Letters (Nabokov) 2, 6, 13–14, 97, 187n
Shadows and Fog (Allen) 10
Shakespeare, William 10, 63–64, 167, 187n
Shklovsky, Victor 184
"Silentium" (Tyutchev) 104, 190n
Sisson, Jonathan 68, 111, 137, 143, 188n, 190–191n
The Song of Igor's Campaign (Anonymous) 129
Speak, Memory (Nabokov) 227, 145–147, 29–31, 34–37, 60–61, 70, 79, 81–82, 84, 103, 109–110, 142, 146–147, 157, 162, 164–166, 169, 188–189n, 191n
"Spring in Fialta" (Nabokov) 42
Stegner, Page 67, 98, 167, 170
Stevens, Wallace 4, 67
Stevenson, Robert Louis 118, 101, 187n
"Stopping by Woods on a Snowy Evening" (Frost) 87, 169–170
Strong Opinions (Nabokov) 4, 6, 9–10, 27, 42, 51–52, 55–56, 68, 81, 84, 86, 156, 178, 186, 189n
Stuart, Dabney 180, 189n, 192n

Tammi, Pekka 5, 7, 117
"Thirteen Ways of Looking at a Blackbird" (Stevens) 67
Timon of Athens (Shakespeare) 167
Toker, Leona 69, 127, 135–137, 150–151, 189–191n
Tolstoy, Leo 9, 14, 32, 39, 113, 118–120
Transparent Things (Nabokov) 143, 106
"Tyrants Destroyed" (Nabokov) 8

Index

Tyutchev, Fedor 104, 190*n*

"Ultima Thule" (Nabokov) 91
Ulysses (Joyce) 15, 18–20

"The Vane Sisters" (Nabokov) 59, 93

Wells, H.G. 129–130, 190*n*
Whitman, Walt 80–81, 87, 170, 189*n*

Wilson, Edmund 55–56; see also *Nabokov-Wilson Letters*
"Wingstroke" (Nabokov) 39
Wood, Michael 9, 29, 35, 54, 65, 78–80, 96, 127, 149, 163, 166
Wyllie, Barbara 123

Yeats, W.B. 63–64

www.ingramcontent.com/pod-product-compliance
Lightning Source LLC
Chambersburg PA
CBHW032058300426
44116CB00007B/793